GETTING OFF AT GATESHEAD

GETTING OFF
AT **GATESHEAD**

The dirtiest words
and phrases in English
from Ass-end to Zig-zig

JONATHON GREEN

CONTENTS

A LEFT-HANDED LEXICON

'Arseholes, bastards, fucking cunts, and pricks ...'
Ian Dury, 'Plaistow Patricia' (1977)

Fuck it. Let's start where we mean to begin, not to mention continue. The so-called obscenities, from the Latin word *obscaenus,* inauspicious, ill-omened, filthy, disgusting, lewd and ultimately, though this may be but a folk etymology, from *scaevus*, left-handed, or even *casenum*, mud. Dirty words indeed. Words that are found, as often as anywhere, in pornography, from the Greek, and meaning 'that writes about whores'. Or smut: German *schmutz*, dirt, Blue, crude, foul, offensive, profane, scatalogical, spicy, unwholesome ... go search your thesaurus. Or your slang dictionary. Or indeed mine. The filthy lemmas bespatter the pages. *Cunt* and its compounds, three-and-a half columns, *arse* the same, and add the same again for America's *ass*, *crap* three, *shit* and *fuck* eight apiece. And so it goes. And the synonyms, the synonyms. 1750 copulations, 1300 penises, 1200 vaginas, 1200 homosexuals, 1100 whores and pimps, 950 varieties of self-abuse, 650 anuses and 550 voidings of human waste. Rough figures, of course. Very rough.

The peerless US stand-up, the late Lenny Bruce, used to do what he called a 'bit' about figurative dirt. As described by the moral of mind and pure in heart. His supposed stock in trade, the 'dirty toilet joke'. He died on one, a needle in his arm, but they were not of his repertoire. Those he left to 'family' entertainers. In any case, how could a toilet be of itself 'dirty'? Figuratively. Likewise, how can words, simple aggregations of consonants and vowels, from the monosyllabic fuck to the oedipal polysyllable motherfucker, how can words be 'dirty'? If beauty is in the beholder's eye, so too is 'filth', and both take their cue from lust.

7

It comes, it would appear, from taboo. The earliest taboos, when the bearded old boys in the sky held even more gruesome sway than today, were blasphemous. Breaching commandment three: taking the name of your Lord in vain. They sound funny now – *gadzooks* (god's hooks), *'snails* (God's or again rather Christ's nails), *godsprecious* (heart, that was) – but at the time such locutions represented a conscious desire to resist a fall into lexical sin. Paradoxically the filth of the future remained pretty much on-limits. certainly the bodily functions. Shit, piss, and turd, among others, raised nary an eyebrow. Prick and arse likewise. The Enlightenment saw off God – at least among the enlightened – and to a great extent saw off the power of blasphemy too. Our bodies, it appeared, were the new taboo. Their parts and what we did with them. Genitals, defecation, and copulation. Enough said. Today one might expect such fears to have vanished. Hardly. For a diehard and tediously vocal group, the traditional terms still exercise their magic. Still, there is hope: the young, it does appear, have decided that the language of other taboos – racism, sexism – is more worthy of suppression (and the young and their standards and their vocabulary grow older every day). And women, once en-pedestalled as a race apart from indecency, are as likely to swear as any man.

So what are they, these rancid, purulent, unwholesome terms? Despite the almost uncountable synonymy that slang can offer, we actually have a list of the hardcore hard core. Thanks to a performance by another US stand-up, in this case George Carlin. In October 1973, appearing before a live audience in a California theatre, Carlin recorded a 12-minute-long monologue entitled 'Filthy Words.' It featured, as he put it, 'the words you couldn't say on the public, uh, airwaves, um, the ones you definitely wouldn't say, ever.' He then proceeded to say them: *fuck, shit, piss, cunt, tits, cocksucker, motherfucker, fart, turd, cock, twat* and *ass.* On 30 October the monologue was broadcast by a New York radio station. The shit duly hit the fan.

It might be suggested that in our allegedly enlightened world such agglomerations of vowels and consonants, synonyms for parts of the body or what we do with them, should no longer inspire terror in the hearts of the adult (children, however much we pretend otherwise, use them all the time), but of course they do. So, in an attempt to let everyone, libertarian or censor, know something for once about that upon which they orate, what follows is a look at the dirty dozen, their etymological backgrounds and the many words and phrases to which they have given birth. And alongside, since even 12 letters do not an alphabet make, are some of themes that have informed slang, it seems, since the first glossaries were laid down more than four centuries ago.

One general point: most of these terms did not begin life as slang. They described bodily functions and were not taboo. But not for long. Sex was more contentious than defecation, and those words were outlawed first; by the eighteenth century, when an ever-more powerful nation sought to reflect its importance by cleaning up its language, they began to move to the linguistic margins. And after that the great dark age of evangelical Christianity, backed by the wholesale feminisation of Victorian society, remade language as it did so much else in its own meanly limited image, and what had been acceptable was consigned to the outer hells. They did not, of course, vanish but, excluded from polite society, they became slang by default.

A note for readers: the aim of the book is to lay out the slang lexicographer's stall. In other words to show what Carlin's list, and a number of thematic relations, e.g. dirt or disease, have to offer. I have not, on the whole, offered dates or geographical labels, other than when it seems useful. This is partially a matter of space, but more because what is on offer here is what I would describe quite unashamedly as the magnificence of the vocabulary, rather than its detailed chronology. For that information I would, equally unashamedly, recommend my *Chambers Dictionary of Slang*.

A
IS FOR
ARSE
ARSEHOLE
AND
A LITTLE PIECE OF
ASS

Nearly 50 years ago I was taught, I cannot recall quite what, by a man who, admirable pedagogue though he doubtless was, tended to address his charges not as X or Y or even Z, but as 'arse'. 'You, boy, you stupid arse…', 'Are you an utter arse?', and on special days when his memory for individuals was working, 'Green, you're a complete arse' (in which assessment if, as I suspect, the subject was maths, he was wholly correct).

Later I wondered: was he really, c.1960, calling 11-year-olds 'arses'? Maybe not. After all, this was a man who carefully placed the emphasis on the final syllable of Nelson's final battle, i.e. Tra-fal-*gar* (not to mention making dedicated mockery, and how we little racists laughed along, of the names – Lumumba, Kasavubu – of the main players in the contemporary Congolese war). Maybe I'd heard it wrong. And in restrospect it was probably all enunciation: it wasn't arse at all, but a drawling, long-a-ed 'ass', a donkey and hence a fool. No matter. Arse stuck (are thus slang lexicographers made?).

As indeed it should. **Arse**, like bollocks, is one of those 'Anglo-Saxon' words that really is. And like bollocks (see under **B is for Bollocks**, p.22) it makes its first printed appearance in Abbot Aelfric's Latin–Anglo-Saxon dictionary of 1000, where he defines the Latin *nates*, buttocks, as 'ears-lyre'. As such inclusion implies, arse was standard at coinage, but it moved gradually into slang. Its sources include a variety of words found in several Teutonic and Scandinavian languages. The nearest relation is the German *arsch*, and there are definite links back to the Greek *orros* and *orsos*. In English it dates at least to 1000, when it was spelt **ars**, **ears** or **ars**. The modern spelling appears c.1300.

ARSES, ASSES AND ELBOWS

Once rendered taboo, arse was to be resisted in polite conversation and printed only after the exclusion of crucial consonants, typically by Francis Grose who, as was his wont with such terms, in his *Dictionary of the Vulgar Tongue* prefers a hyphen, i.e. *a–e*, to the full-blown word. It remained off-limits, at least in print, until 1929, when Frederic Manning used it in full in his First World War memoir *Her Privates We* (itself a slightly bawdy pun, and slightly more accessible than his original and equally punning title, *The Middle Parts of Fortune*). Since then the word has become relatively acceptable, and such phrases as **arse about** or **not know one's arse from one's elbow** (see below), while not exactly standard, no longer have the correspondents grabbing at their pens.

That said, arse (and its American equivalent **ass**), remains one of those 'filthy words' cited in 1978 by the US Federal Communications Commission as indecent, if not actually obscene. As regards this US spelling (which has been appearing increasingly in the UK since the late 1990s), it is often interchangeable with arse, especially in compounds, although of course certain usages are nation-specific. It might also be noted that ass is not some kind of independent American neologism (although its relative simplicity of spelling might well have been created by Noah Webster, the American lexicographer who gave us color, theater and such like): Shakespeare, for instance, opts for ass, often in a punning context, on several occasions. Nor was it unknown to a later UK audience: take this thigh-slapper from *Nancy Dawson's Jests* (1761): 'An old woman had a jack ass run away … she called out to a man in the road, stop my ass master, stop my ass. Take a cork you old whore, and stop it yourself, says he.' Indeed. It's the way, if one may plagiarise a rather more modern jokesmith, that they tell 'em.

The primary meaning of arse is the buttocks, initially in a non-sexual context. From there the words extended to mean the vagina (and occasionally the penis); as a ballad of *c*.1600 puts it: 'I had some hope, & to her spoke, / "sweet hart, shall I put my flesh in thine?" / "With all my hart, Sir! your nose in my arse" / quoth she', and we can be sure that it was neither his 'nose' nor her buttocks of which she spoke. More recently it has meant sexual conquests; and is thus generic for a woman when viewed purely as a sex object, often as a **bit of arse**. It can denote the rear of anything (human or otherwise). Almost equally popular, at least as regards the phrases that follow, is the concept of a generic arse: one's person, one's body, a use that originated in the mid-eighteenth century, as one highwayman, frustrated of his prey, remarked in Johnson's *History* of his profession (1734): 'I was as much plagu'd to take one William Ryland ... I was dangling after his Arse a Fortnight, without any Success.' Other definitions have included an unpleasant person, especially a fool (wherein, if such it was, lies my early encounter), or a worthless, unpleasant place.

In figurative uses arse can mean (originally in Australia) cheek, effrontery, luck and courage (which last works on the same pattern as the figurative, non-testicular **balls**). As **the arse** (and the **big A**) it means the sack, dismissal, though the enforced parting can be from a relationship as well as a job and usually appears as **get** or **give the** (**big**) **arse**. It can be a comparative: e.g. **cold as arse**. Derivatives include **arseness**, wilful stupidity, and **arsewise**, either back-to-front or ludicrous and wrong. An **arser** is a hunting or riding term that means a fall onto one's behind.

ARSING ABOUT

Arse can be found as a verb. The unadorned version variously means to reverse a vehicle, to push or shove, to drink or consume and, as in so many arse-related terms, to dismiss. To **arse about** is to turn round or to waste time, to wander idly or to fool around. To **arse it**, **arse out** or **arse off** are to leave at speed and to **arse up** is to ruin, to make a mess of. **Arsed** as an adjective means bothered or concerned, almost invariably as a negative: 'I can't be arsed'. It also means fed up and, as **arsed up**, confused. As a suffix it appears in Aelfric's dictionary and is spelt **earsode**. Since then it has been used either directly, as a description of someone's figure, thus **short-arsed**, **bare-arsed** or **hopper-arsed**, and the figurative **smart-arsed**, or as a figurative description of a type of person, e.g. **cheeky-arsed**, **hot-arsed** and **ragged-arsed**, in which form it echoes the far more widely used US qualifying suffix **-ass**.

To go back to first principles, the arse = buttocks definition gives various add-ons. The **arse-strings**, dating to the late sixteenth century, represent a metaphorical part of the body, supposedly holding the buttocks in place and related, though perhaps not in *Gray's Anatomy*, to the **twattling strings** (the sphincter); like them they can be 'bust' with horrible results. An **arse like a working bullock** is a large one, at least in New Zealand, while to **hang an arse** is to hang back, to be afraid to go forwards. To **give someone the arse**, i.e. to turn one's buttocks and thus one's back to them, is to treat with contempt, to reject. What one shows is one's **arse-end** (or **ass-end**), the rear, a phrase best known in the condemnatory **arse-end of the universe** or **of nowhere**, an especially godforsaken, unlovely spot. And while arsehole is dealt with below, one can usefully add the synonymous **arsehole of the universe** (or world, or creation). The first use – or near-use – appears to be a 1660 description of Holland as 'the Buttock of the world, full of veins and blood, but no bones in't', but given the title of the book in which this appears, *A Brief Character of the Low Countries*, it makes one suspect a laboured pun, **low countries** being another term for posterior not to mention vagina (**low** and **cunt**, geddit?). Perhaps its most apposite use is that of the chemist, writer and concentration camp survivor Primo Levi, who described Auschwitz, albeit in Latin but completely recognisably, as *anus mundi*.

MORE ARSE THAN A TOILET SEAT

Arsewipe (also a term of abuse) and **arsepaper** are lavatory paper, and **arsepapered** means thrown away. An **arsewiper**, like an **arselicker**, is a sycophant (and occasionally and literally, licker of the anus). This in turn gives **arselicking**, sycophantic or servile, and **arselick**, a toady. To **kiss someone's arse**, and such compounds as **arse-kisser**, are equally intimate, and equally grovelling, as is the idea of having one's nose up or in someone's arse. Long gone now is **arse-cooler**, the bustle on a mid-nineteenth century lady's dress. **My arse is dragging**, I'm exhausted, is simple enough – **my arse is a red cabbage** less so. This is another phrase of dismissal, and may refer to haemorrhoids (**arse-cabbage** or **arsegrapes**). Other anal adjuncts are **arsenuts**, faecal matter found clinging to the anal hairs and buttock cleft, and **arse-piss**, diarrhoea. Charming.

Neither one's arse nor one's elbow is a synonym for neither one thing nor another, and an inability to discern the buttocks from some otherwise obviously different object underpins a number of phrases. 'We're rednecks,' sang Randy Newman on his *Good Old Boys* album (1974), 'we can't tell our ass from a hole in the ground'. And that phrase, or others like it, have been around since the mid-nineteenth century. They include the suggestions that one doesn't know one's arse from a **hot rock**, an **adding machine**, an **avalanche**, **ice cream**, **third base** and, of course, **one's elbow**. A fool also **doesn't know if their arse is on fire**, and might **lose their arse if it were loose**. When one **can't see someone's arse for dust**, it means that they have left very swiftly.

The bandbox, a light cardboard box used to contain millinery and the like, is long gone, at least as a name, but it wouldn't have been very secure as a seat and **mine** or **my arse on a bandbox** implies that something offered is inadequate for the purposes required, i.e. 'that won't do'. **Not a sixpence to scratch one's arse with** meant absolutely impoverished; it does not seem to have been succeeded by a decimal version, but one can always opt for being **on the back** or **the bones of one's arse**, in both cases equating with poverty and lean-ness. For something to **be one's arse** implies that it will cause one trouble and lead to inevitable punishment, e.g. 'do that and it's your arse.' The offending posterior will, literally or otherwise, be kicked. To be **in someone's arse** is to nag or scold them; **up** someone's arse is literally to stand immediately behind them and thus figuratively to provide a source of irritation. To be **up one's own arse** is to be self-important, otherwise to **think the sun shines out of one's arse(hole)**, while the simple **up to one's arse** or **up to the arse (in)** is to be completely overwhelmed by.

Although the arse can be found as both vagina and penis, the sexual terms in which it appears tend to refer back to the basic rear end. To **give one's arse a salad** (in the early eighteenth century) was to have sexual intercourse outdoors; to **polish one's arse on the top sheet** was to have sexual intercourse, as the image implies, in the 'missionary' position; to **shake one's arse** is to move vigorously as in sexual intercourse or dancing. The nineteenth-century **arselins coup** combined arse with the suffix *-ling*, implying direction, and *coup*, a fall: it means intercourse and is something that a woman **gets**. A man on the other hand, if sufficiently successful, gets **more arse than a toilet seat** (as well as **more arse than a married cow playing snooker**). The female equivalent is **more pricks than a second-hard dartboard**.

HITCH-HIKERS ON THE HERSHEY HIGHWAY

The world of homosexuality, where amidst its other slang stereotypes the buttocks play so central a part, offers a number of terms. The **arse jockey**, **-shagger**, **-bender** (itself using **bender**, a gay man) and **-stabber** are all **hitch-hikers on the Hershey highway**; the **arse-wedge**, **-opener** and **-poker** represent the penis. The **arse** (**arsehole** and sometimes **anus**) **bandit**, perhaps the best known of all these, is another **turd-burglar**, and **arse-banditry** is generic for homosexuality or homosexual activities.

Those who take the passive role in anal intercourse **take it up the arse**, as well as the **arsehole** and **bum**. In figurative terms it means to be victimised, treated unfairly or harshly and as such parallels such terms as **fucked, screwed, shafted** and so on. One response is to **take the foot out of one's arse**, to rid oneself of ill treatment, of victimisation, exploitation. A **split-arse** was both a woman and a gay man, while a **split-arse mechanic** was a prostitute.

The buttocks provide further compounds: **arseache** (and **pain in the arse**), when not literal, is a general insult or a bad temper; an **arse-kicker** is an aggressive, violent person though, adopting the sexual senses, it is also a successful seducer. An **arse-crawler** is a groveller, as is an **arse-creeper**; both terms can work as nouns with an -er suffix. An **arsepiece** is an all-purpose insult. The seventeenth century's picturesque (and repellent) **arse-worm** is another term for a sycophant, but in this case one of small stature. **Arse-rugs** are trousers (from one of two meanings of standard English *rug*, a covering or a coarse material more usually used for cloaks). **Arsepants**, however, is not a noun but an adverb and means slyly or covertly. Another adverb, **arse-splittingly**, implies excess. During the Second World War, Londoners attempted to mitigate the menace of these prototype missiles by nicknaming the German V-2 rockets **arse-alights**, from the flames that poured from their tail.

MORE ARSE THAN CLASS

A number of phrases imply a state of being back-to-front or head-over-heels: **arse about face**, **arse over apex**, **arse over appetite**, or over **ears, head, kick, kite** (or simply **k**), **teakettle, tip** or **tit**, and **turkey**. **Arse over header** is not quite the same: as Australian rhyming slang, it refers to the Varsovienna or Varsovienne (from Varvosie, the French name for Warsaw), a dance that had been created in France and was said to resemble some of the Polish national dances. **Arse up** is another variety of upside down, but **arse upwards** means lucky, often as **rise** or

raise arse upwards, to be lucky. Apparently getting up from a fall in this manner was believed to be lucky, and it certainly gives the punning **Mr R. Suppards**, a very lucky man. Whether Mr S. has **more arse than a paddock-full of cows** (which also puns, this time on the standard English *cheek*), and is otherwise very cheeky, is unknown – but given his good fortune it may be assumed that he has **more arse than class**, more luck or effrontery than style. Slightly expanded terms that mean much the same are **arsey-boo** (boo being an abbreviation of **buggered**) and **arsey-tarsey** (which may imply a confusion of the arse and **tarse**, i.e. the penis), both antipodean terms for being in a state of chaos or incoherence, or just plain wrong. Best-known is **arsey-varsey** (also **arsey-versey**, **arsy-versy**, **assy-turvy**), which models itself on standard English *vice-versa*; prior to the mid-sixteenth century it too was standard. As well as upside-down (one can fall arsey-varsey), before and after 1700 it also meant contrary, perverse and preposterous.

More luck comes with **arsey**, **arsie** or **arsy**, which term is used in Australia. This is an abbreviation of **tin-arsed**, itself from **tin-arse** (or **tin-back** or **-bum**), used to describe an extremely fortunate person and referring to **tin**, meaning money, though there is an element of the metallic tin as something that will protect one (however marginally) from harm.

PLAYING THE ARSE

There are a profusion of other phrases. To **catch arse** is to find it hard to make enough money to live; the Australian phrase to **die in the arse** is to be struck rigid, motionless, usually through terror. To **make an arse of** is to make someone ridiculous, while to **play the arse** is to play the fool and to deceive. To **– the arse off** is a general intensifier implying energy, usually sexual, e.g. screw the arse off, as is the similarly variable **– someone's arse off**, e.g. tear someone's arse off. More aggression can be found in **kick someone's arse** or **kick the arse out of**, to surpass, to defeat comprehensively, and **knock someone's arse in**, to defeat in an argument or a fight. Still arguing, we find **put someone on the arse,** to criticise or berate, and the phrase **shut your face and give your arse a chance,** or the simpler **shut your arse!,** both of which are ways of telling someone to shut up. To **carry one's arse** is to leave, and to **bring one's arse to an anchor** to come to a halt, to sit down. To **do one's arse** is to bet heavily and unsuccessfuly, hence to lose all one's money.

Like its 'filthy' peers, arse naturally comes in handy in a variety of exclamations. On the whole they all emphasise rejection, dismissal and disdain. They include **lick my arse!** (long preceding Bart Simpson's **lick my shorts!**), **dry your arse!,** stop whining! stop complaining!, **not on your arse!,** no way! on no account!, and **in your arse! My arse!,** which has implied contempt since the seventeenth century (in 1679 a witness at the Old Bailey explained how 'He replied, then you are Rogues: Upon which one Jenkins, somewhat scurrilously, return'd a foolish ill-bred Phrase, Mine Ar— upon you.'). Similarly dated and similarly contemptuous is **my arse to … !** (or **for** or **on …!**). **Devil my arse!** is an Irishism, as is **my arse and Katy Barry!,** an expression of disbelief which commemorates the keeper of a celebrated shebeen, an illicit ale house, in 1930s Dublin. **Your arse!** is another way of demonstrating the same lack of interest, while **what, why, where** and **how the arse** are all ways of intensifying a basic query.

FROM ARSEHOLE TO BREAKFAST TIME

And where is arse, there too must be **arseholes.** Amongst the many early glossaries that the Victorian philologist Thomas Wright included in his *Volume of Vocabularies* (1857) is a fourteenth-century example that like Aelfric translated Latin into Anglo-Saxon; in this instance Latin's *podex* becomes **arcehoole.** Thus it has stayed, meaning the anus, the end or back of something and, as noted above, the least appetising, poorest, most rundown and possibly dangerous area of a city or town or place. And like arse, it can mean courage. Its derivatives include **arseholed**, very drunk or in other contexts sacked from one's job – to **arsehole** being to dismiss (the image being one of being 'kicked out'); **arseholey**, sycophantic; and **arseholishness**, acting like an idiot and/or being annoying. **Arseholes!** has meant rubbish! nonsense! since the late nineteenth century, while **my arseholes!**, another exclamation of disdain and arrogant contempt, is two centuries older.

To **arsehole crawl** is to grovel unashamedly, to play the sycophant, giving such compounds as **arsehole-crawler** and **-creeper**. According to Peta Fordham, writing on the UK underworld in 1972, 'Anglo-Saxon ruderies are rare in the underworld, which mostly uses rhyming slang or gypsy expressions … [Arsehole creeper] is the greatest word of condemnation in underworld parlance.' The **arsehole polisher** is another crawler, while the **arsehole perisher** (from standard English *perish*, to suffer the cold) is a short jacket. To **give someone arseholes** or **the arsehole** is to infuriate or to attack verbally. To be **unable to know if one's arsehole is bored or punched** is to be an absolute fool, in other words **stupid as arseholes**. **From arsehole to breakfast time** or **-table** implies utter confusion as well as meaning all the way, all the time and completely. To **talk through one's arsehole** is to talk nonsense, while to **tear one's arsehole out** is to work furiously. The promise to **tear someone a new arsehole** is a violent threat, while to be **up arsehole street** (presumably running hard by **shit creek**) is to be in a far from enviable situation. Finally, a pair of comparatives: the seventeenth-century **white as midnight's arsehole**, totally black, utterly dark, and Australia's blithely non-PC **dark as an abo's arsehole**, a description of a moonless night.

As noted above, **ass** is synonymous with arse and has been America's spelling of choice for many years. Space, sadly, renders it impossible to probe ass to the extent it might require, but let us at least venture a few terms, at the head of which is the notional superlative: **assholingest**. An **asshole-breath** is a person to avoid, although different standards pertain to an **asshole buddy** (or **A-hole buddy** or even plain **asshole** – but check that context!) who is an extremely close friend; if there once were gay connotations, they seem to be carefully overlooked. That said, the phrase maintains a gay-only use: normally heterosexual men who, deprived for whatever reason of women, enjoy anal intercourse, both as an active or passive partner.

Asshole also provides a few phrases that its UK cousin has overlooked: to **break out into assholes** or to **fall through one's own asshole** is to become terrified, to be extremely surprised or utterly shocked. To **have a paper asshole** is to be a weakling or coward or to talk excessively, especially when that talk is meaningless. To **keep a tight asshole** evokes the propensity of intense fear to loosen one's bowels and means to maintain emotional control (unsurprisingly it was coined by the military). To **lock assholes** or **asses** is to fight, as is to **snap assholes**. **Out the asshole** (or **ass**) is a general intensifier, i.e. blatantly, excessively, totally, reprehensibly, in large quantities. **Up the asshole** implies involvement to the greatest extent. To **not know one's asshole from one's piehole** is to be stupid and, finally, one who **thinks their asshole squirts perfume** has a high (but quite unjustifiable) view of their own abilities.

B

IS FOR

BOLLOCKS

OR

BALLOCKS

OR

BALLYX BOLIX OR BOLLUX
BOLLIX BOLLOX

NOT TO MENTION

BALLS

Among the various euphemisms used to sidestep what would otherwise be termed 'dirty words', is the adjective 'Anglo-Saxon'. Whether Britain's eighth-century conquerors thought of their Teutonic tongue as especially coarse did not, one imagines, concern them then, or the historians later. And certainly their saga of Beowulf, as so far translated, has yet to reveal much naming of naughty bits alongside all the hacking and slaying.

But the idea of that language as 'plain, unvarnished, forthright' (OED) remains a given. George Orwell, for instance, was a great champion of the idea that Latinisms only over-embellished one's language: good solid Anglo-Saxon was what was needed. Some would agree, but now when 'Anglo-Saxon' is linked to 'language' it has come usually to imply obscenity. Thus a report of 1927: 'Several Laborites were suspended in the House of Commons ... to the accompaniment of the hurling of bald Anglo-Saxon epithets traditionally classed as unparliamentary.' Even if, given the all-embracing linguistic gelding that underpins 'unparliamentary language', one suspects that these were still some way from hardcore. Nonetheless the idiom, and the term, remains: usually as a slightly shamefaced excuse.

And in the case of **bollocks**, it's true. Going back a millennium to one Abbot Aelfric, who in 1000 was compiling an Anglo-Saxon/Latin glossary, there it is. Latin: *testiculi* – Anglo-Saxon: *beallucas*. The case rests. As for bollocks (or **ballocks**, be my guest), like so many terms relating to the testicles its origins lie in the simpler **ball** plus in this instance the suffix *-ock*, which means 'little'. It is thus linked to **stone** which, with examples reaching back to the 1100s, is the earliest word for ... bollocks. Not to mention a variety of slang equivalents, such as **acorns**, **apples**, **bangers**, **clackers**, **clappers**, **marbles**, **pebbles**, **nuts**, **rocks** and **swingers**. One might even add **frick and frack**, echoic of the 'balls' knocking together. But the original Frick and Frack sported the rest of their bodies too, as a 1920s–30s Swiss comedy skating team who performed to vast acclaim in the US and Europe. (Frick (Werner Groebli) and Frack (Hansreudi Mauch) were famous for a routine where they would put the heels of their skates together, bend their knees and skate in large circles with their bodies leaning outwards. Their choice of names came from Frick, a Swiss village, and frack, the frock-coat worn by Mauch on the ice.) Nor are they only balls: the term is found to describe two inseparable people, or a pair of fools.

THE DOG'S BOLLOCKS

Bollocks are unsurprisingly a slang staple. Other than the obvious, it can mean nonsense, a clergyman (i.e. he who talks it), a confused or stupid person or be a term of affection and, in Ireland, of malice ('a right old **bollix**'). Like stones, bollocks can mean courage. To **drop a bollock** is to blunder; to **do one's bollocks** is to make a great effort; to **have one's brains in one's bollocks** is to be particularly dumb. On the other hand, one who **has his bollocks in the right place** is an admirable figure, deserving of praise. **Ballocks in brackets** is a bow-legged man. A **bollocks worker** is overbearingly unpleasant. **Bishop's bollocks** are the number 88, perhaps the top halves of the eights represent his well-fed stomach – or is that, as another clerical phrase has it, **all gas and gaiters**?

In standard English, compounds include **bollock-hafted**, a knife, otherwise known as the less than appealing **bollock knife**, which has a handle with a knob. (Terry Pratchett fans will recall that fine old refrain, 'A wizard's staff has a knob on the end'.) **Bollockwort** is a variety of orchid, which plays on a number of terms based on the Greek *orchis*, testicle (thus *orchidectomy*, castration by a flowerier name); **bollock grass** is another, in this case one that has tubers that look like testicles.

Best-known of all bollocks are the **dog's bollocks** and **bollock-naked**. The former, describing something outstandingly good (though bollocks alone knows why – popular etymology suggests the phrase **sticks out like a dog's bollocks**) came on stream around 1920 when it meant 'something obvious'. Today's meaning, of excellence, is a 1980s coinage. Of somewhat older vintage is **bollock-naked**, which may be expanded as **stark bollock-naked**, **stark bollick naked**, **stark bollux naked**, **starbolic naked**, **starko-bollocko**, **stark rollock naked** and even **starbolic**. It can certainly be found in James Joyce's *Ulysses* (1922). There's even a very early example, although it's very likely euphemistic, from a poem entitled 'Fryar and Boye', dated around 1660: 'Some in their shirts, some in their smockes, / & some starke belly naked.'

BALL GAMES

And then there is (or are) **balls**. Obvious in its etymology, the term was coined, or at least first noted, around 1500 in a Scottish 'flyting', a kind of poetic insult competiton (the distant ancestor, no doubt, of today's 'dirty dozens', not to mention the 'dissing' that can be found in a variety of rap lyrics): 'Haill, forever senyeour! thy bawis hingis throw thy breik', or to bring it up to date, 'your balls are hanging out of your trousers.' Setting testicles aside, balls can mean the female breasts, nonsense, a blunder, courage (and these days women can **have balls** too) and nothing at all ('What did you get?' 'Balls.') And like the similar use of **arse**, among others, one can **work one's balls off** or indeed **knock** or **kick the balls off** someone else.

When it comes to compounds and phrases, balls **knocks the bollocks off** bollocks. Like the rest of a man's genitalia, they're continually under threat from **ball-breakers**, **–crushers**, **–cutters** and **–tearers**, all of which are of course dominating women who 'emasculate' their partner, usually a husband. (Her genitals are of course made of sterner stuff, and he is **pussy-whipped**.) That said, all those **ball-busting bitches** can be rendered gender-free, with the alternative definition of all these terms as daunting and demeaning tasks, usually physical. Nor does **ballsache**, to whinge, have any sexual link. And man is not wholly finished: the **ball-clanker** boasts, probably without much justification, of his sexual conquests of amorous girls who are **swinging on his balls**. To **ball slap** is to have sex, while **balls-ass** and **ballsy** mean tough and macho. To **go balls-out** is to commit oneself unreservedly. Like the 'senyeour' above, this may mean a man having his **wedding tackle** hanging out, but **balls to that**. He's a real man and certainly not **ball-less** nor yet **one-ball** and, heaven forfend, an impotent **dry-ball**.

ALL BALLS AND
BANG-YOUR-ARSE

There are many phrases inspired by balls. To **have balls on one like a scoutmaster**, popular since the 1930s, means to have large testicles; the link is obviously to a stereotypically paedophile occupation, but is there any proof? It did not, one imagines, offer a badge. **All balls and bang-your-arse** embellishes the balls-as-nonsense meaning; to **get one's balls in an uproar** offers an alternative to those twisted knickers; to **have someone by the balls** means to establish one's complete control, as does the promise to **have someone's balls for breakfast** (not to mention **sauteed**, and the same buffet can also include **nuts** and **butt**), while the threat **I'll wear your balls for a necktie** may be anatomically challenging and maybe less than ideal catwalk fodder, but the meaning is quite clear. Nor have the unfortunate gonads done with suffering; like some menu of sado-masochistic indulgences, one can **get one's balls off**, achieve orgasm, **have one's balls in the fire**, be in serious trouble, **have one's balls twisted**, be stupid but outspoken and **have one's balls under one's chin**, be terrified. To **put someone's balls in a knot** is to irritate, while to put them **in the fire** is to excite or agitate. If, after all that, one has **swollen balls** it's hardly surprising, but the phrase, in US prisons, means to lust after. A case, perhaps, of **blue balls**, intense sexual frustration, although it can also refer, one trusts not as a literal description, to certain varieties of veneral disease.

Like the orchidaceous scoutmaster, the **man with the fuzzy balls**, an African–American usage of the 1950s, has earned himself a place in language. He is a white person, and by extension accomplished and expert. Why this should be is unproven, but it is worth noting that the fuzzy has been put forward as the root of **fuzz**, meaning a policeman (although **fuss**, as in 'he makes a … ' is equally feasible).

Paradoxically, **balls-to-the-wall** – meaning all-out, no-holds-barred – does not, for all that it really ought to, come from what rhyming slang terms the **Alberts** (Albert Halls) or even the **betty swallocks**. Its origins are explained by Oxford lexicographer Jesse Sheidlower: 'The expression comes from the world of military aviation. In many planes, control sticks are topped with a ball-shaped grip. One such control is the throttle – to get maximum power you push it all the way forward, to the front of the cockpit, or firewall (so-called because it prevents an engine fire from reaching the rest of the plane). Another control is the joystick – pushing it forward sends a plane into a dive. So, literally pushing the balls to the (fire)wall would put a plane into a maximum-speed dive, and figuratively going balls to the wall is doing something all-out, with maximum effort.'

RED SAILS IN THE SUNSET

And after balls, **blood**. And not just any blood, chaps: chance'd be a fine thing. What's the line? 'A bloody waste of fucking time.' 'Open Dracula's lunchbox.' Ho, ho, bleedin' ho. Because it's that time of the month, it's that most literal of loony (or rather lunar) tunes, it's menstruation.

And while blood can be blue, not down this alley it isn't: the word is red. **The reds**, **red Mary** (or **bloody Mary**), the **red tide**, the **crimson wave** (which the woman **surfs**) or the **cardinal**, who **is at home** (presumably adorned by his traditional red hat and vestments). The toothsome **cherry pie** for once sidesteps the usual cherry–virgin link and merely accentuates the colour (**pie**, of course, already meaning vagina). The **blob**, i.e. of blood, plus **on the blob** or **on a streak** (again of blood), means menstruating. The **communists** are of course 'the reds' as well, and the otherwise obscure **flying baker** refers to nautical signalling where B, the flag signifying the second letter of the alphabet, is red. And among biker gangs the **red wings** are awarded to those who achieve cunnilingus with a menstruating woman (with, natch, your mates gathered round agog). Were the woman black, then the wings would be **brown** ones. And on what their fans would doubtless consider a more charming note is **red sails in the sunset**, originally a 1935 song-title and as such a hit for Bing Crosby, Nat King Cole and others of the crooner elite. Then back down the market, or at least up the match, where **the reds are playing at home** (the game being **blood sports**). A menstruating woman is a **red dog**, or a **red knight on a white horse** (i.e. the tampon or sanitary pad).

RAGS, FLAGS AND THE BIG X

The need for tampons, pads or towels gives a variety of central terms, all based on rags and flags. The **rag** or **red rag** (otherwise the tongue) or **fanny rag** all represent a menstrual cloth or sanitary towel and **flash the red rag** means to menstruate. **OTR** means **on the rag**, which means both menstruating and irritated, testy or bad-tempered (and need not apply only to women). Similarly, to **have the rag on** is both to be menstruating and to act foolishly or eccentrically, or to be annoyed. To **share the rag** is to be hostile, to place blame on someone else.

And with rag, thus with **flag**, another term for the sanitary towel. The **flag-day** is the menstrual period, **flagging** is menstruation and to **fly the flag** is to menstruate (an earlier use referred to a prostitute, walking the streets looking for trade). If the **flag is up**, or **in port** or **out**, or **the danger signal is up**, she **has** or **has put the flags out** and **it looks like a wet weekend** –

he can forget about sex while she's still on a **beno**, be no fun that is.

Wet weekends being what they are – and they can sometimes go on for a **wallflower week** – she'll be staying in: a good thing since there seems to be a whole queue of visitors, all signifying **that time of the month**, starting with the simple **visitor** itself. Then comes **my (little) friend**, who seems to rejoice in such names as **A.B.** ('Annie Brown'), **John**, **George** (who **is calling**), **Tommy** and **Monica**. **Grandma**, **granny** or even **grandma George** are among the party – **granny grunt** personifies a painful period – but it's aunts who seem to have the monopoly of the door bell. There's simply **aunt** or **auntie** (who **is coming to town**), **Auntie Jane**, **Aunt Rose**, **Aunt Flo** (who **is visiting**, as are **Aunt Lilian** and **Aunt Minnie**), **Aunt Jody** (who **has come with her suitcase**) and my **red-headed aunt** (who **has just arrived**). It is also possible to **entertain the general**. And last but not least to knock at the door is the **captain**, who would seem to be Greek (no, not that way) since **the captain is at home** or **the captain is come** both play on the Greek *catamenia*, monthly. The regularity of periods also offers the **monthlies** or **monthly bill**, **old faithful** and **the dog days** or **the big X**, which is the way in which they are marked on the calendar. And when one is thus **poorly** or suffering from **d.a.s** (domestic afflictions) you're **back in the saddle again**.

WHEN THE RED IS OVER THE PINK, GO FOR THE BROWN

There is a **flood** (i.e. a heavy flow) of euphemisms relating to menstruation: all those visitors aside, a menstruating woman can be **road-making**, **so** or **so-so**, **squiffy** (more usually drunk), have **fallen off the roof**, be **out of order**, **up on the blocks** (hands up all those who describe their car as 'she'), suffering the **whatsits** or the ultra-genteel (not to mention dated) **flowers** or **roses** or an encounter with **mother nature**. The period itself can be the blasphemous **holy week** and while we're keeping it biblical, perhaps best known of all, **the curse** (of Eve, that is).

The tampons and towels have their own, linked, lingo. The **coyote** or **jelly sandwich** gets us back to blood, as does **jam rag**, where jam is the blood, **jamming**, menstruation, and **show** (i.e. the blood upon it). A tampon is a **snatch-mouse** (**snatch**, vagina, plus its string 'tail'), while **snatch pad** and **mouse mattress** are pads. A **hammock** is a sanitary towel as applied to a 'lazy cunt' – 'lazy' because it is not available for intercourse. The image of the tampon as a plug gives **spark-plug** and the rhyming **little brown jug**. Other towels or pads include the **submarine** ('it goes down in the wet') **brillo pad**, **saddle-blanket**, **manhole cover**, **diaper**, **clout**, **window-blind** and what might be termed a less than predictable use of **Teddy Bear**. A pair of figurative uses give two of the Caribbean's most venomous descriptions; the **bambaclaat**, **bumbo–claat**, **bombo–claat**, **bumbo–cloth** or **bumbo-cloth** – literally the **bum cloth**, the **blood claat** (the 'blood-cloth') – and the **raas–claat**, which has nothing to do with Selassie-I, but means **arse–cloth**. The practical use of such 'cloths' gives a variety of phrases; **ride a/the cotton horse**, **a/the white horse**, **the cotton pony**, **the rag** (or **wear the rag**) and **ride the red horse**.

The menstrual blood is also seen as the basis of some merry sexual romps. At least by some. When **there's a letter in the post office** our young lovers have the opportunity of enjoying a **strawberry kiss** or **strawberry Sunday** (surely **sundae**), both terms for cunnilingus or intercourse with a menstruating woman, while the **cherry blossom kiss** restricts the action to oral sex.

So there we are. All you wanted to know ... and don't say slang is just a bunch of words and phrases – there's lifestyle advice too. As the lads say down the Sheffield Crucible: **when the red is over the pink, go for the brown**. Thank you, and good-night.

C IS FOR CUNT

OR COYNTE

CUNTIE, CUNNY, OR QUAINT

COCK

O f all of George Carlin's canonical list (see Introduction, p.8) only one word failed to make the chronological cut, not moving from the middle English of pre-1500 to the 'modern' English that succeeded it. **Cunt** persisted, but now only in taboo. It may have been, as Eric Partridge noted in 1931, six years before he entered it into his own dictionary, albeit bowdlerised of its vowel, 'a very frequently used word – one indeed used by a large proportion, though not the majority, of the white population of the British Empire' and as such 'a basic part of the English language', but upfront and accessible it definitely wasn't.

Predictably it had been excluded from mainstream dictionaries until the OED supplement of 1972 embraced it. Despite rumours to the contrary, this was a first: Sir James Murray, the OED's initial editor, had no more had the word researched, only to be stymied by the puritanism of late-Victorian England, than he did **fuck**. (**Prick**, on the other hand, presented no such problem; nor did, inter alia, **shit**.) Following the original OED's lead, other, lesser dictionaries on both sides of the Atlantic showed themselves equally coy and many otherwise authoritative American tomes, hamstrung either by the religious right or the politically correct left, have yet to break the taboo. The canting glossaries of the sixteenth to eighteenth centuries sidestepped it – justifiably, as it was hardly an exclusively criminal term – but in 1788 Francis Grose, in the second edition of his *Classical Dictionary of the Vulgar Tongue*, offered 'C—t, a nasty word for a nasty thing.' He had, on the other hand, blithely included 'cunny-thumbed' a few entries earlier. He suggested roots in the Greek *konnos* and the Latin *cunnus*, and lists the French synonym *con*. Therein lies a paradox: cunt can mean a fool and so can *con*, but while the former remains taboo, *con* and its derivative *connerie* (meaning foolishness or idiocy), and such phrases as *ne fais pas le con* (be reasonable), are almost standard French, certainly uncommented-on colloquialisms. Nationalist clichés are unavoidable; we shall resist them – though one might note that in gendered French, the female genitals are labelled 'le', i.e. masculine.

FROM GROPECUNTELANE TO VAL CAVA

Once the OED sets out to include cunt, the first use it can find appears c.1230, when **Gropecuntelane** is listed among the streets that made up the 'stews' (brothel area) of Cheapside. Given the primary commodity of the area, it must be assumed that the term was already in general use. It would also appear from subsequent early citations that the term, while vulgar, was descriptive rather than obscene. The medieval surgeon Lanfranc, for instance, used it while writing his *Chirurgia Magna* on surgery in 1363. But by the end of the fifteenth century cunt was unacceptable and two centuries later it was deemed legally obscene, and to print the word in full rendered one liable to prosecution. Its most notorious appearance in the dock came in 1960 in the trial of *Lady Chatterley's Lover*. It appears in that list of linguistic shame trotted out by the prosecution counsel, as he urged the jury to hold hidden from 'your wives and servants' a book that contained: '30 "fucks or fuckings", 14 "cunts", 13 "balls", six each of "shit" and "arse", four "cocks" and three "piss".' It has yet, if ever, to return to grace. Even rap, hardly one for tugging its lyrical skirt over its knees, seems to opt for 'pussy' or the dehumanising 'it'.

As Grose suggested, the word can be traced back to the Greek, although Partridge disputes whether *konnos* – a trinket, a beard or the wearing of the hair in a tuft – is actually linked to the Latin *cunnus*, which meant both vagina and, like such metonymous English terms as **crack, slit** and **pussy**, the woman (especially if seen as promiscuous) who possesses it. More likely Greek roots are *kusos* and *kusthos*, which are both related to the earlier Sanskrit *cushi*, meaning ditch. *Cunnus* itself, setting a pattern for its descendant, was already outlawed as obscene in

Rome. Horace used it, Cicero did not. While the French, more heavily influenced by Latin, have *con* (and the Spanish, *coño*), with its obvious links to *cunnus*, the English 'cunt' or *cunte*, as found in Middle English, takes its immediate inspiration from a variety of German (*Kunte*) and Scandinavian (*kunta, kunte*) terms. It would appear, in this form, to be a combination of the ultimate root *cu* (which also lies at the basis of **cow**), which appears to imply quintessential femininity, and the *nt* of the European synonyms. One can also note **val cava**, 'used', as the late sixteenth-century lexicographer John Florio explained in 1598, 'by Boccaccio for a woman's private parts, a hollow cavity or valley'. On that basis there may also be a link to Welsh *cym* (pronounced 'coom'), a valley.

One of the charms of the great obscenities is their versatility. They're just so useful, so pliable, so ready for exploitation, and cunt is no exception. As well as the obvious, the word denotes a woman, whether derogatively or when considered purely as a sex object. It can also encompass commercial sex and prostitution. Camp gay use turns the physiology back to front, using the word to mean anus and/or buttocks. It can be the crease inside the elbow into which one injects a narcotic or, as **cunt splice** (latterly reformed as **cut splice**) a form of knot based

on making a vagina-shaped hole in the rope. Following Captain Grose, the 'nasty thing' can extend to cover any infuriating object, often mechanical, or something very difficult or unpleasant to do or achieve. It can apply to any person or indeed thing, and by no means always negatively, although the implication is that a non-vaginal cunt is a fool at best and probably a seriously unpleasant or undesirable individual or thing. Finally, like a variety of its peers, it can be used to mean the 'essence', the 'daylights' ('knock the cunt out of') and stand in as a synonym for 'damn'.

TALKING CUNT

That's the noun. Alongside it are such derivations as **cunt-struck**, obsessed with sex; **cuntish**, either stupid, unpleasant or effeminate; the insults **cunting** and **cuntless**; **cunt-eyed**, used of one with squinting eyes; and the unashamedly misogynistic **cunt-bitten**, a sixteenth-century term meaning syphilitic. Cunt's many blends stick firmly to the genital. They are, one might say, merely descriptive, but not since the fifteenth century. Thus the penis is variously a **cunt-buster**, **cunt-hook** (though cunt-hooks are also fingers, as are **cunt-scratchers**), **cunt-plugger** (hence **cunt-plugging**, intercourse), **cunt-rammer**, **cunt-stopper** or **cunt-stretcher**. The female pubic hair is a **cunt-curtain**, **cunt-fringe**, **cunt-rug**, **cunt-wig** or **hair** (and a **cunt's hair** is an infinitesimally tiny distance). A **cunt-chaser**, **cunt-hound**, **cunt-hunter** or **cunt-man** is a womaniser. A **cunt-teaser**, the male equivalent of the better-known **cockteaser**, excites a woman but – albeit implausibly – stops short of intercourse. A **cunt-rag** is a sanitary towel, while a **cunt-swab** is a pair of knickers.

As for the rest, it's the same sad old story. He fancied her younger sister, and tried **talking cunt** (nudge-nudge, wink-wink) to her but as they say, **that's not cunt it's peehole** (she's under-age) and it all went **cunt-up**. Too **cunted** to see straight he's caught in a **cunt-collar**, trapped by the elder's overwhelming sexuality. Back in his **cunt-wagon**, a flashy car designed to ensnare the impressionable opposite sex, he can tell she's turned on by her **cunt-stand** (the antonym of her partner's **cock-stand** – even if both seem irretrievably Victorian) and her stimulated vagina exudes **cunt juice**, moistening her **cunt-lips** (the labia), especially after attentions from his **cunt-tickler**, his moustache. But he proves to be a total **cuntprick** and indeed a **cunthead**, neither to be admired, and what's worse, a **cunt-pensioner**, a pimp. Not only that but he turns out to be a **cunt-starver**, in other words denies her maintenance payments as proscribed by Australia's Deserted Wives & Children's Act, known in that land of directness as the **Cunt Act**. 'Stick it up your cunt' he sneers, **coming the old cunt**, and she finds a new life with her girlfriends, a pair of **cunt-sucking cunt-munchers**, who initiate her into the delights of mutual **cunt-lapping**. Alone, wearing his **cunt-hat** (a trilby, and so called either from its distinctive crease or from its being made of 'felt'; a similar pun underpins the uses of **hat** to mean vagina, both being 'frequently felt'), and bedevilled by his foul **cunt-breath** he has a single recourse: the **cunt-book**, a piece of porn.

COCKS OF BRASS

And **cock**. A cock is a penis, as is well known and is discussed below, but a **cock** is also a cunt. Not a lot of people know that. Or not a lot outside the African–American community and the southern states of God's Own Country. This vaginal cock, to be sure, lacks the pedigree of its masculine counterpart, but it's put in the mileage. Its origins lie in the French *coquille*, a cockleshell, which it allegedly resembles. Like many such slang 'resemblances' it requires a degree of delusion, but no matter. It first appears in the 1830s, hence these lines in a piece of smutty 1833 doggerel 'The Turncock': 'Her husband used to do her jobs, but since he closed life's business, / Her cock had been neglected, which oft caused her much uneasiness.' It remains wholly current, appearing in a variety of contemporary rap lyrics. Indeed, it is the male version which seems bizarre to southerners: for instance in Gini Sykes's *8 Ball Chicks* (1997) one finds a group of harder-than-nails gang girls sniggering over so exotic a usage.

The female cock gives a number of compounds. The **cock-hammer** or **cock-opener** is a penis, and cock easily substitutes for cunt in **cock book, cock hound** and **cock wagon**. To **cock it up** is for a woman to offer herself for sex. **Long-cock** refers to a large vagina and is seen as an insult. **Cock pluck** is to stimulate the female genitals, after which, if things work out, one **gets some cock**. The **cock show** is a striptease.

But for the remainder of the English-speaking world, a cock is a penis. 'Pistol's cock is up and flashing fire will follow.' That Shakespeare, laugh a line, eh? Not to mention those laboured nineteenth-century vocational rhymes: 'Here's to the plumbers, / Who are the chaps for a lass, / For their balls are of copper, / And their cocks are of brass.' The root is simple: Latin's *cuccus*, the male domestic fowl; in standard English *cock* represents any object that resembles a cock's head. As far as its use as a sexual term is concerned, this cock mixes the basic image of the cock as rooster (itself a nineteenth-century US euphemism) and the cock's head seen as a tap-like shape, this secondary aspect emphasised by its function in 'pouring' semen (or urine). Tabooed subsequent to Queen Victoria's coronation, it has yet to return to the mainstream. As Partridge put it in 1937, 'always standard English but since 1830 a vulgarism' and the OED (in the late nineteenth century) notes 'the current name among the people, but, *pudoris causa*, not admissible in polite speech or literature'.

ALL COCK AND RIBS LIKE A MUSTERER'S DOG

Pudoris causa (for modesty's sake) or not, cock remains one of the primary terms in the slang lexicon. It means the penis, man as a sexual being, and man as a plucky fighter or an expert. For a while, when Tyburn's gruesome 'triple tree' held sway over villainy, it defined one who died bravely on the gallows. It means the clitoris, often seen as an attenuated penis (and as such has no link to the vaginal cock), as well as intercourse and the moment of orgasm. In figurative uses it covers a show-off, a self-promoter, an offensive man and one who is easy to sponge on, especially one who buys more than his necessary share in the pub.

But it is as the penis that it bestrides the slang vocabulary. **All cock and ribs like a musterer's dog** is Antipodean for a very thin person; to **step on one's cock** (also **trip over one's cock**) is to get oneself into serious trouble, to make a major blunder; to **have one's cock on the block**, **get one's cock caught in one's zipper** and the terse **cock up**, mean much the same. **That cock won't fight** (as well as **that cat won't fight** and **that dog won't hunt**) is a phrase used to demolish the previous statement – 'that won't do', 'you must be joking', 'I'm not having that'. **Beat the cock off**, **give someone the cock**, **pull someone's cock** and **put the cock to**, all offer variations on the basic theme: give someone a hard time. And the cock must encompass sex, as in **cop a cock**, to fellate; **cream** or **pull one's cock**, to masturbate; **go cock-fighting** and **have a bit of cock**, to have sexual intercourse. To **cock-block** is to ruin another man's sexual activities by stealing his woman or interrupting his seduction.

UP COCK ALLEY, DOWN COCK LANE

And where comes the cock, there lies the vagina, the **cock-trap**, **cock-pit**, **cock-inn** and **cock-holder**. And **cock alley** and **cock lane**, which imply, a 'road', like many vagina words – in the case of the latter reinforced by the real-life Cock Lane (near London's Smithfield Market and St Paul's Cathedral), which in the fourteenth century was the only street where London's prostitutes were licensed to ply their trade in public. The Great Fire was supposed to have stopped at its junction with Giltspur Street, while in February 1762 thousands of the curious (including Dr Johnson, the duke of York and other grandees) flocked to number 33 Cock Lane to hear the scratchings and knockings of the alleged 'Cock Lane Ghost'. It proved, surprise, surprise, to be a hoax, even if it entered popular mythology, appearing in Dickens, Melville and most fittingly Charles Maclean's *Catalogue of Extraordinary Popular Delusions* (1841).

Returning to anatomy, the **cock socket** is the anus. A **cock manger**, meanwhile, is a urinal (Pony Club members may best appreciate the supposed similarity). **Cock puke**, **sauce** and **snot** all mean semen; **cock cheese** (which rarefied dairy product is also found as **dick-cheese, knob-cheese, knob yoghurt** and **prick cheese**) is smegma. **Cock rot** is VD and the man who treats it is a **cock doctor**. **Cock-rotted** means broken down or useless – the clap is not obligatory. The literal translation of **cock-bawd** is 'man-whore', but she's all-woman, either a madam or simply top of her game. A **cocktail** also meant a working girl until around 1940; after 1970 too, but the 'girl' was now a boy who catered to his gay peers. Equally gay, the **cock-diesel** or **cockstrong** is a straight piece of beefcake, or his gay equivalent. The **diesel** appears to be that used for his sapphic sister, implying the solidity and power of Rudolf Diesel's invention. A foolish young man is **cock-brained**, in contrast to his sophisticated cousin a **cock-artist**; a nervous young woman is **cock-shy**, while a sexual zealot is **cock-struck**. A fellatrix is a **cock-smoker**, **cock-scratchers** are hands and **cock-knockers** and **cock-monkeys** are unpleasant, worthless people, though the first can also mean a gay man.

Finally comes the punning **cock ale**, that is, ale mixed with the jelly or minced meat of a boiled cock, plus a few other ingredients. Take, suggests a seventeenth-century writer, 'eight Gallons of Ale; take a Cock and boil him well.' Predictably it is seen as an aphrodisiac. Equally predictably it was probably the alcohol, not the boiled bird, that did the trick.

D

IS FOR

DiRTY

AND

DISEASE

Like Shakespearean humans, some words are born dirty, others become so and some have their dirtiness thrust upon them. Let us take **dirty words** as such as read: they are, after all, the topic and content of the book you are holding. But here we have dirty as in disease, and not just disease, but venereal disease, specifically gonorrhoea and syphilis – literally the diseases of Venus, the goddess of love – with all their rotting bubos, oozing pus, aching joints, abbreviated noses and male acts of urination reminiscent of an attempt to dispose of an entire Boots warehouse of razor-blades via the never-so-narrow confines of the penis.

What's so remarkable, however, is that if we are to take our slang sources seriously, none of these nasty diseases seem to have originated in the UK. Of course our hapless fellow-countrymen and women, often in the course of their professional lives, have suffered them, and been forced to face a range of what, prior to antibiotics, were less than pleasant, nor indeed especially efficient, 'cures'. But, like the plague, brought in by some filthy foreign cabal of death-ridden rats, venereal disease was strictly an import.

KNOCKED WITH
A FRENCH FAGGOT-STICK

Which – although I'm loath to harp on our cross-Channel neighbours without whom, remember, we would lack that vital component of sexual fulfilment, the *capote anglaise* – brings us yet again to the French (see also under **N is for Nancy**, p.154). It's so useful to have an all-purpose national enemy – even if they have been our ostensible allies since 1815. But the truth will out, and there are more terms for VD evoking France than of any other variety. They include **French chilblains** (referring to the swellings that accompany syphilis); **French goods**; **French gout**; the **French crown** (properly known as *corona* *veneris*, the ring of spots that appear around one's forehead); the **French cannibal** (whose favourite dish is the genitals); a **French loaf**; **French marbles** (from *morbilles*, small blisters); **French measles**; **French mole** (it 'burrows' into the flesh); **French morbus** (Latin *morbus* meaning sickness); the **French pig**, usually the syphilitic pustule or bubo (Latin *bubo*, a swelling in the groin) which can also be a **poulain** (from the synonymous French – its parallel meaning is of a horse under three years and may therefore link to **horse**, see p.51) or a **marble**; plus **French pox** and the **French razor**. All these are primarily syphilis, which was the first form of venereal disease to appear on these shores and which flourished in the seventeenth century; thus, a **French welcome**, a dose of syphilis. **Frenchified** means diseased, though on a more positive note it also refers to a sexually adept woman. To **learn French** or **take French lessons** means to contract a venereal disease, while **piled for French velvet** means suffering a venereal disease. (To **tell a French joke**, however, means to stimulate the anus with one's tongue.)

Less obvious is **goodyear**, meaning especially gonorrhoea. It comes from *gouge*, a French army term for a soldier's companion or, as the OED puts it, 'a common Camp-Trull'. The mid-twentieth century **running range**, the discharge from the penis or vagina that accompanies gonorrhoea, comes from standard English *running*, plus French *reins*, the kidneys. Finally, one may sustain a **blow with a French faggot-stick** or **cowl-staff**, meaning the loss of one's nose through syphilis; those who are thus marked out have been **knocked with a French faggot-stick**. A *faggot-stick* is one used for lighting a fire – and thus a pun (see below). A *cowl-staff* was a pole or staff used to carry burdens, supported on the shoulders of two bearers; thus the popular punishment for a pussy-whipped husband who was abused either verbally or even physically by his wife, **riding the cowl-staff**, which involved him being sat on a pole and carried in derision about the streets.

ITALIAN TRICKS, SPANISH BUTTONS AND AFRICAN TOOTHACHE

Yet it may be — historically, that is, rather than simply nationalistically — that we are abusing the French unfairly. Another version is a **blow with a Naples cowl-staff** and it is equally possible that the world's **dripping johnnies** originated there rather than in France. Still, give a dog a bad name … Nonetheless, we find the adjective **Italian**, already seen as a synonym for anything 'dirty' or 'foreign', meaning simply syphilitic in the late sixteenth century, some decades prior to anything French entering the picture. **Italian tricks** refer to hetero- or homosexual anal intercourse, possibly productive of health problems. Thus the seventeenth-century riddle commencing 'I've two holes in my Belly and none in my Bum / Yet me, with much pleasure, Italians do thrum … ' (**thrum**, literally play upon, meaning to have intercourse). The rest of Italy appears immune, and it is the **Naples canker** or **scab** that describes syphilis, as do the **Neapolitan favour**, **bone-ache**, **button**, **court** and **disease**, as well as the **Neapolitan running-nag**, **scab** and **scurf**. A simple **Neapolitan**, therefore, is one who has syphilis, though it too can refer to the disease. Another term is **scabbado**, a 'Spanished' version of standard English *scab*. The Spanish, England's primary national enemy during the sixteenth and seventeenth centuries, turn out to be equally pustulant; thus, **Spanish buttons**, syphilitic sores, and the **Spanish gout**, **pip**, **pox** or **needle**, all rendering the disease itself.

Other 'national terms' include **Scottish fleas**, which — while the Scots are often associated with bodily invaders — refers yet again to syphilis. So too do the **Scotch** and indeed **Welsh fiddle**. More recent is **African toothache**. Then comes **go under the South Pole**, a sixteenth-century phrase meaning suffering from syphilis or venereal disease, and based on the belief that those who went on long sea voyages suffered from fevers, underpinned by the image of the genitals being in the 'southern' part of the body. Less obvious is **flapdragon**, otherwise a game noted in 1755 by Dr Johnson 'in which they catch raisins out of burning brandy and, extinguishing them by closing the mouth, eat them'. In this case the term means a German or Dutchman, who are seen as all display but no substance and therefore as belonging to races that for all their external show can be 'eaten up' by any Englishman; by extension – of course – these foreigners are equated with venereal disease. Last of the 'foreigners' was the famed **Saigon Rose**, much mentioned, if not actually contracted by Vietnam-era grunts, a form of super-VD, what others might term a **bullhead clap**, from which no recovery was even dreamed.

COVENT GARDEN AGUE

But for all the careful attribution to 'abroad' of the problems faced by those who, having **taken a turn in Cupid's alley** and **beaten Cupid's anvil** (and the vagina also claims **Cupid's cloister, cupboard, feast, furrow, hotel**, and **warehouse** as its nicknames, while **Cupid's kettledrums** are the female breasts) have ended up with a touch of **Cupid's itch**, it just ain't necessarily so. A whole new set of terms evolved, these still geographical, but now much closer to home, focusing on London's centres of prostitution. (Such centres doubtless exist countrywide but, as ever, slang remains a very metropolitan construct.)

Covent Garden was the first among these. The **Covent Garden ague** (*ague*, any form of acute or violent fever, usually involving shaking; synonyms included bone-ache, bone-ague and bone-breaker) or **gout** (a term used as much as a euphemism as a conscious

synonym) were VD, and one obtained them from a **Covent Garden lady** or **nun**, a whore, who may well have worked for a **Covent Garden abbess**, a madam in, logically, a **Covent Garden nunnery**, a brothel. The name can be abbreviated to Garden, thus **Garden gout**, in this case the fruit of a liaison with a **Garden goddess**. It was also possible to **break one's shins against Covent Garden rails**, although **break shins** (from the Russian tradition of beating the shins of those who refused to pay their debts) meant to borrow money, especially during an emergency, when one is forced to run from person to person in the hope of a loan.

Drury Lane represents the eastern border of Covent Garden. It too gives its name to a variety of **ague**. Further west, and chronologically slightly later, lies Piccadilly (so named from the piccadills or ruffs once manufactured there). The early eighteenth century saw the arrival of the **Piccadily cramp**, in this case carried by a **Piccadilly daisy** or, from around 1900, **commando** (the term commando being widely popularised during the contemporary Boer War), a term that lasted until the Street Offences act of 1959 saw the girls thrown off their beats and into the small-ads and phonebox fliers. **Piccadilly weepers** were not, however, remorseful clubmen, bemoaning their aching parts, they were the long side-whiskers worn without the then usual beard, which gained a temporary fashion from the mid-to-late nineteenth century.

Given the usual hypocrisies, the great whoring centre of London of the years prior to the eighteenth century, featuring such brothels as the intriguingly named Hollands Leaguer, was placed deliberately beyond the city walls and indeed on the other side of the river in Southwark, for many years the only part of London to be developed 'across the water'. This area, modern Bankside, was owned by the Bishops of Winchester, who were thus the largest brothel-owners in the country. This gave the **Winchester goose** or **pigeon** and lay at the root of a popular seventeenth-century proverb, referring to a well-known whore: 'No Goose bit so sore as Bess Broughton's'. It was perhaps not coincidental that nearby Battersea, equally transpontine, gives the term **Battersea'd**, meaning to have one's penis treated for venereal disease, in this case using the hopefully curative herbs that grew in the area's market-gardens. Clapham is also south of the river and occurs in the punning **haddums**, a term that means had 'em (i.e. the pox) and is found in the phrase **been at had 'em and come home by Clapham**.

'A CUNT AND A CLAP'

Even more specific was the late eighteenth century's **blue boar**, another name for a venereal bubo. This took its name from the notorious Blue Boar tavern in London, sited on the corner of Oxford Street and Tottenham Court Road; this area, long since destroyed by moralistic town-planners who replaced it by New Oxford Street and later Centre Point (which if nothing else is phallic), lay next to the **rookery** or criminal slum of St Giles, named for the adjacent church. St Giles itself has no venereal connections but it did give **St Giles' Greek**, a synonym for criminal slang, and **St Giles' breed**, criminals as a class. The Blue Boar was extended to the **blue boy** and **blue board,** presumably variant pronunciations. (Still blue, prostitutes at one stage were forced to wear **blue gowns** and known generically as such: whether this had any bearing on their potential as disease carriers is unknown.) Geography provides a couple of final terms and both, for a change, outside the metropolis: the **Barnwell ague** came from Barnwell near Cambridge, 'a place of resort for characters of bad report' as B.H. Hall put it in his *College Words* (1856). The university had long recognised the problem, and had issued a decree in 1675: 'Hereafter no scholar whatsoever ... upon any pretence whatsoever, shall go into any house of bad report in Barnewell, on pain ... of being expelled from the university'; it would appear that many young men remained undeterred, to their cost. A **Tetbury portion** (doing little for the image of the town of Tetbury in Gloucestershire) was sexual intercourse that is followed by a dose of venereal disease, or as Grose put it in 1788, 'A ******** [cunt] and a clap.'

WHAT A POX!

All this geography remains, however, very much in the past. If one were to select any terms that remain definitive of venereal disease, they must be these two: the **pox** and the **clap**. Pox is no more than an abbreviated spelling of the standard English *pocks*, the eruptive pustules on the skin that are a sign of syphilis. The pox does exist in standard English, but there it means smallpox; in addition syphilis was also called the **great** or **grand pox**, to distinguish it from 'lesser' venereal diseases. Pox gives a number of compounds: the specialist **pox doctor** who works in the **pox hospital**, which in turn specialises in sexually transmitted diseases and deals with those who are **pox-eaten** or **poxed up**. The unpleasantness of syphilis rendered **pox! pox take – !** or **the pox on – !** a useful curse from the mid-sixteenth century. Pox can also be used as a substitute for fuck, hell and so on in such interrogative phrases **who the pox?**, **how the pox?**, etc. Further exclamations of annoyance and irritation are **what a pox!** and **with a pox!** The seventeenth to eighteenth century **horse-pox** was considered an especially vicious strain.

While pox itself is perhaps less common than once it was, it has become the root of a number of rhyming slang terms. They include: **band in the box**, **royal**, **Surrey**, **Whitehaven** or **Tilbury docks**, **boots** or **shoes and socks**, **collie knox**, **cardboard box**, **coachman on the box**, **goldilocks**, **crab on the rocks**, **jack in the box** and **johnny rocks**. There are also a number of real-life individuals, safely dead, who would probably not have relished their 'honour': **John Knox** (?1514–72), the Scottish Calvinist theologian, the Catholic clergyman **Ronald Knox** (1888–1957) and the comedians and members of music hall's Crazy Gang **Nervo and Knox** (Jimmy Nervo (1890–1975) and Teddy Knox (1896–1974)). Syphilis, or rather **siff**, offers **lover's tiff**, **bang and biff** and **Wills' Whiff**, otherwise encountered as a small cigar. One last specimen of rhyming slang is Australia's **bumblebee**, VD.

And alongside the pox, the **clap**. Indeed, this takes us back to the unfortunate French, although on a linguistic rather than a patriotic basis. The word comes from Old French *clapoir*, a venereal bubo; thus **clapoire** or **clapier**, a place of debauchery and the illness one can contract there. The term appears as standard English in the late sixteenth century but starts appearing in cant/slang lists a hundred years later. Cotgrave, in his *Dictionary of the French and English Tongues* (1611) defines **clapier** as a rabbits' nest as well as a name for 'old time Baudie houses'; it was thus a pun on the standard English word *coney*, a rabbit, as well as its slang equivalent – a man might catch the disease from the diseased vaginal **cony** of a whoring **cony** who was working in a **clapoir**. Clap too has its compounds; the **clap-clinic**, one that specialises in venereal diseases, also known as a **clap-shack**, and the **clap-trap**, a less than complimentary, if all too predictable, slang synonym for the vagina (as well as a brothel). Thus the transitive verb **to clap** means to infect with venereal disease, while **clappy** (but perhaps not happy-clappy) means to be suffering from venereal disease and a **clapster** is a regular sufferer and, logically, a promiscuous man. Clap has its rhymes too: **handicap** and **horse and trap**.

COCK-ROT, CRINKUM AND THE BOTS

There are many other names. **Cock-rot** offers no illusions. A **cold**, as in **I've got a bit of a cold**, tries to. So do the **new consumption** (although consumption – TB – was hardly an easy option for seventeenth-century sufferers); **et-caetera**, which can also mean intercourse or the vagina; **noli me tangere** ('don't touch me'), another genteel Latinism; and a **dose** (and thus **dosed up**), which sounds as much like a medicine as a disease – doubtless for one's sins. **Crinkum** can be found, between the seventeenth and nineteenth centuries, as **crinkums**, **grincam, grincom, grincome, grincum, grinkcome, grinkham**, and **grinkum**: they all suggest the sense of twisting pain that accompanies the disease. Back amongst the euphemisms is the **gentleman's disease** (sixteenth century) and its modern successor the **gentleman's complaint** (both encountered in the **gentleman's pleasure-garden** – the vagina). The costermongers' **kertever cartzo** comes from Lingua Franca (a form of showbiz Italian) and means literally 'bad cock'. Modern America offers the blackly humorous **gift that keeps on giving**. Other names include Australia's **the jack** (thus one is **jacked up**), **nag** (like the standard English an undeniable term of abuse), **nap**, **scrud** and **yook** (a nineteenth-century use which long predates the modern **yuck**, even if both tend to the disgusting).

Syphilis has its own sub-group: **big Charlie**, **boogie-woogie**, **the bots** (usually a disease of horses caused by infestation of botfly larvae in the digestive tract), or **the pip**, 'a disease of poultry and other birds, characterised by the secretion of a thick mucus in the mouth and throat, often with the formation of a white scale on the tip of the tongue' (OED). There is the resignedly affectionate **old dog** (who 'bites' the sufferer) or **old joe**, **old rail** (or **old ral**, **old rall**, and **rall**), all from the dialect *rail*, to stagger, to reel – reflecting the fact that the development of the disease gradually impairs mobility. Gambling informs **big casino** (gonorrhoea being **little casino** and both referring to card games), **deuce** (i.e. the two and thus the lowest or least lucky card or dice throw), while a **full hand** (poker's 'full house' – one pair plus three of a kind) means a simultaneous dose of both syphilis and gonorrhoea (or an infestation of both head and body lice).

BUBES, BOTCHES AND BROPHYS

A number of terms relate to the symptoms that accompanied one's encounter with **Venus's curse**. The actual swelling or ulcer was the **bube** or **shanker**, **pig**, **flankard** (from the hunting jargon for a wound in a deer's flank or side), **pintle-blossom** (from **pintle**, the penis) or **blue balls**. It can also be a **botch**, which refers to non-venereal sores too; thus this from Deuteronomy 28:27: 'The Lord will smite thee with the botch of Egypt, and with the emerods, and with the scab, and with the itch, whereof thou canst not be healed.' Don't ever say we didn't warn you. The **dumb watch** is another term; it seems obscure but uses standard English *watch*, meaning a sentinel, to suggest that the silent bubo is now keeping watch on any further sexual misadventures. The diseased genitals were a **dirty barrel**, while **flyblown** – a description sometimes applied as well to a woman who is no longer a virgin – describes one who is suspected of carrying venereal disease. One who has just got it might be called a **fresh cow**. The **dropping member** is the flaccid penis, rendered ineffective through disease. To **break one's boltsprit** is for one's nose to rot away as a result of syphilis (the bolt- or bowsprit being a large spar extending from the stem of a vessel).

It can be **the itch** or **itching**, but VD is usually known as a source of unpleasant discharges such as **glue** (a dirty prostitute is **glue-necked**), **the whites**, **the yellows**, **the sauce** and **the stick** (i.e. stickiness). **Gleat**, from Old French *glette*, slime, filth or purulent matter has been used for urethritis since the late seventeenth century and in modern Australia it is a venereal infection in the rectum. Ireland's **brophys** are a nickname for the supposed insects, relations of body lice or crabs, which allegedly carry the disease. The **dripper** has been used since the late seventeenth century to describe both the disease and the discharge and the term can also apply to an allegedly diseased woman; more recent are **drip**, **drips** and **dripsy**. A **running**, in the sense of oozing, **horse** is presumably not to be caught. Standard English *token* means a sign, in this case of a disease, and to **tip someone the token** was to pass it on.

The pain that accompanies urination is indicated by **nail** and **pick up a nail**, and also by the image of **pissing broken glass**, **pins and needles** or **razor blades**. To **piss out of a dozen holes** is to be infected with syphilis and refers to the rotting penis. That sorry organ is also known as a **lulu**, while the ring of ulcers around the diseased genitals that indicate syphilis are a **wreath of roses**.

KNIGHTS OF THE BURNING PESTLE

Above all, if the slang has checked with its GP, VD burns. **Burn** means to infect someone else, and to **burn one's tail** or **poker** means to get a dose. The eighteenth-century Navy offered its own joke: **to be sent out a sacrifice and come home a burnt offering**, to be sent off to fight, but to return carrying venereal disease. A **burner**, otherwise a cheat or dwindler, is VD itself, and to be **warm**, **hot**, **sunburned** or **peppered** is to suffer (**to pepper** or **spice someone** else is to infect them, while **pepper-proof** means healthy). Although **scald** seems to offer the same image, it comes from sixteenth-century dialect *scald*, meaning scabbed, afflicted with the 'scall' (any scaly or scabby disease of the skin, especially of the scalp; **dry scall** was psoriasis, **humid** or **moist scall** was eczema).

Pestle seems less obvious, but it stems from Francis Beaumont's play *The Knight of the Burning Pestle* (*c.*1607);

knight of the burning pestle is someone who has contracted VD, as well as meaning the apothecary who offers a cure. A more recent version is to be **one of the knights**. As Ned Ward wrote in 1699, 'The Doctor undertook to extinguish … all Venereal Fires that had unhappily taken hold of the Instruments of Generation' and **fire** is a logical candidate for inclusion; a **frigate on fire** is a diseased whore, triple-punning on **frigate**, **frig** and **fire**. A **fireplug** is one who is suffering from a venereal disease, a **flame** is the disease and **flaming**, diseased. **Glimmer** and **glim** both originally referred to fire; they too were enrolled to describe the 'hot' disease (**to knap the glim** was to catch it). The mid-eighteenth-century sufferer was **hot-tailed** or had their **tail on fire**. They could also be **high**, usually said of a prostitute, although the term implies as much the 'high' of rotten meat as that of the temperature. A syphilitic prostitute might also be a **barber**, a term that plays on the role of a barber as a primitive surgeon (who might treat syphilis), the red-striped, bloody and phallic barber's pole and the fact that his shaving water/her vagina is 'hot'. She might also be a **queer mort**, literally a bad girl or 'a dirty Drab, a jilting Wench, a Pockey jade' (B.E. c.1698). A last and laboured pun comes with **in for the plate**: in horse-racing jargon, horses that qualify for the plate (the main race) have first won the **heat**.

PLACKET-STUNG IN THE POWDERING TUB

If all that is not enough, a selection of terms for the sufferers: one can be **between the two Ws** (i.e. wind and water), **get a knob**, **take a leak** (that holed penis again), or **load up**, **cop a packet** (the original packet being the 'packet' of gauze and lint that comprised the First Field Dressing, as applied to wounds during the First World War, when it initially appeared as slang for a wound) or be **placket-stung** (the **placket** being officially the slit at the top of an apron or petticoat, facilitating dressing and undressing and thus enslanged as the vagina). One might be **shot**, either **in the tail** (in which one might also harbour a **maggot**), or **betwixt wind and water** (a nautical term for that part of a ship's side that is sometimes above water and sometimes submerged, and in which part a shot is particularly dangerous). And Australia's all-purpose -o, as found in **milko** or **garbo**, works just as well for **sypho**, a syphilitic.

One must not be overly pessimistic. Today's clap clinic had its predecessors, although their 'cures' were debatable. They often took place inside a **lock hospital**, first noted around 1698, which was what it said: a locked place, wherein patients were quarantined until (in theory at least) they were rendered sound, i.e. clear of disease.

Also known as the **cornelian tub**, a pun on the **horn** (see under **H is for Horns**), which was presumably less than currently functional, was **Mother Cornelius's tub**: this was the sweating tub that formed the basis of the cure. There may have been an actual Mother Cornelius, whether a nurse or a procuress; however, one should note the masculine 'Cornelius' in the 'Water Poet' John Taylor's 'Travels to Bohemia' (1620): 'Or had Cornelius but this tub, to drench / His clients that had practis'd too much French' (i.e. venereal disease). This has been seen as a possible reference to the physician Henry Cornelius Agrippa (1496–1535), a leading advocate of hot baths for medicinal purposes. A further etymology may lie in 'the wood of *Cornus mascula*, celebrated for its hardness and toughness, whence it was anciently in request for javelins, arrows, etc.' (OED). Such a hard, dense wood would have been necessary to withstand the heavy salt brine used in 'pickling' patients; also known as **cornel-wood**, there may be one more pun involved – on **cornel**, **cornuted** and the cuckold. Another name for the 'tub' was the **powdering tub**, originally the name of the pickling tub in which the flesh of dead animals was pickled or 'powdered'; it was also the nickname for a specific lock hospital near Kingsland, London. Another hospital was **Job's ward** or **dock**, the venereal disease ward at St Bartholomew's Hospital in London, in which one was **laid up**. The use of Job suggests that VD patients suffered as much as did the biblical figure. In 1785 Francis Grose offered another, though linked, use of dock: 'Docking: a punishment inflicted by sailors on the prostitutes who have infected them with the venereal disease, it consists in cutting off all their clothes, petticoat, shift and all, close to their stays, and then turning them out into the street.'

YEOMEN OF THE VINEGAR BOTTLE

The doctors who worked in such clinics were **nimgimmers** – sadly the etymology thereof remains elusive. Those who took the cure were known as **yeomen of the vinegar bottle**, a reference to the use of vinegar as a 'cure' for the disease. As well as internal or external use, some doctors suggested that the mercury used in the treatment of syphilis should first be boiled in vinegar. The use of mercury gives **blue butter**, coloured by the substance on which it was based. By the nineteenth century victims were also known as **dock-shankers**, from the medical dock in which they were berthed and standard English *chancre*, a venereal ulcer.

The treatment itself gave **sal**, a clipping of standard English *salivation*, and thus to **be in a high sal** meant undergoing treatment for syphilis. To **play a game at loll-tongue** was to have one's saliva checked for traces of syphilis. More recently, but still prior to penicillin, are a couple more phrases relevant to undergoing treatment for VD – **ride the silver steed** and **take the bayonet course**, both of which refer to the course of injections of bismuth subcarbonate and neoarsphenamine for venereal disease that was continued weekly over a period of years. To **bumfuck**, meanwhile, is to massage the prostate as a way of diagnosing and treating gonorrhoea. Finally, even in the 1950s, there was the **snakebite remedy**, the post-coital washing of the genitals in potassium permanganate, supposedly a prophylactic against venereal disease.

E IS FOR ERECT

OR OTHERWISE

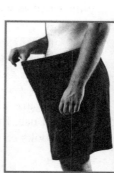

Four stiff standers,
Four dilly-danders,
Two lookers,
Two crookers,
And a wig-wag!

Well, the nursery rhyme experts Peter and Iona Opie, and who is to gainsay their expertise, claim that this riddle is multinational, several millennia old and describes … a cow. If you say so. But as Mandy Rice-Davies said of Lord Denning (no, children, if you don't know, *look it up*): they would say that, wouldn't they. But if, as does your author, one basks in the polluted waters of a mind that, while perhaps not dirty, is linguistically attuned to shall we say the *potential* of a word, then it is hard not to spy that **stiff**, those **standers**, not to mention that naughty **wig-wag**, and … wonder.

No matter. The point is hard. Hardness. Prolonged rigidity. Surging. Thrusting. Rampant. Daddy has to put his boat in Mummy's harbour – flabby doesn't make it. The erect penis, still banned from most public and media display, even though apparently considered less needy of protection than the female genitals, has marked out its corner of the slang lexicon. The image, as suggested, is of hardness, though what goes up must come down (and may not get there in the first place) and if E is for the glories of erection, then, by extension (or perhaps diminution), it has also to include the miseries of impotence as well.

THE STANDING AGUE

What you see is what you get, and the hardness is what erections are all about. Nonetheless when it comes to first recorded use, the image is of what the penis does, rather than how it looks or feels. And what it does is stand up straight and a **stand** has meant an erection since the early seventeenth century. Even older is the verb, to stand (erect), the earliest example of which can be found – like many such vintage versions of our lexicon – in the poems of the Scot David Lyndsay, in this case the *Pleasant Satyre of Thrie Estaitis* in 1540: 'Fair Damessell, how pleiss ye me? I haif na mair geir nor ye fie. Swa lang as this may steir, or stand, It fall be ay at your command.' The **standing ague**, in which the ague points to the quivering, lust-engorged member, is an early synonym for sexual excitement.

And although the over-riding image is one of hardness, when it comes to terminology, on a chronological basis hard must give place to **stiff**, which as **stiff and stout** is the first slang term for an erection that has been recorded. Sir Thomas Urquhart, whose translation of Rabelais' *Gargantua & Pantagruel* in 1653 introduced so many new terms to the language, included it in one of the many wonderfully inventive lists with which the original, and thus his book, is filled: 'And some of the other women would give these names … my lusty live sausage, my crimson chitterlin, rump-splitter, shove-devil, down right to it, stiff and stout, in and to, at her again, my coney-borrow-ferret, wily-beguiley, my pretty rogue.' It was another translation of Rabelais, published by Motteux in 1694, that gives a further synonym: the **stiff deity** (plus an accompanying term for the vagina: 'her natural Christmas box'). Given the physiology involved the image must certainly be even older, and while such language was rarely set down in print, we do have a ballad of 1650 explaining that 'I am now stiff-standing / And Cupid with his dart hath me at his commanding.' A century later an unmodified stiff did the job, with such later developments as **stiffer**, **stiffy**, the **stiff lock** (which rhymes on **cock** and means an erection on waking up), the **stiff-stander** or **bit of stiff**, and a couple of phrases for becoming erect; **crack a stiffie** and **sport a stiff**.

Given slang's propensity to annex the coarse and vulgar in our lives and offer a range of words and phrases to fit, it's surprising that the link of **hard** to erection doesn't seem to have come on-stream till the mid-nineteenth century. Indeed, hard itself is first recorded in 1890 (a **hard bit** is roughly contemporary), while **hard-on**, still the most widely used term today, is recorded 30 years earlier, with an example from a doggerel verse, 'A Roué's Apology': 'If I have said or done too much, / I humbly beg your pardon; / The magic of your thrilling touch / Has given me a hard-on.' And a few lines later the subject of his lusts responds delightedly, 'Bless me, you've a hard-on … Old Reuben's head is bobbing high up to your vest.' Hard remains a candidate, but hard-on rules the linguistic roost. As well as an erection it can mean passionate, lustful feelings, an obsession – usually a hostile one – and thus aggressive feelings towards someone; and a bad temper, irrespective of its possessor's gender. It can also be used as a term of address, generally a sarcastic one and aimed at deflating someone's high self-esteem; it can mean a despicable individual, a tough, aggressive person and in extended senses a difficult task. To **get a hard-on** obviously began life as meaning 'to have an erection' but it later came to mean 'draw a pistol' or 'desire someone', in which case it usually takes the word **for**, as does the 'opposite' definition: to dislike someone intensely. A **hard-up** can also be an erection, which is therefore **on the hard**, while to **give (a bit of) hard for (a bit of) soft** is to have intercourse, from the male point of view; the woman's experience is to **give soft for hard**.

BETHLEHEM STEEL AND BRITANNIA METAL

With our **stonker** safely **pitching a tent in our shorts** so solid **that a cat couldn't scratch it**, it's time to look at some alternative descriptions. The **bar**, presumably of steel, is an erection and to **have a bar on** or to **bar up** to is to become erect. **Steel** also underpins such terms as **Bethlehem steel** and **Britannia metal**, in standard English use an alloy of tin and regulus of antimony, resembling silver in appearance: as such it was less than dependable and the slang term has been used to describe anything fake. However, those who associate it with the penis prefer to concentrate on the metal bit. Steel can mean a knife or gun – both themes that lie behind so many penis synonyms, and the **pink steel** is the erection. While the **rocks** are usually associated with the testicles, when you **get rocks** or someone **gives you rocks**, then **John Thomas** is duly springing to attention. After that, you do what you can: **get your rocks off**, **pop**, **shoot** or **blow your rocks** all imply ejaculation; to **give someone big rocks to hold**, on the other hand, is for a woman to make a date with a man when she has no intention of keeping it, and thus to trick a suitor in any way. The diamond, a form of rock, is yet another variation on hardness: **diamonds** are the testicles and the erect penis is the **diamond cutter**.

The penis is the **bone**, and a **boner** or **bone-ache** is an erection. To **bounce one's boner** is to masturbate and a **mad boner** is a sex addict. And before moving on, let us take a brief diversion through the sexual boneyard: **bone-eater**, **bone-gobbler**, **bone-hog**, **bone-stroker**, and **bone queen** are all devotees of oral sex, the last alone being solely gay, as is the **bone smuggler**, in whose life the bone is contraband and its 'hiding place' the anus – he is often a transvestite. The **bone phone** is the penis, while a **bone-in-a-valley** is a very thin individual. To **give someone a bone**, **ride the bone**, **bone down** and **throw the bone to** all mean to have sexual intercourse. To **bury the bone** does too, and when it is extended to **bury one's bone in the back garden** or **in the back yard**, the intercourse turns anal. To **bite the bone** means to fellate (as does **smoke** or **gnaw someone's bone**), but it also means to be a loathsome, repellent person. Finally, to **knuckle the bone** is to masturbate.

FIXED BAYONETS AND POCKET ROCKETS

Given the identification of the penis with so many forms of gun, club, knife, bludgeon and much similar, it must be assumed that virtually any of those terms can, with such verbs as **get** or **have**, imply its erection, for instance to **get a rod on**. There are some, however, where the erection seems to pre-empt the penis, typically **wood**, which after all is rooted in solidity. To **get (good) wood** is to have a strong erection; to **give** or **slip someone wood**, is to have sexual intercourse, as is **put the wood to**; to **buff the wood** is to masturbate. To **catch wood** is to get an erection and thus figuratively to become extremely excited; to **give someone wood** is to make them erect and to **sport one's wood** is to wave the thing around. **Morning wood** is the erection that often, thanks to a desire to pee, accompanies one's waking. Synonyms include **morning pride** (or **pride of the morning**) and **pee-** or **piss-hard**. **Morning glory** can also mean intercourse before getting up, as well as a junkie's first injection of the day. Wood leads to **woodie**, which can also encompass non-sexual excitement, and to **juice one's woody** is to masturbate; a woodie is another thing one can **sport**, though one wonders as to the cause of so much exhibitionism. **Woodrow**, surely not memorialising the somewhat puritan US president Woodrow Wilson, is just another play on wood and is usually found as **slip (her) the woodrow**. The **wooden spoon** in fact predates all these by some 30 years, but one must assume that it is the shape, as much as the rigidity, that produces the image. The **broom-handle** and **clothes-prop** are also made of wood, and also serve as erectile synonyms, as do the **spike**, the **prong(-on)**, the **jackhammer**, **panhandle** and **jackhandle**, **scope**, **stalk**, **bonk(-on)**, **mast** or **flag**, **mountain**, **rajah**, **roger**, the **horse's handbrake** and the **anteater**, which refers specifically to the circumcised **roundheads** rather than the uncircumcised **cavaliers**. A final parade of less than deadly weapons gives

pocket rocket, **guided missile**, **truncheon**, **fixed bayonet** and **ten-hut!** (i.e. stand to attention!).

As one might expect, rhyming slang has its part to play: For the most part these refer to **horn**, sexual excitement (see under **H is for Horns**, p.100). Such rhymes include **Marquis of Lorne**, **mountains of Mourne**, **frog-spawn**, **popcorn** and **Sunday morn**. In addition are the **colleen bawn**, an anglicised version of Irish *cailín bán*, the white or fair woman; Colleen Bawn was the heroine of the hit opera *The Lily of Killarney*, first produced in February 1862. Horn also offers **September morn**, a term that appears to pay homage to an early twentieth-century scandal: 'September Morn' was the title of a painting by Paul Chabas of a young woman bathing nude, which was first exhibited at the 1912 Salon in Paris. Censors attempted to ban a reproduction of the picture from public exhibition in the US, a farcical effort that led to the sale of more than seven million reproductions – appearing on dolls, statues, umbrella handles, tattoos and many other places – and the assurance that Chabas need never work again. A **full-blown stallone**, paying homage to the self-image of the fading Hollywood hardman Sylvester Stallone (b.1946) rhymes with **bone**, and **Yasser** is an abbreviation of the late Palestinian leader Yasser Arafat, rhyming with Australian **crack a fat**, to get a hard-on.

ENGLISH GUIDANCE AND IRISH TOOTHACHE

On the whole an erect penis is an erect penis, wherever you find it, but there are a couple of 'geographical' links. One is the **English sentry** – presumably getting set up for a bit of **English guidance** (B&D) or sex via the **English method** of non-penetrative rubbing between the closed thighs (known across the Atlantic, in honour one assumes of various extra-curricular practices at one of the Ivy League's greatest universities, as the **Princeton rub**).

And then we have the Irish, a group who, with the greatest respect, score less than elevated marks when it comes to the table of slang's national sexual stereotypes: the **Irish inch**, for instance, is not the size

of penis of which one might boast, nor is the **Irish disease**, which refers to the state of possessing so diminutive a member. However, the miniature **mickey** must have some value, since the **Irish** or **Paddy's toothache** are defined as an erection, as is the **Irish toothpick** (though there's another cruel hint at something wanting). For herself to **give a hot poultice for the Irish toothache** is to have sexual intercourse. Other Irishisms include: the **Irish dip** and **Irish whist**, an arse-about version of cards — stereotypical no doubt of the much-maligned Emerald Isle — where quite against usual practice the **jack**, i.e. the penis, takes the **ace**, i.e. the vagina; the **Irish fortune**, the vagina (presumably in the context of prostitution); an **Irish promotion** or **Irish wedding**, masturbation; an **Irish virgin**, one who is a virgin and is likely to remain one; and the **Irish way**, meaning heterosexual anal intercourse, seen as an acceptable form of contraception for Catholics otherwise forbidden by an infallible pontiff to use artificial means. And to maintain the negative feel, the **Irish horse** and the **Irish rise** mean penises that will neither 'run' nor 'stand up'.

FLABBERS, FLUFFERS AND FUMBLERS

Impotence. Oh the horror of it all, and oh, how slang revels in man's inevitable fall. It's a condition generally associated with the old, though **stage fright** — sexual nerves — can afflict anyone, young as well as aged. So let us first of all consider the flaccid penis, which from an early date became predictably synonymous with the impotent old codger who owns it, the **flapper**. **Flap-doodle, doodle-flap** and **floater** are close, albeit later cousins. Just as old, maybe older, is **chitterling**, as seen on your local butcher's slab in the form of the small intestines of various animals, especially pigs. The penile version has far less to offer: addressing one hapless 'Tom Farthing', a ballad of 1675 sneers, 'Rivel'd up like Chitterlin, Thou'rt sometimes out and, sometimes in / And all thou dost's not worth a pin.' And even in 1686, when the assumption is that the act requires a little solidity, one cannot be too sure when the earl of Dorset writes in 'A Faithful Catalogue of our most Eminent Ninnies' how one unfortunate and possibly impotent fellow 'by the help of an assisting thumb / Squeezes his chitterling into her bum.' Three centuries later he would have had some help from the **fluffer**, that essential figure on any porno set, ready to urge an erection on the least willing of parts, or indeed the **stunt cock**, not some form of strap-on, but a person, capable of erectile magnificence on demand.

The penis may not be so able anymore, but it may not yet be a total write-off. The semi-erection can be just that – a **semi**, a **dobber, half a mongrel**, a **lazy lob, huby** or, for Australians who appreciate that the name is that of a town half-way between Melbourne and Ballarat, a **Bacchus Marsh**. But enough procrastination. Back to our sorry catalogue. Among other weedy specimens are **dead meat**, the **hanging johnny**, the **lobcock** (alhough at least this one is large), the **dropping member** and the **porridge bird** (a matter of consistency, one assumes, though maybe it's something to do with the semen – to **stir the porridge**, after all, is to have sexual intercourse with a woman immediately after she has had sex with another man, especially used of the final man in a gang rape). To take a quick tour around the breakfast buffet, porridge also features as the **blue-veined porridge gun**, the penis, which can equally well appear as the **blue-veined custard chucker, havana, junket pump, piccolo, root-on, yoghurt-gun, steak**, or **trumpet** – all of which presume an erection. All those blue veins suggest a neat link to

Roquefort or Stilton, and thus to **cheese** and thence smegma and beyond, but the blue vein is probably no more than that which nature has provided the virile flesh. Nor, anyway, is it always that virile.

The names given to those who have neither **lead in their pencil** nor **ink in their pen** are rarely compassionate. These include **dry-balls, broken arrow** (and his penis is one too), **bungler**, one who is sexually inadequate if not actually impotent, **dead pecker** (perhaps playing deliberately on **wood-**pecker), **capon** (a 'castrated cock'), **apple-john** (shrivelled and old), **flapper, flat tyre, softy, stuffed eel-skin** and **freak**. He's **past it, yitten, topher**, and plays as much part in sex **as the cocky on the biscuit tin** – Australia's old tins of Arnott's biscuits had a picture of a cockatoo, which was thus 'on' the tin but not 'in' it. To **fumble** is to indulge in sexual foreplay, and that's the very best the **fumbler** can manage once he's **free of** (i.e. has nothing to do with) **fumbler's hall**, the vagina, although fumbler's hall can also represent a metaphorical place where impotent men might be confined as punishment for their failings and in this case to be 'free of' it is to go there as often as he wants. The real problem would be to leave. He's a **bobtail** (a horse or dog with its 'tail' cut short) and a **dominie do-little** (literally, a useless schoolmaster) and neither his **dead rabbit** nor his **sleeping beauty** can do anything but **shoot blanks**. And like the political **mugwump**, who withdraws his support from any group or organisation, he has withdrawn his support from sex – or rather it has given up on him.

IS FOR FUCK

And did anyone have any other choices? Fart maybe, or fellatio. They may have their moment. But F is for **fuck**. It is, after all, the **F-word**.

I quote from the net, *c.*1999:

> 'Did you know? In ancient England single people could not have sex unless they had the consent of the king. When people wanted to have a baby … the king gave them a placard that they hung on their door while they were having sex. The placard had F.U.C.K. (fornication under the consent of the king) on it. Hence that's where the word fuck came from.'

Or it could be 'under Charles the king', 'Christ the king', 'the crown of the king', or 'forbidden under charter of the king', 'for unlawful carnal knowledge'; or there was 'forced unlawful carnal knowledge' and 'file under carnal knowledge' (as apparently marked on rape files in Scotland Yard).

Yeah, of course it could. And the cheque's in the post and of course I'll respect you afterwards. Where do they get this stuff? And worse still, why in hell do they believe it? It's not a matter of point-by-point refutation – I mean why **polish a turd** – but that irresistible fascination: why do they need, because it does seem to be need, this level of bullshit?

THE FUCKING FUCKER'S FUCKING FUCKED

Fuck is undoubtedly a problem word. Not in its use – the problem there is not to find examples, but to attempt the tracking down of all the variants, compounds and whatever – but in its origins. If one is to be scrupulous then the whole thing is reduced to that dull dismissal 'etymology unknown', but let us at all accounts attempt, well not a solution, but a suggestion. The word is old, recorded since at least 1508, when it appeared in William Dunbar's poem 'In Secreit Place this Hyndir Nycht': 'He clappit fast, he kist and chukkit ... Yet be his feirris he wald haue fukkit.' It was undoubtedly older, and certainly not restricted to Dunbar's Scotland. As laid down in the latest revision of the OED's entry (2008), it is obviously linked to a number of European words: 'Dutch *fokken* to mock (fifteenth century), to strike (1591), to fool, gull (1623), to beget children (1637), to have sexual intercourse with (1657), to grow, cultivate (1772), Norwegian regional *fukka* to copulate, Swedish regional *fokka* to copulate' (and note Swedish regional *fock*, the penis). But beyond that? Like Eric Partridge, the OED suggests some form of Indo-European root (Partridge linked Latin *pugno*, I fight; the OED opts for *pugnus*, a fist) and there may have been a Middle English word *fuken* – but there are no records. Given the plethora of euphemisms equating intercourse or penetration with striking or hitting (bang, knock, screw, hammer, poke, etc.), the sex = violence equation seems highly feasible. But ultimately, over and beyond any other of its 'dirty' peers, fuck leaves us in the etymological dark.

As regards its status, fuck may technically have started life as standard English, but as the OED labels it, it was soon 'coarse slang', and very likely ever more shall be so. At least in 'respectable' use. After Dunbar and a number of other sixteenth-century examples, the first dictionary listing is by John Florio, whose Italian–English *Worlde of Wordes* (1598) was the first to list, by way of its translations, many as yet unglossed English terms. His entry runs '*Fottere*, to iape, to sard, to fucke, to swive, to occupy.' *Sard* is long gone, and *swive* exists only in conscious archaism. As for *jape*, well, it puts a whole new interpretation on all those merry schoolboy romps in the dorm at Greyfriars (Bob *Cherry*? Johnny *Bull*?). *Occupy* (a whole new take on occupational therapy, dare one suggest) is another of those terms that started off quite respectable, before moving into slang; it is used, for instance, some ten times in the

Authorised Version of the Bible. But by the end of the sixteenth century it had fallen from grace, a fact that Shakespeare notes in *Henry IV, Part II* (1597), 'A captaine? Gods light these villaines wil make the word as odious as the word occupy, which was an excellent good worde before it was ill sorted.' It was too late: by now **occupying** was an act of sexual intercourse and an **occupying house** a brothel.

'SHE HAS FUCKED, I BELIEVE, THE WHOLE SCHOOL'

But **fuck** is always with us, even if by the eighteenth century, if the word was printed at all, the form was usually *f—k*, typically in the keen but cautious Francis Grose's dictionary entry: 'F–K, to copulate.' It could be found in porn, of course, and there are cites a-plenty in magazines like *The Pearl* (1880): 'She has fucked, I believe, the whole school', or *My Secret Life*, the anonymous sexual epic which in later editions has been attributed to one 'Walter': 'Ain't you green ... a girl's hole isn't called a cock, it's a cunt, they fuck with it' (but see under **C is for Cunt**, p.32). The term returned to literary use with James Joyce's much-banned *Ulysses* (1922) although such books as e.e. cummings' First World War memoir of the same year, *The Enormous Room*, still played it safe: 'A little later he came rushing up to my bed in the most terrific state of excitement ... and cried: "You f— me, me f— you? Pas bon. You f— you, me f— me: – bon. Me f— me, you f— you!"' Ultimately it has remained taboo in the popular media and in 'polite' speech. This position has been eroded ever since, with the term and its compounds appearing today in films, books and on television, although the press, especially the tabloids, pretend to a continuing squeamishness. 'Officially', for all that the realities of everyday speech (irrespective of class) disprove the theory, **fuck** remains an outlaw in conversation.

As suggested elsewhere, there is no characteristic so evident in the obscenities as their wondrous flexibility. Fuck is definitely no exception. Let us take the verb first, since its citations make clear that at least as recorded it predates the noun form by a good century and a half. Sometimes euphemised as **fug, fugh, eff** and similar, it means to have sexual intercourse, originally and for centuries usually of a man, but now increasingly of either sex; it can also refer to anal intercourse, for which there are examples thanks to the libidinous earl of Rochester showing his indifference as to 'Whether the Boy fuck'd you, or I the Boy' as early as 1675. In figurative senses it means variously to harm irreparably, to cheat, to victimise, to betray, to deceive; to stop, abandon or give up (on); to trifle with, to mess around, to interfere with; to blunder, to make a mess (of); to kick, to stomp on; to throw; to use or exploit for one's benefit or to dismiss, to expel. It been used as a synonym for to hell with, and the derivative **fuckish** means sexually forward. **Fucksome** is sexually desirable, a **fuckaholic** is obsessed with sex and the West Indian **fuck-a-bush** (literally, one who fucks in the bushes) means promiscuous. **Fuckability** is sex appeal and **fuckable** means both sexually desirable and available. A **fuckathon** (from *telethon* and ultimately *marathon*) is a long sexual encounter or an orgy and the seventeenth-century **fuckation** was sexual intercourse. A **fuck-a-rama** is an orgy too, though it can also mean a **fuck-up**, i.e. a disaster, while as an exclamation it signals frustration and/or annoyance. **Fucky** means nubile, ostensibly sexually enthusiastic and usually describes a woman (though possibly a young gay man). And the noun **fucky-fucky** (also **fuck-fuck, fucky-sucky, fuckee-fuckee**) is sexual intercourse, especially as used in Asia, often by prostitutes who doubtless 'love you long-time'.

Although **fuck along** means no more than walk (away) and **fuck away** means to squander, most fuck phrases are straightforwardly sexual. There are the comparatives: one can **fuck like a bunny** (**rabbit**), a **mink**, a **rattlesnake** (which may equally **root** or **shag**) or a **stoat**. *Wind in the Willows* was never like that, but up-for-it Mr Toad's cross-dressing as a washerwoman may indicate other preferences. Among the most widely used is **fuck one's/the arse/ass off**, which can be varied as **fuck one's/the arse/ass out**, **fuck one's/the brains**, **hump one's ass off**, **fuck one's head off**. Despite the presence of arse or ass, and the usually male subjects of the phrase, there is no implication of anal intercourse or homosexuality; the reference is merely to the woman considered, as ever, as merely an aggregation of 'naughty bits'. The phrase means to copulate enthusiastically, from the male point of view and often as the wishful thinking voiced by a young man watching a passing woman; it can also simply mean what it says: to make one's partner the object of enthusiastic or aggressive love-making. Nor more supposedly gay, though one might wonder, and certainly just as aggressive is **fuck the crap out of** someone (similarly **fuck the shit out of** someone, **fuck the cum** …).

YOU CAN FUCK ME BUT YOU CAN'T MAKE ME LIKE THE BABY

Other phrases include **fuck that/this for a lark!** (plus **fuck this for a geg!**, **fuck this lark!**, **shag that for a lark!**) which is variously an exclamation of derision, indicating something is not working, or another way of excusing oneself from involvement in what the speaker sees as an absurd idea or situation. **Fuck this** or **that for a laugh** is synonymous. Slang's resolute refusal to move into the modern world ensures the persistence of **I wouldn't fuck her with a borrowed prick** (and the selfless **I wouldn't fuck her with your prick**), a general term of masculine distaste spoken on seeing what is considered an unattractive or unpleasant woman. And in Australian prison slang one finds the defiant **you can fuck me but you can't make me like the baby**:

in other words, a prisoner may endure his punishment but need not necessarily enjoy it. Masturbation gives **fuck Mrs Palmer** (she of the **five lovely daughters**), **fuck one's fist** and **fist-fuck**, (although that usually refers to the generally gay occupation of forcing the fist into one's partner's anus). One may add **fuck one's knuckles**, the choice of cadets at Australia's military college, RMC Duntroon. To **fuck** (**someone**) **out of** is either to cheat someone (out of something) or in Ireland to eject or throw out. To **fuck someone's head** is to confuse. To **fuck the dog** (and **sell the pups**), otherwise known as **f.t.d.**, **finger the dog**, **fug the dog**, **feed the dog**, **screw the dog** or **walk the dog** all mean to idle, to waste time, to loaf on the job or to bungle or blunder. To **fuck** or **stroke the duck** mean the same (and are probably no more than a matter of hearing dog as duck.) **Fuck-your-buddy week** (another US military coinage) is a response to any moment or act of betrayal, usually as the embittered comment 'So it's fuck your buddy week then … '.

Fuck is also the source of many exclamations, starting with **fuck!** itself, a useful accompaniment to misplaced hammer blows, intimations of disaster, frustration, anger, resignation and anything else that requires a verbal expulsion of emotional steam. It can even equate to a sigh of pleasure: 'Fuck! That was good.' Given the opacity of the past one cannot say whether or not such apparent euphemisms as **feck!**, **feckins!**, **fecks!**, **fegs!**, **faugh!**, **faw!**, **figh!**, **fogh!**, **foh!**, **fough!**, **hough!**, **paugh!**, **phoh!**, or **po'gh!** really stand in for fuck! Were our ancestors really so potty-mouthed? Probably. Unequivocal is **for fuck's sake**, as frustrated a phrase as one might imagine, often with a slight overtone of resignation, and **fucks to**, albeit slightly juvenile (as in **sucks to**), means the hell with. **Fuck it!** (also **fug it!**) is used as a verbal punctuation, with no real meaning, thus such phrases as **do I fuck!** (also **do I hell!**, **do I nick!**, **will I fuck!**, **will I shit!**) making clear one's absolute rebuttal, i.e. the hell I will! or no I certainly won't/don't!; it also works with all the other pronouns.

FUCK MY LUCK!

High on the list of exclamations is **fuck 'em all!**, used for dismissal, bravado, and as a 'harder' alternative to 'to hell with them'. It emerged in the Second World War and provided the original chorus for the soldiers' song that has been bowdlerised as 'Bless 'Em All'. **Fuck** or **frig my days!** expresses surprise or annoyance, while **fuck my luck!** stands for I don't believe it! **Fuck my old boots!** (also **blast my old boots!** and **fuck my old slippers!**) denotes astonishment; this originally military term sometimes appears as **seduce my ancient footwear**. **Fuck that**, whether all alone or modified by such additions as **for a bowl of cherries, for a comic song, for a top hat** or **for a game of soldiers!**, which can in turn appear as **bugger that for a game of soldiers!** or **feck this for a game of cowboys**, implies derision, indicating something is not working; it is often bowdlerised as 'blow this ... ', 'sod this ... ', etc.

Another group of exclamations deal with people. **Fuck the begrudgers!** is an Irish term of defiance or scorn; **fuck them all but six!** (or **eight!** or whatever number the speaker chooses) is another military coinage, a general oath of annoyance and hostility, that is often extended with ' ... and save them for pallbearers'. **Fuck yourself!** (alternatively **go fuck yourself!**, **go fug yourself, go diddle yourself, go fiddle yourself, go flog yourself, go jerk yourself, go shoot yourself!, take a fuck to yourself!**) is surely self-explanatory. **Go fuck a duck!** (also **go fuck a dog!, go kiss a duck!, go fuck a fishnet!**) is an exclamation of dismissal or disbelief, while **go fuck your mother!** (or **your sister!**), is another dismissive, and generally seen as being as offensive as you can get.

AWA' TAE FUCK!

That fuck as a noun, meaning first and foremost an act of sexual intercourse, does not seem to come on stream until the mid-seventeenth century, and then as a supposed nickname, may simply be no more than a failure, given the taboo nature of the word, in its collection. This early use, taken from the October 1654 edition of the prototype 'newspaper' *Mercurius Fumigosus* ran thus: 'A delightfull Mask or Dance is presented between Fatt Fish-wives, and leane Fisher-men, with all their Rodds, Tacklings and Baytes, Madam F—k-at-a-venter being chief Lady of that nights Revells.' After that the record remains patchy until the twentieth century, although one must, on philosophical grounds alone, note the radical politician John Wilkes' dictum, delivered in his *Essay on Woman* (1763): 'Life can little else supply / But a few good fucks, and then we die.' And that undaunted devotee of all things lubricious, the earl of Rochester, used the word regularly in his smut-ridden play *Sodom, or the Quintessence of Debauchery* (1684) – sample characters 'King Bolloxinion' and 'Queen Cunitgratia'.

The old **in-and-out** aside, fuck has a predictable selection of sexual uses: a person (usually a woman but of both sexes since the 1970s) considered purely as a sex object (thus a good/bad fuck, someone who is seen as a sexual adept or incompetent), semen, a penile thrust and anal intercourse. Still in the realm of the personal, albeit sexually neutral, it can describe a person, usually negatively, as in a dumb fuck or useless fuck. Like the verb, it offers a number of figurative definitions, the first being anything at all, usually in the negative phrase **not give a fuck**. (Americans, for reasons of their own, see no need for the not, just as they 'care less', where we 'couldn't' or 'don't' do much the same.) It can mean nonsense or rubbish, it can be used to indicate quantity, usually excessive and in comparisons, e.g. fat as fuck, hurts like fuck, bigger than fuck. The adverbial **like fuck** can either imply derision or commitment. Like such equally coarse peers as shit or crap, fuck can mean the essence, the spirit, 'the daylights', e.g. **beat** or **kick the fuck out of**. Such 'daylights' are also found in **scare the fuck out of**, to terrify, although **throw a fuck into** means simply to have intercourse. It can indicate difference or importance, usually in the negative, e.g. **that don't make a fuck**, and mean nothing, e.g. **I don't do**

fuck. A last image is of ill-fortune, a piece of bad luck, e.g. I lost the gig, **ain't that a fuck**.

Constructed with **the**, fuck gives such questions as **who**, **why**, **when**, **how** and **where the fuck?** Also **the fuck I care**, i.e. I don't care at all, and such intensives as **get the fuck out!**, go away. **Get to fuck!**, variously **get to fuck out of here!**, **get to fuck out of it!**, **get to the devil out of it!**, **get to Falkirk!**, **get to Jesus!**, **get to shite off!** and the Scottish **awa' tae fuck!**, all represent the harsh demand that one leaves at once.

FUCKFESTS, FUCK-INS AND FUCKOS

Compounds with the noun have a predictably sexual accent. The gay **fuck-bar** is one which provides a back room for sexual activity. Grose describes a **fuck-beggar** as 'an impotent or almost impotent man whom none but a beggar-woman will allow to "kiss" her'; a **fuck-fist** or **fuck-finger** is a male or female masturbator; a **fuck book** is written pornography – a **fuck film** or **flick** is the animate sort; a **fuck show** is a live sex performance. A **fuck boy** is a young gay man, a catamite, and can also mean one who is victimised by his superiors or associates. A **fuck buddy** – male or female – is one with whom has a sexual, but no deeper relationship, while the **fuck–eye** is a flirtatious, sexually encouraging glance and a **fuckfest** or **fuck-in** (aping the Sixties' hippie love-in) an orgy. **Fuck flaps** are the labia, **fuck handles** are excess rolls of fat (they presumably give one something to hang on to) and the **fuckhole** is the vagina, although it can be found meaning an unpleasant, disgusting place or a contemptible, unpleasant person. A **fuckpad** is a room or apartment that a man keeps for seductions and sex, and if one is not available, there's always the back of your **fuckmobile** or **fuck-truck**, a car that improves one's attractiveness to the more gullible members of the opposite sex, who if female, boast **fuck udders** and if hot to trot, may be a **fuckdog**. **Fuck sauce** is semen and when ejaculated in a display of the **lonely art**, it may well end up in that particularly repellent item of any young man's wardrobe: the **fuck sock**. The **fuck rubber** is a contraceptive sheath and the **fuck plug**, ladies only, a diaphragm. The penis can be a **fuck muscle, fuck-pole** or **fuckstick** (the latter also being a term of dislike or even of address). **Fucko** is another term of address: despite its root, it is not necessarily abusive, although used as a personal description it is. Finally there are a couple of derivatives: **fuckstruck** and **fuck-nutty**, both describing one who is obsessed with sex.

In the non-sexual sense a **fuckload** is very large amount (about the same size as a **shitload**), as is the phrase **a fuck of a**, usually followed by **lot**. **Fuckbag** is a general term of contempt for an unpleasant, disgusting person, although Australia's Royal Military College, Duntroon, that valuable source of macho verbosity, uses it to categorise a woman believed by cadets to be a 'good fuck' and/or readily available for sex. Other derogatives include **fuckball, fuckbrain, fuckchops, fuckdust, fuck-knuckle** (from **knucklehead**), **fucknob** (**knob** meaning penis and thus a fool), **fuck-nut, fuckpig** (usually of a woman), **fuckwad** and **fuckwit** (also **shitwit**). In pretty much every case the person is seen as not merely unpleasant, but stupid too.

TALKING FUCK

Fuck also gives such phrases as the ever-useful **fuck knows?**, a general intensifier, underlining one's ignorance or disinterest; **get the fuck**, an Australianism for losing one's job; **on the fuck**, working as a prostitute; **sure as fuck**, absolutely certain; and **talk fuck**, to murmur or shout obscenities during sexual intercourse for the gratification of one or both partners.

And on it goes. Fuck can exist as a suffix, implying the destruction of the appended noun and something that overturns order and promotes subversion; hence **clusterfuck**, **gender-fuck**, **head-fuck**, **mindfuck** and **rat fuck**. To **fuck about** (otherwise found as **fuck around**, **fug around**, **fugh around**, **feck about**, **fuck round**) can mean to mess about, to waste time, to fool around as well as, transitively, to annoy, to inconvenience, to waste someone's time; further uses of this convenient phrase mean to wander about aimlessly, to have sex outside one's primary relationship and to astonish. As a noun, it means time-waster, or something considered time-wasting. To **fuck a duck** is to live a sexually promiscuous life, and in exclamatory form expresses surprise, disbelief, dismissal or rejection. It is occasionally cited as rhyming slang, but it is more a matter of assonance.

Fuck all (also **feck all**, **fok-all**, **fugh-all**, **shit-all**, **eff-all**, **bollock-all**, **shag all**, **piss-all**, **stuff-all**) has meant 'none' or 'nothing' since the 1910s, and as such can condemn a second-rate or worthless person; it also works as a negative measure, similar to a damn, e.g. I don't give fuck-all, or as a synonym for hell, e.g. who the fuck-all does he think he is? It can be coupled with else, e.g. there's fuck all else to do around here, and it can be an exclamation, simply an extension of fuck! **Fuckarse**, as a noun a general term of contempt, becomes to play the fool, to act stupidly, as a verb. **Fuckshit!**, to blend another pair of obscenities, denotes anger. A **fuckerware party** (a play on a Tupperware party) is a party organised for the sale of erotic 'toys' and clothing. The suffix -ery denotes 'a place where an indicated article or service may be purchased or procured' (OED) which meant that a nineteenth-century **fuckery** was a brothel. That interpretation is now redundant, but fuckery remains in use in modern Britain where, based on **fuck-up**, it stands for unfairness, ill-treatment; treachery and nonsense.

FUCKED UP, OVER AND OUT

Fuckface (and its adjective **fuckfaced**) plus **fuckhead** (and **fuckheaded**) are insults denoting worthlessness, though fuckfaced can also mean drunk, bleary-eyed or half-awake. A **fuckee**, using the suffix -*ee*, denoting a recipient, describes the 'passive' or recipient person during copulation and in figurative senses one who is treated badly, one who suffers harm or punishment. The idea of victimisation further underpins **fuck-job** (also an insult): one is **fucked** (**over**), from **fuck over**, used of people, meaning to harm, to beat up, to hurt emotionally, to act cruelly, to interfere, to mess around with and, of ideas or objects, to adulterate. A further suffix, -*ster*, implying agency or 'doing', gives **fuckster**, a promiscuous man or occasionally woman. Logically, the **fuckstress** (incorporating the suffix -*stress*, a female agent or 'doer') has been a prostitute, a female sexual sophisticate or that much-prized object of male dreams, a nymphomaniac. She is possibly **fuckstrated**; he, recovering from her ministrations, may be **fucked out**, i.e. exhausted, especially from fucking. One can also **fuck something out** or, using **out** to mean 'elsewhere', have sex other than with the primary partner.

Nor is fuck itself fucked out yet. Far from it. Setting aside the as yet unlisted phrasal verbs (the ones that end in a preposition, i.e. **fuck off**, **up** and **with**), there are a number of 'fucks' to consider. In the first place is the adjective **fucked**, which has a whole subset of uses all its own. Like the verb from which it stems, fucked can mean having had sexual intercourse (or having had it thrust upon one) but its primary uses are figurative. And negative. People who are fucked are exhausted, unhappy and wretched; they can be cheated, tricked, defeated or deceived. Fucked things are broken, out of order, ruined or spoiled. They – and indeed people, circumstances or ideas – can be very bad, offensive, rotten or unfair. Returning to people, the term encompasses a state of serious trouble, of being hugely intoxicated either by drink or drugs, of lacking in good sense (and escalating to simple craziness and onwards to psychological maladjustment) or more mildly, being somewhat bothered.

Thus the attendant phrases offer little or no hope. One can be **fucked by the fickle finger of fate**, **fucked to a fair-thee-well** or **fucked and no Vaseline** (underpinned by the use of Vaseline to facilitate sexual, usually anal, intercourse). One can be **fucked over** (though that can also refer to the not invariably unpleasant effects of a stimulant), **out**, **up** and **off**, which last means angry. A **fucked duck** was once one who was about to, or doomed to, die. **Get fucked** is one of the least polite terms of dismissal and a cry of **I'll be fucked** (or **frigged**) refers not to incipient sexual delights, but is a general exclamation of surprise, frustration, and anger. A conditional fucked, as in **fucked if ...** , implies a refusal or rejection. It can sometimes be extended by a pronoun, I'll be ... , she'll be ... , and so on. The compound **fucked up**, sometimes euphemised as **f'ed up**, is equally common. It means much the same as the shorter form, and describes the miseries, pains (emotional and physical), disappointments, failings and inadequacies of people and things with equal pessimism.

UP TO FUCK

In common with fucked, **fuck-up** can deal with animate and inanimate objects, people included. The meaning is always that of failure, bungling and incompetence. He, she or it can all be fuck-ups, just as they can be fucked. It works as an adjective; thus something can be the superlative **fuck-up-est** (though the comparative **fuck-up-er** seems to have missed the boat). Above all, however, it is found as a verb, and was coined as such during the First World War, as reported by Frederick Manning in his memoir *Her Privates We* (1929) where he recalls a song that ran in part 'And they'll call up all the women / When they've fucked up all the men.' It means to ruin, to destroy; to make a mess of and gives **fucker-up**, that which ruins or destroys; in intransitive senses it means to blunder, to fool around, to go wrong, to malfunction, to break down or to waste. Transitively, to fuck up is to confuse, to confound, to hurt or injure, to cause problems for someone, to kill, to thwart, to render drunk or drugged and to infect with a venereal disease. As an exclamation it means shut up!, stop it!, and in the phrase **fuck up someone's pussy**, it means to interfere with a rival or a companion's efforts at seducing a woman.

From fuck up to **fuck off** (also **fack off**, **fuck out**, **feck off**, **frig off**). Basically defined as to leave or go away, and widely used as such as the exclamation **fuck off!** or **fuck off out it!** (and which can also equate with a rather more aggressive form of 'don't be silly') it is equally popular, sometimes as **f.o.**, as meaning to waste time, to idle, to avoid one's duties; thus the noun **fucking off**, wasting time or acting lazily and the adjective **fuck-off**, idle. Other meanings include to waste, to squander, to disregard, to brush aside or to put off, to miss out on something through one's own or another's ineptitude, to expel or reject, to stop or to annoy. A **fuck-off** is a lazy or inefficient person, who prefers to 'fuck off' rather than work. It can also stand for a gesture of contempt, a statement of prohibition or an irritating or frustrating situation. As an adjective it seems especially popular in the sense of arrogant or ostentatious, e.g. a great, fuck-off Maybach, often appearing in the phrase **fuck-off money**, enough money for one to say 'fuck off' to the world (and more specifically to one's employer). This can also be **fuck-you money** – the only thing different is the phrase.

Fuck with, yet again, can mean to enjoy intercourse with a partner, but, yet again, tends to the negative, implying senses of messing about (with), involvement with and interference, often by physical or mental intimidation. Other meanings include to impress, to overwhelm, to manipulate, to play around or associate with. To **fuck with someone's head** or **mind** is to disturb and harm them emotionally.

FACKER, FECKER, FUCKER

As one might expect, the noun **fucker**, for one who has sexual intercourse, is almost as old as fuck itself. It is listed by John Florio at *fottitore*, though unenterprisingly he merely adds an *-er* suffix to each of the *fottere* list cited on p.68. It then vanishes until the nineteenth century, but for a single line in Dekker and Webster's 1607 play *Northward Ho*: 'Min vader bin de grotest fooker in all Ausbrough'. And given that the speaker is a heavily caricatured Dutchman, and the name Fugger happened to be that of the then greatest bankers in Europe, it is at very best a highly laboured pun. But that's it for fucker (on the page at least) until – no surprises here – it re-emerges in 1894 when Victorian pornographer 'Walter', reminiscing over yet another bout of commercial satiation, tells his readers, 'I had till then never known what a high-class, well-practised professional fucker could do.' This fucker is of course a woman (James Joyce's use is also woman-centred, in a 1909 letter to his beloved Nora, whom he also addresses as 'my naughty wriggling little frigger, my sweet dirty little farter'); however, the male of the species plays his part. As Charles Devereux put it in his pornographic novel *Venus in India* (1889), 'I must leave it to my male readers, especially to those who have been real ardent and constant fuckers.'

And fucker has more to offer. In concrete terms it can mean both a pimp and his stock-in-trade, the vagina; more usually it is found as a term of abuse, and spelt variously **facker**, **fecker**, **fugger** or **fugher**. With another set of alternatives – **fugger**, **fugher**, **fogger**, **fecker** – it can be an unspecified object, irrespective of its qualities, and an animal. In addition it is a difficult or irritating thing or task. It can also be a person – probably male – no judgement implied, though it can also mean one who sets out to cause harm. Australians, who had already fallen for America's **cocksucker** (see under **G is for Gob**, p.85) also seem, if W.H. Downing's glossary *Digger Dialects* (1919) is to be believed, to have considered that fucker meant, with absolutely no frills, a private in the English army. They may have been right, but still … and like **mother**, fucker can mean an extreme example, whether positive or negative.

ABSOFUCKINGLUTELY FANFUCKINGTASTIC

Fucking, as we know, is a town in China, but it can also denote the act of sexual intercourse, not to mention harsh and unfair treatment. It is most widely used as an adjective, where it is a found in a variety of somewhat half-heartedly euphemistic spellings, such as **facquing**, **facking**, **farking**, **fecking**, **focking**, **fugging**, **fughing**, **fogging**, **fucken** and **funking**. While it can refer to sex, it is more usually an intensifier, and while, again, it can suggest pleasure ('that was fucking wonderful') it is more likely to take the negative route, synonymous with vile, despicable, unpleasant, corrupt and dirty. It is sought after as an infix, i.e. something tossed into the middle of another word as an emphasis: examples include **absofuckinglutely**, **fanfuckingtastic** and the reassuring verb to **guaran-fuckingtee**. The almost equally cumbersome **fuckingly** can substitute for extremely, very much or damned.

For reasons that as yet elude the lexicographers – or at least this one – fucking can be combined with two women's names to make a pair of quasi-jocular exclamations: **fucking Nora!** and **fucking Ada!** The first remains obscure (could there be a link to that same fucking, frigging, farting Nora Barnacle, Joyce's suitably named one and only); the second, best heard on Ian Dury's eponymous song which ends the *Laughter* album (1980), where he and the Blockheads lovingly intone it over and over again until they're faded out, is probably an extension of fucking's own intensifer, **fucking-A**. On the other hand, it may be no more than a softening of the more aggressive **fucking arseholes**, or then again a toughening up of the comparatively restrained **fucking hell**. In both ladies' cases, **bloody** can substitute for fucking. It might also be noted that in actual use the 'fu' may be deliberately abandoned, thus giving **'kin' 'ell! 'kin Ada!** and so on. **Fucking-A!, fugging-A!, fuggin' ay** and **fucking A-OK** are almost always positive (though the noun form means very little, as good as nothing, e.g. I don't know fucking-A about it) and works (with alternatives **bricking-A, mucking-A**) as an adverb ('You're fucking-A right') or an exclamation meaning either emphasis – absolutely! definitely! – or to denote astonishment, dismay, acceptance, praise or recognition.

FUCK ME GENTLY (WITH A CHAINSAW)!

At least as regards its exclamatory uses, **fuck me!** is not an invitation to a spontaneous instance of wham-bam-thank-you-mam. It is, rather, a way of expressing one's surprise, astonishment or resignation. It can come on its own, but often arrives with an adjectival or adverbial companion. Thus **fuck me rigid!, fuck me insensible!, fuck me dead!, fuck me blind!, fuck me gently (with a chainsaw)!, fuck me pink!, fuck me ragged!, fuck me hard!, fuck me sideways!, fuck me days!** and any other images – on the whole less than obviously linked to copulation (at least in its vanilla formats) – the speaker happens upon.

It is as an adjective, however, that fuck-me returns to the world for which it ought to be best suited: an open invitation to join the speaker in unrestrained rumpy-pumpy. Otherwise, but rather weedily, found as **do-it-to-me**, the word means outrageous, especially when extremely sexy. The usual context is footwear: **fuck-me pumps, fuck-me's, hump-me pumps, fuck-me boots** or **booties, FM boots, come-fuck-me's** or **follow-me-and-fuck-me shoes**. One is loath (or is it embarrassed?) to slaver; suffice it for me to direct interested readers to the nearest Manolo Blahnik catalogue. However, the original **f.m.'s** were by tradition those adorning the feet of movie goddess Joan Crawford (1906–77), who sashayed her ankle-strapped, wedge-heeled shoes through the 1930s and beyond. For those who care, the phrase even goes beyond shoes, giving **fuck-me-** or **fuck-eyes**, a modern replacement for the relatively coy **bedroom eyes** but like them indicating flirtatious, sexually encouraging stares or glances. And the shoes can also belong to a gay man, at least as written by Armistead Maupin in one of his *More Tales of the City* (1980).

FUCK YOU, JACK, I'M ALL RIGHT!

And from fuck me to **fuck you**. It works as a noun – a statement of dismissal or aggression – or as an adjective – aggressive, dismissive – but the real thing is the exclamation. **Fuck you!** (also **fug you!**, **fugh you!**, **fuck yourself!**, **f.u.!**) has been a general exclamation of dismissal and contempt since at least the 1930s and works as a distinctly more robust version of such phrases as I don't believe you! go to hell! nonsense! or don't make me laugh! It is extended as **fuck you, Charley!**, which in turn is often reversed as **Chuck you, Farley!**, but nobody's fooled.

Finally, **fuck you, Jack, I'm all right!** This began life as a nautical catchphrase, denoting utter selfishness and disinterest in the plight of anyone else; the **jack** was both a generic and a nickname for **jack tar**, a sailor. By the First World War it had spread across all the UK services and thence made its way to civvy street. The best known use is bowdlerised in the film title *I'm Alright, Jack* (1959), which burlesqued bloody-minded industrial relations and promoted itself as 'One Big Laugh Riot!' The pertinent line was rendered 'Blow you, Jack, I'm all right'. It may be assumed that the American definition of **blow** had yet to cross the Atlantic, though the film is solid with nudge nudgery, typically a stuttering shop steward who has trouble with words like 'c-c-c-lot' and 'f-f-f-ork lift truck'; not to mention a pneumatic factory girl who specialises in 'spindle polishing' as well as having a devoted interest in 'commercial intercourse with foreigners'. How we laughed.

G

IS FOR

GOB

The **gob** is the mouth and has been since the mid-sixteenth century. It may come from Gaelic and Irish *gob*, beak, mouth, but yet again it is a slang term that defies easy research. No matter, because here we require the mouth for a single function, and it's not etymological: the provision of oral sex.

It gives us **gob job**, fellatio, and by extension **gobble** both as a noun, an act of fellatio, and **gobble**, to fellate. Gobble in turn can be found as **gobble the gook, the goop, the goose** or **the gravy**. A **gobble-prick** is a sexually voracious woman, though it may be her **nether lips** that consume, rather than her mouth. Playing on that, one finds **gobbledegoo**, fellatio, or a whore who offers it. Gob job can also pun, offering the gay term for fellatio performed on a sailor. Gob here is not the mouth but the sailor himself, so-called from gob, a lump of spittle, and the fact that, according to the lexicographers Farmer and Henley in 1890, 'When a meeting [between sailors] takes place the men indulge in a protracted yarn and a draw of the pipe. The session involves a considerable amount of expectoration all round, whereby our friends come to be known as gobbies.' Spittle-bedecked or otherwise, **jack tar** has always occupied a favoured role in gay iconography. One recalls the sailor in the Velvet Underground's gay bacchanalia 'Sister Ray' (1967) who's been 'suckin' on his ding-dong'. Thus such invariably punning terms as **chicken of the sea** (the brandname of a US variety of canned tuna), the young sailor as a sex-object – and **tuna** itself is synonymous; **salt-water taffy**, a sailor's penis as an object for fellatio (in a simpler world it is merely a US sweetmeat that one licks and sucks); and **shore dinner**, another sailor who offers himself for fellatio – though a standard shore dinner is simply **seafood**, itself slang for … a sailor who is 'eaten'. Gobbling also gives **goop-gobbler**, **goop** being any slimy, sticky viscous matter, in this case semen.

EATING AND MUNCHING

Eat, is of course the pertinent term. The word alone means to perform hetero- or homosexual fellatio or, more usually, cunnilingus. It can also mean anilingus, that is, **licking the chocolate starfish**. The compounds, based on a variety of sexual nouns, mainly refer to cunnilingus: one can eat a **furburger**, **hair pie**, **box lunch**, **taffey**, **pie** and **poundcake** (which all-purpose sexual menu also refers to coprophilia – OK, shit-eating; maybe the so-called dead languages do still have a part to play – and anilingus). To **eat at the Y** may hint at the gay goings-on traditionally associated with the YMCA, but the reference here is to the woman's spread – and thus Y-shaped – legs. One can **eat** (a woman) **out**. To **eat**, or indeed **suck** (someone's) **dick** is to fellate a man (though both terms can mean to toady or grovel). The **dicklicker** (or **dickylicker**) is thus both a fellator, or fellatrix, and an unpleasant person. The punning **man-eater**, otherwise a sexually predatory woman, is a gay man and thus a fellator.

Munch is a variation on eat, and to munch is to perform oral sex. **Munching the trunch**, or **truncheon**, is unequivocally fellatio, while **munch the carrot**, i.e. the female pubic hair, refers to (lesbian) cunt-sucking. Australia's **nunga-muncher** is a fellatrix, from the Nhangka (a language of southwestern South Australia) word *nhangga*, meaning a person. **Gnaw the nana** (the penis) means to fellate. The Yiddish word **nosh**, from *nashn*, to eat dainty food or delicacies, joins the party and a fellator or fellatrix is a **nosher**. Yiddish also gives **fresser**, from *vress*, to eat. Other 'eaters' include the **glutton for punishment**, a fellator who continues sucking the penis even when orgasm has been reached; **iron jaws**, an exceptionally competent fellator; **nibbler**; **guzzler**; **muzzler** (from **muzzle**, the mouth); and **raw jaws**, someone who is still a novice as a fellator, thus an inexperienced street prostitute, and his or her antithesis the **mighty mouth**.

DEEP THROAT
AND LIP SERVICE

The mouth, of course, plays an important role. The **mouth artist** offers both varieties of oral sex, and is considered an expert at them; the **mouth worker** or **queen** only fellates; a **mouth fuck** and a **mouth job** are fellatio and **mouth music** cunnilingus, although the **hummer** or **hum job** refer only to female ministrations to a male, the pleasure being intensified by her simultaneously sucking and humming; this may be linked to the synonymous **blow some tunes** (though that may simply extend the more general **blow**). A whistler can also be a fellator, though this may be coincidental. A **gator-mouth** and a **yuck mouth** are both extra-proficient fellatrices, though given the root of the latter – **yuck**, something disgusting – she may be less than wholeheartedly devoted to her task.

The mouth, or part of it, also gives one of the most celebrated varieties of fellatio: **deep throat**, in which the penis is taken not simply into the mouth, but down the throat. The term was first popularised by the 'art porn' film *Deep Throat* (1973), starring Linda Lovelace as the girl with her clitoris in her throat; it was also used as the nickname of the then anonymous source who helped journalists investigate the Watergate Affair (1972–4). 'Deep Throat', it transpired in 2005 when he finally came clean, was W. Mark Felt, in 1972 second-in-command at the FBI. From the mouth to the lips, especially to **DSL** or **dick suckin' lips**, seen as well-suited for the performance of fellatio, which can in turn be referred to as a **lip lock**, **lip action**, **lip service**, **lip dancing** or **lip music**. To **lip read**, of a lesbian, is to perform 'cunning linguistics'. To perform an **ice job** the fellator has ice cubes in his/her mouth. Another part of the mouth that is the source of a number of further slang terms is the gums, providing proof, we may assume, that age is no bar to adventure: **gum-job**, **gummer** (the act rather than the actor) and the verb **to gum** all involve a person removing their dentures before performing fellatio. A **suck-queen** and a **suck-prick** are both gay fellators; a **suckstress** is a heterosexual female one. And **s.m.s.** does not always mean 'short message service' or texting; it can also abbreviate 'suckle my sac', yet another variation on our theme.

SOIXANTE-NEUF AND SOIXANTE-HUIT

Behind the lips lies the tongue: hence the **tongue-job**. A **tongue party** is synonymous with **soixante-neuf**, where each partner sucks the other, while the punning **tongue sandwich** refers to anilingus. To **tongue lash** means to lick either the genitals or anus. A **tongue bath** involves licking and sucking a partner's body, including the genitals and sometimes the anus, the 'amateur' version of the prostitute's **around the world** (or **horn** or **universe**) – licking and sucking the partner's body, including the genitals and sometimes the anus (thus **halfway around the world**, fellatio and licking of the anus only). Other licking terms include **lick** itself; **lick-box**, a male homosexual; and **lick the holy ground**, perform cunnilingus (a play on **hole**, the vagina). To change languages, but not imagery, there is **tollie-lekker** ('penis-licker' in Afrikaans), meaning fellatrix. Enthusiastic licking, it is assumed, will impart a shine to that which is licked, thus the contemporary UK **shine** or **shiner**, fellatio, as well as New Zealand's **polish** and the West Indies' **polish and shine**. Sucking is also the basis of **hoover (up)**, suggested – although one fears that the proprietors may be less than keen – by the brandname of Hoover vacuum cleaners, here used generically as meaning to vacuum, thus to 'suck up'. Those ever-inventive Australian cadets add **vac flaps**, a first-rate fellatrix or her lips.

In terms of mutual pleasuring, the *echt*-term remains **soixante-neuf** or **sixty-nine**, from the supposed resemblance of the two entangled bodies. This gives the jocular **sixty-eight**, defined as fellatio and explained 'you suck me and I'll owe you one'. Numbers also feature in **181**, which mathematicians will note is the metric equivalent of 69 and as such recommended for continental European holidays. They are absent, however, from the alternatives **saddle up**, playing on **ride**, and **vice-versa**.

RUSSIAN SALAD PARTIES AND WHITE HOUSE CIGARS

More exotic — and perhaps an act of faith on behalf of those who merely read of these things — are activities such as the **lick and shine**, defined as the act of smoking crack cocaine while a prostitute performs fellatio on you. This leads to the **double master-blaster**, the orgasm reached through this enhanced variety of fellatio. Other 'specialist' areas include **blumpies**, female-to-male fellatio while the man is seated on the toilet, **fifty-fifty**, a sexual act in which the two partners alternately perform fellatio and sodomy on each other, and **half-and-half**, as offered by a prostitute, fellatio plus full intercourse (alternatively, in a gay context, fellatio plus anal intercourse). Nationalism is always reprehensible, as are its stereotypes (see French, p.42) and one must leave to others an assessment of their truths. Nonetheless one must note **Russian high**, simultaneous fellatio and anal intercourse, and, while not strictly oral, the **Russian salad party**, an orgy in which all participants are covered in baby oil (a Russian salad being a mix of chopped or shredded vegetables and mayonnaise, and, in this case, people).

Two-way is a generic term for 'non-standard' sexuality. Thus a **two-way man** is a male prostitute who is willing to act as passive or active partner in sodomy or fellatio. Such a man can also be known as a **goofer**, although the term originally described a clumsy fool. And although it is usually found in quite different contexts, a **stool-pigeon** (in this case playing on **stool**, excrement as well as the standard *seat*) is one who loiters in men's lavatories in order to offer fellatio. (The possible hint of police entrapment that was once so constant in such **cottages** is probably coincidental.) While not especially exotic, **zipper sex** or **zipper dinner** refers to quick, spontaneous fellatio without even dropping one's trousers, just unzipping and whipping it out.

Stretching a point, lips lead us to **smoke** or **smoking**, yet another synonym. Smoke itself plays on **pipe**, the penis, and one should note the synonymous French argot *faire une pipe*. The verb enjoys various forms: **smoke a horn**, **smoke the bald man**, **smoke the big one** and **smoke the white owl**. For a while these were embellished by **smoke the White House cigar**, a souvenir of the Bill Clinton/Monica Lewinsky liaison, but that has surely vanished, Bush Junior preferring the smoke of real-life weaponry. A **smoker** – gay or straight – fellates. As regards pipe itself, it gives **pipe job, pipe smoker** and the phrases **blow** or **clean someone's pipe**. A **cocksmoker** partially euphemises cocksucker.

HEAD ARTISTS AND FACE PAINTERS

Perhaps even more than the mouth the head and the face play a vital role in the linguistics of oral intercourse. **Head**, quite unadorned, means oral sex and to **give head** is to offer it. It also creates the rhyming slang **blood red** and the punning **brain**. There is no gender preference any more than there is in an equally well-used term, **go down on** (or **get down on**). The **head job** is the act, while the **head artist**, **head chick**, **head queen**, **head jockey** and **head worker** are the actors. A **head hunter** swaps a suck for some drugs, as does the otherwise oddly named **strawberry**. This coinage of the crack era specifically refers to one who barters sex for crack, as the 1995 song 'Based on a true story' has it: 'She call a Strawberry, and everyone knows ... Strawberry, Strawberry is the neighborhood hoe.' Why? Good question. The prevailing theory is that 'she' spends so much time on her knees that they get scars – which, just about, resemble strawberries. The role of the knees is also found in **kowtow chow**, the act of performing fellatio while kneeling in front of one's partner. It comes from standard English *kowtow*, literally meaning 'knock the head', and defined as 'the Chinese custom of touching the ground with the forehead in the act of prostrating oneself, as an expression of extreme respect, submission, or worship' (OED). **Chow** is food, originally in the US military – with which institution in mind, one finds **army style**, oral sex followed by beating up the fellator, presumably to prove one's 'masculinity'.

The face too serves its role in mouth-to-genital diversions, usually as **get** or **give face**. **Face pussy** and **face job** mean fellatio, while **face-painting** is the ejaculation of semen over a female partner's face – the semen itself is **face-cream**. To **face the nation** is to perform cunnilingus, which may or may not amuse the watchers of the similarly named US Sunday-morning political interview show, a staple of TV since 1954. **Face fucking** is of course fellatio (though note the comment at **skull fuck**, below), while to **sit on someone's face** is for a woman to position her vagina directly above her partner's mouth, either literally sitting or squatting above their face, in order to facilitate cunnilingus; it is also used, as a synonym for enjoying man-to-man fellatio, by males. Thus the game of Carnival: 'where you sit on my face and I guess your weight'. There is as yet no multiplayer version.

The skull is synonymous with the head and plays the same role in slang. Apart from **skull** (or **skully**) itself, oral sex is a **skull fuck**, although Bruce Moore, in his 1993 study of Australian military cadet slang, suggests 'not altogether synonymous with "fellatio", for where fellatio implies activity by the woman on a (perhaps) passive male, a skull fuck implies activity by the male on a (perhaps) passive woman'. Still, a **skull job** is definitely oral sex, while to **give some skull** or **whip some skull on** mean to fellate. **Skull pussy** is a fellatrix. With the subtlety and restraint so typical of slang, we can also enjoy **skull-buggery**.

GIVE THE DOG A BONE

Other than describing the bodily organs that perform it, words for oral sex further break down into two areas, focusing on the penis and on sucking (whether of the penis or vagina). Some combine the two.

If effeminacy (see under **N is for Nancy**, p.154) is one stereotype of homosexuals (all the macho clones — anyone for a Village People reunion? — that followed Gay Liberation notwithstanding), then another (setting aside **bum-banditry**) is fellatio, or **cocksucking** as the uncompromising slang prefers it. As listed by George Carlin (see Introduction, p.8), one word for a gay man is **cocksucker**, a term that leaves nothing to the imagination and reflects the in-your-face vocabulary of a less self-censoring age. (It fails the political correctness paper, but this is, never forget, slang.) Cocksucker is first listed by Farmer and Henley in their late nineteenth-century slang dictionary, and they define it as 'a fellatrix', i.e. the female of the party. By 1919 the possibility that both parties were chaps was acknowledged, and it finds its first printed record (at least so far uncovered) in a court testimony, where a witness admitted that 'I never told anyone that I was a queen or a cocksucker or a pogue.' The most appealing example of the term comes in a couple of glossaries of Australian soldiers' slang — W.H. Downing's *Digger Dialect* and A.G. Pretty's *Glossary of ... A.I.F Slang* (largely a copy of the first book), which appeared respectively in 1919 and 1924. The entry, without any modification, appears thus: '**carksuccer** an American soldier.' One wonders which doughboy was the first to pull that one on his Anzac buddy. Not to mention how remarkably gullible, at least on this occasion, the usually sceptical down under troops must have been.

Along with cock come other penis-based words. **Bird** gives **eat**, **swallow** or **gobble someone's bird**; to **cop a bird** is to fellate, usually as performed by a prostitute; **bird-washing**, however, is mutual cunnilingus. **Bone**, productive of a whole range of compounds, such as **bury one's bone in the back garden** (also **bury one's bone in the back yard**), to sodomise, gives **bone-gobbler, bone-eater**, and **bone-queen**, all of which mean a male homosexual, and by stereotype a fellator. A **bone hog** (on the pattern of **tush hog**, a sexual athlete) is a dedicated and enthusiastic fellatrix. And one can **gnaw** or **smoke** one's partner's bone. To **give the dog a bone** is to have sex — although not especially with a **dog**, an ugly girl — while the **nodding dog**, as probably not seen on the back shelf of one's car, although perhaps on the back seat, is indeed a plain girl doing her oral best.

The decline of camp gaiety has sadly diminished the currency of gay slang, but any review of terms referring to the penis must include **basket**, also **basketful of meat**, **basketwork** and **picnic basket**, which since the 1940s have all referred to the male genitals and more specifically the bulge caused by their display in tight trousers. Paradoxically, the earliest slang uses of basket refer to the vagina and thus a woman in sexual terms as well as sexual intercourse or **basket-making**. However, the gay lexicon has long since taken it over with: **chicken with a basket**, a 'well-hung' teenager; **basket days**, a spell of fineweather, permitting one to wear light clothes that reveal one's genitals; **basket lunch**, fellatio; **basket party**, a man with large genitals; **basket picnic**, **basket-shopping** and **basket-watching**, all staring at other men's genitals while wandering the streets; and **basket weaver**, one who wears tight trousers for sexual display.

Knob is the source of a variety of terms, and the reader is referred to its general coverage at K. The **hose** — otherwise provider of that lust-worthy **horndog**, the **psycho hose-beast**, a very attractive, sexy, and presumably promiscuous girl — gives **hose job**. Deliberately or otherwise **pickle**, the penis, maintains the 'eating' imagery (although there is an obvious equation of shapes), and **pickle-chugger** and **-kisser** mean a male fellator. (To **pump** and **paddle the pickle** are to masturbate.) Other penis terms include the **piccolo-player**, the **pole-pleaser** or **pole-smoker**, the **snake-charmer** and the **spigot sucker**.

BLOW JOBS AND SNOW JOBS

Why the act of sucking should be described as a **blow job** remains mysterious, and the naïve but enthusiastic girl puffing fruitlessly on her partner's penis is a staple of sexual folklore. The term, however, is perhaps the most popular, with its abbreviations **b.j.** or **b-job**, synonymous with **biting the crank**. In time, anyway, she will become a **blow job artist**, although her brother, the **blow-boy**, opts for boys only. Contemporary black slang offers **puffy**. The same imagery underlies Australia's **clarinet-player** and perhaps the **flute-player** or **fluter** who plays a tune on the **one-holed flute**. No blowing with cunnilingus, or not linguistically. It doesn't work with a **box**, i.e. a vagina (and an anus). Instead we find the **box-biter**, a lesbian who likes to **lick a box**, the **box lunch** and a **box tosser**, a sexually enthusiastic woman. The **box screw**, on the other hand, is a bank guard, even if the **screw**, meaning key, comes from the same root as **screw**, meaning fuck. Also female-orientated is **brush (the beaver)**, to perform cunnilingus. Back with the chaps, one finds **dick-sucking** and **dick-licking** (and **dick-licker**, though that can simply be a put-down), although **dick-kissing** implies flattery and **taking the hard out of someone's dick** is purely figurative: to take an unfair share. **Joint** is also a penis and to **cop one** is to fellate. Prick offers **pricknic**, **pricklick** and **pricklicker**. **Batsucker** comes from **bat** (often as **bat and balls**), while **choadsmoker** applies to either sex. The **peter-eater** fellates, while **peter puffer**, who does the same, takes us back to the world of blow. **Turkey gobbler** is a further synonym; that which is gobbled is the ever-tasty **turkey neck**. Quite how one equates glass with the penis is perhaps a secret, but the punning **blow one's glass** is a popular phrase. The role of the **sword-swallower** is self-evident and suggests the capacities of one who can **deep throat**, and while the **swallower** is happy to consume the ejaculated semen, the **spitter** is not. The **sperm-burper**

presumably does just that, while to **spit out of the window** is to spit out one's partner's semen after fellatio.

Semen unsurprisingly has its place. The **scumsucker** and **semen demon** are both fellators, as is an **icing queen**. To **spray someone's tonsils** is to ejaculate in one's fellator's mouth; that which is sprayed is a **milkshake** or **white swallow**. If, far from gentlemanly, one ejaculates in the young lady's eye, one is a **sniper**; to ejaculate on her neck is to give her a **pearl necklace**, the **pearls** being drops of semen. Other pearl terms tend towards cunnilingus: the pearl itself being both semen and what Roger Mellie's magnificent *Magna Farta* (2008) terms the **clematis**, and include **pearl diving** and **pearl-fishing**. Colour underlies **snow job**, i.e. the 'whiteness' of semen, although the term is better known as insincere, albeit persuasive speech. Perhaps the best-known synonym for semen is **come**, or as spelt in pornography, and elsewhere when one wishes to note the sexual context, **cum** (for which see **J is for Juice**, p.110).

'COME AND GAMAHUCHE THE GENTLEMAN'

Outside its primary themes, there are many random terms for oral sex and its practitioners. Among the earliest was the decidedly euphemistic **larking**, which in 1785 Francis Grose defined as 'a lascivious practice that will not bear explanation'; indeed so lascivious was it that he omitted it from subsequent editions of his dictionary. It reappeared, still coyly, in Farmer and Henley, who label it 'venery'. A century later, as fans of nineteenth-century porn will know, the word was **gamahuche**, otherwise **gama**, **gamaruche**, **gamaroosh**, **gamahoosh** or

gamahouch. Thus the somewhat detumescent line from the porn-publisher Edward Sellon's *New Epicurean* (1865): '"Quick, quick, Blanche!" cried Cerise, "come and gamahuche the gentleman."' ('Oh all right, if I really must ... ') Sellon does make amends: his biography, much-banned and little available, is entitled *The Ups and Downs of Life*; shortly after its publication in 1867 he took a Piccadilly hotel room, wrote a final note – 'Vivat Lingam, Non resurgam' or 'Long live Cock. I shall not return' – and shot himself. The origins of gamahuche are obscure; it may be from the Greek *gamos*, wedding, or the Northumbrian dialect word *rouched*, meaning wrinkled or puckered. It lives on only as an abbreviation, **gam**, and in rhyming slang where it is the root of **slice** or **plate**, i.e. **of ham**, though both terms could equally rhyme on **meat**, and thus eat. Paired with **gamahuche**, which usually refers to fellatio, is **minette**, to perform cunnilingus. Its root is the French *minette*, pussycat.

Other terms, and there are indeed many, include the **dog's dinner**, the implication being that the fellator is a **bitch** (whether male or female); **moofty-poofty** (perhaps playing on both **muff**, the pubic hair, and **poof**); **trapeze artist**; **skin diver**; **felicia** (from the mutual initial, and of course the 'fell-ay-shee-o' rather than 'fell-ah-tee-o' pronunciation of the word); and **boss**, which refers only the female-to-male act and thus points up the man's dominant role. **Spam**, usually a proprietary name for a brand of pork luncheon meat, has been used to mean vagina (otherwise the **spam alley, chasm** or **purse**) – and thus to have a **spam supper** is to 'eat meat'. To attain the vagina, one must go **way down south in Dixie**, a use of the popular synonym of the southern states of America that its coiner, the 'blackface minstrel' Daniel D. Emmett (1815–1904), who first sang the song 'Dixie Land' on 4 April 1859, had probably not envisaged. **Steam clean** suggests a very energetic act, while **talking to the mike** (think hen nights, karaoke) is available to girls only. For a gay male prostitute to **do someone for trade** is to perform fellatio without expecting anything sexual in return. To **woof it**, as in the standard *wolf*, to eat ravenously, is to perform fellatio energetically and voraciously. And lastly, the otherwise mysterious **derb queen** presumably puns on head, i.e. the derby hat that sits on it.

FRENCH TRICKS

Or not quite last. Because when it comes to sex, and particularly oral sex, one must never, ever forget the French. Setting aside the French involvement with disease (see under **D is for Dirty**, p.41) – and let's just say that it's not for nothing that **learn French** means to contract syphilis – what we are considering here is the stereotypical Frenchman's filthy habits as regards the application of mouth to **minge**.

The equation of **French** (otherwise **French art**, **Frenching**, the **full French** or a **Frenchie**) with fellatio is first recorded in H.N. Carey's manuscript dictionary of *Venery* in 1916, although the former brothel madam, Nell Kimball, writing her memoirs of life in late nineteenth-century America, cites **Frenching** as the main name for oral sex among her girls and clients. Similarly a 'Tijuana Bible' (an eight-page pornographic comic) of 1930 has a professional ask 'What do you want honey? Straight, French or any other?' To **speak** or **talk French** was to fellate.

The **French pox** aside, the main use of French has been in the context of oral sex, and usually its male-to-male variety. Fellatio itself can be a **French bat**, **French culture**, a **French date** (as well as a prostitute's client), a **French** (**head**) **job**, an act of **French love**, **French polishing** (hence **French polisher**, a fellatrix), and the **French way**, all of which are performed **French-style**. Perhaps the oldest example is the all-purpose **French tricks**, a general euphemism for degeneracy and debauchery, in which oral activity gradually took pride of place. **French language training** was a gay term defined as teaching another person fellatio. Once tutored, they became a **French language expert**. The fellator is a **French artist**; a **French active** is the passive (i.e. sucked) partner in fellatio, while **French**

passive denotes the fellator, otherwise known as a **French girl** or **lady**. To **be French by injection** (the 'needle' being of course the penis) is said of anyone considered particularly well-versed in fellatio; it has also served to identify any American prostitute who opts for foreign customers. Other linked French terms include **French dressing** or **French-fried ice cream**, semen in the context of fellatio; the **French embassy**, any location, especially a gym or YMCA, where homosexual activity is extensive and unchecked; and **French stuff**, any 'unusual' sexual activity. The **French revolution** was the movement for homosexual rights, although it was just that revolution that sent all these camperies straight to the linguistic guillotine.

The French, as anyone who has eaten there (yes, in this case, actual food) knows, may sell vegetables but they never seem to turn up in quite the same profusion on one's restaurant menu. It is fitting therefore that our last, and for some indeed least, variety of consumer is the **vegetarian**, a female prostitute or male homosexual who will not 'eat meat'.

H
IS FOR
HORNS

O n the whole, slang is seen from the male point of view. But there is one area where men for once receive the stick's shorter end. H stands for **horns**, perhaps the *echt*-term when it comes to adultery. In a world of speedy divorce, of serial monogamy, of the singleton, the freemale and of the increasingly enthusiastic acceptance by both genders of the single state, adultery seems almost quaint, even if its results can still be all too often painful. But, historically, it was numbered among the sins and as such has been irresistible to the slang confessional.

The immediate link between horns and adultery might appear to be **horn**, the penis, and that may well have come to underpin it, but ultimately it lies elsewhere. The term apparently comes from an old German farming practice: the grafting of the spurs of a castrated cock on the root of the severed comb. These transplants would grow into horns, sometimes several inches long. Thus the German word *Hahnreh* or *Hahnrei*, meaning cuckold, originally meant capon, a castrated cock. This is accepted today, although an older theory linked the term to the posture of 'missionary position' intercourse, in which the man represented a head and the woman's legs, spread and raised, were his horns. The literary innkeeper Ned Ward seems to play on both in his poem 'The Dancing School' (1700): 'I should hate a Husband with horns, were they even of my own grafting.'

WEARING THE HORNS

The horn–adultery link is old. Among those lost, almost pagan celebrations that once played a role in popular life, was the **Horn Fair**. In slang it came to mean the state of being cuckolded; or a figurative gathering of cuckolds, but it was once an absolutely tangible event. It was held on 18 October, St Luke's Day, once a year from the twelfth century and for the last time in 1768. (It has been relaunched, however, backed by Greenwich council, on a site named Hornfair Park.) St Luke bears the evangelistic sign of the ox; in other words, he 'wears the horns'. According to Francis Grose (in 1785):

> 'The vulgar tradition gives the following history of the origin of this fair; King John, or some other of our ancient kings, being at the palace of Eltham, in this neighbourhood, and having been out a hunting one day, rambled from his company to this place, then a mean hamlet; when entering a cottage to inquire his way, he was struck with the beauty of the mistress, whom he found alone; and having prevailed over her modesty, the husband returning suddenly, surprised them together; and threatening to kill them both, the king was obliged to discover himself, and to compound for his safety by a purse of gold, and a grant of the land from this place to Cuckold's Point, besides making the husband master of the hamlet.'

It is more likely, and prosaically, to have started off as no more than a regular weekly market, which lapsed and was co-opted for the burlesque procession.

The 'fair' took the form of a procession of cuckolded husbands and allied revellers, all wearing horns and sometimes masks, who walked from a Thames-side spot known as Cuckold's Point or Haven near Rotherhithe (and opposite modern Canary Wharf), where a pair of ram's horns were set up on a pole, to Charlton in Kent. The link to the saint, however, was where religion stopped. An eighteenth-century eyewitness recorded the scene: 'Those who join in the procession array themselves in strange garments: some are dressed like wolves, some like bears, some like lions, some again, like wild savages, and some like Frenchmen, Spaniards, Russians or the lusty Turk, and some wear fearful masks, but all are alike in this respect, that they wear horns tied upon their heads.' The linking of the deceived husband to all those macho animals seems odd, but perhaps it represented some form of revenge. Certainly any women in the area were not safe from 'indecencies', not to mention whippings and being soaked with pails of water. It may also link the horns to the horned rural god: Herne the Hunter. And the list of foreigners is a surely depressing display of English sexual insecurity. But as we know, in the list of sexual–national stereotypes, 'English culture' involves being beaten. It also seems that the husbands were armed with baskets and pick-axes, and that when they arrived at Charlton, they had to dig gravel. Whether this had the slightest link to their testicular **stones**, is unknown.

Once established as an image, the plays on horns became predictably widespread. To **hornify**, **give horns**, to **plant** or **put horns on** mean to cuckold. The victim **grows** or **wears horns**; he can also **blow his horn**. Those who **take a horn** accept that their partner is having or has had an affair without making an issue out of it. On the other hand, the less complaisant are driven **horn-mad**, even if the term can equally mean lecherous or maddened by lust, thus giving **horn-madness**, the condition of lustfulness, and **horn-madded**, lustful.

As ever in slang, woman, unless suppressed, is a partner's threat, a lover's promise and vehicle of her own insatiable desires. **Horns-to-sell** is the errant wife (as well as the **horn-headed** cuckold) and the **horn-child** her offspring. Her boyfriend, with whom she **horns**, is a **horn-maker** or **horner**. What they enjoy is **horn-work**. Any husband, even a newly-wed, can be a **horn-grower** or **horn-merchant** – his susceptibility, if not now then inevitably later, to her wandering eye and **hot** proclivities being taken as read.

ON THE HORN

One more term for a cuckold is **horny** (**Old Horny** being the devil), but horny as mainly used since the early nineteenth century means randy, lustful, 'up for it'. Used intransitively it can also mean sexually arousing, erotic, pornographic. The **hornies** are sexual desire, as is **horniness**. In this case the horn, while still physical, is the penis, which since the late sixteenth century it has been supposed to resemble. In 1748 John Cleland, always one for gilding the genital lily, had his heroine Fanny Hill hymn 'a column of the whitest ivory, beautifully streak'd with blue veins … No horn could be harder, or stiffer; yet no velvet more smooth or delicious to the touch.'

There's undeniably a crossover with the adulterous lust that creates a grafted forehead. As well as the penis, horn can mean sexual excitement or desire, an erection and a male sexual athlete. It can also mean the nose, an adornment that has often been linked to that other, lower physical projection. It can even mean an ear. In compounds, **hornbag** puts woman in her place as a receptacle for a man's horn. A **horndog** is either sexually aggressive or sexually frustrated and to horndog is to chase sexually, adding in standard English *dog*, to pursue. A **horn movie** is a porno film, while **horn pills** are aphrodisiacs, or that's what they claim. To be **on the horn** is a synonym for horny. **Hornsmoking** is fellatio, and thus a **hornsmoker** is a fellatrix (it doesn't seem to be extended to gay use). The **hornpipe**, a nice piece of sixteenth-century punning, is intercourse, and one naturally **dances** it. Just to confuse matters, such intercourse, at least originally, was usually adulterous. Back in the eighteenth century (and for two centuries afterwards) **horn-colic** was either an involuntary horn, or erection, or male sexual frustration. When that frustration is relieved, a man is said to **scrape** or **cut his horns** (though it can also mean masturbation); the testosterone-filled stag needs little reference.

I IS FOR

I is for **it**. Short word. Short entry. Brief. Focused. To the point. Useful though. It is. So.

It is the ultimate euphemism. One can extend it, as in **whatdoyoucallit**, but 'it' does the job quite satisfactorily, thank you. It has meant the genitals, both male and female; it has meant their coming together for sex; it has meant masturbation; it has meant a chamberpot; it has meant ejaculation and excrement, fools, virginity and sexually available girls. It has meant death, it has meant the acme of fashion and the quintessence of black spirit and sensitivity. For a while it meant sex appeal, which (given the period) rendered many quite over-excited. The traditional source of this variety of it was Eleanor Glyn's supposedly 'hot' (rather lukewarm, really) novel *It*, which appeared in 1927. 'I would like to sin', it was suggested, 'with Eleanor Glyn, on a tiger skin.' Across the Atlantic there was an 'It girl', one Clara Bow (she of the lips to match). But this particular flavour of It, it transpires, may not have come from Ms Glyn's imaginings. In 1904 Rudyard Kipling's short story 'Mrs Bathurst' offered the following: "Tisn't beauty, so to speak, nor good talk necessarily. It's just It. Some women'll stay in a man's memory if they once walk down a street.' Still, there may have been a link: Kipling's friend Lord Milner had once pursued la Glyn; maybe she was already using it in private, Milner passed it on and Kipling merely pipped her to the fictional post.

But the primary use of it is to symbolise the penis, in a variety of more or less aggressive images; either as intercourse or some form of, usually, figurative violence. Sex first. Setting aside those macho greetings of **how's it bouncing?**, **how's it shaking?** or **how's it hanging?** ('low and a little to the left'), what we're dealing with is 'it' and 'in'. And **putting**, **shoving**, **getting**, **popping**, **sticking**, **slipping**, **whacking**, **whipping**, **whopping** or **walloping**. Sometimes – regularly even – 'it' can be replaced by **up**. One can simply **have it**, or **have it off**, **up** or **away** and one can **get it on**, **off** or **off with**. Occasionally, having put or shoved it in, one can then **break it off** (the limp, post-ejaculatory member, that is), although prior to that the aim has been, having **got it up**, to **keep it up**. One can **toss it to** or **put it to** (thus Shakespeare's *Love's Labour's Lost* (*c*.1595): 'If their daughter be capable, I will put it to them').

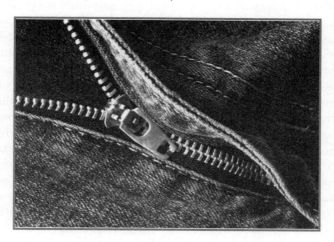

WHIP IT IN, WHIP IT OUT AND WIPE IT

If speed is of the essence one can **whip it in, whip it out and wipe it**, the latter operation necessary since one has just **got it wet** (which can also apply to fellatio, and no matter the context offers the simpler synonym **get wet**). If one likes something more prolonged one can **get down to the ground** (**and move it round and round**); the **crafty butchers** of the party (you know: they like to get their meat round the back) will doubtless **take it up the dirt road**, which anal exploration, from an active point of view, can be to **pop it in the toaster** (this 'toaster', if you were wondering, makes white bread 'brown'). To **fluff it up** is a gay term: to make the penis erect prior to appearing on the street in tight trousers; to **knock it out of the box** (where the **box** is the vagina and one must resist any sort of baseball imagery) is to have sex; to **get among it**, to achieve seduction. Given all this latent aggression it is amazing that the charitable female will either **give** or **lend him a hole to hide it in**.

Thus the literal. How about the figurative. It the aggressor. Unsurprisingly, many of these can mean to sodomise/be sodomised as well: **get it in** or **up the arse**, **ass** or **arsehole**, as well as **up the poop**, all signify to be attacked, victimised or killed. **Take** is synonymous, and adds **bum** to the list of receptacles; to **tuck**, **stick** or **jack it up someone's arse** is to betray, let down or humiliate. To **tell someone where to shove it**, **stick it** or **put it**, is to wave them a less then affectionate farewell: its most likely destination being **where the sun don't shine**. The arse itself is the 'it' in **shake it like a polaroid**: to move vigorously as in sexual intercourse or dancing. To **shake it up** (or **shake it, shake her up** or **shake oneself up**) is to walk in a provocative manner.

TAN PON IT LONG

But it can be a vagina too. Thus, to **put it about, go it, bash it** (though **bash it up you!** means go away!) and the antipodean **crack it for a quid** (long before Australia went decimal) all mean to work as a prostitute. For a woman to offer herself for intercourse can be to **cock it** or **cock it up, fling it up** or **lay it out**. To **see if it fucks**, on the other hand, does not involve sex, merely asking whether some inanimate object works. For a pair to cohabit is to **dab it up** and the Caribbean **tan pon it long** ('stand on it for a long time') refers to his sexual stamina. The scenario behind **leave it wet** (**for**) is presumably a gang-bang, while the response **I'm knocking it back with a stick**, renders the vagina generic, and implies that a man has simply too many horny women queuing up for his favours. Such men, to move from the vaginal to the anal, are probably **spinning it out of their arse** or **spreading it thick**: boasting or exaggerating – this time 'it' is bullshit and the response may well be **shut it!**, i.e.

one's mouth. Nothing daunted, he asks her **are you saving it** or **keeping it for the worms?** (i.e. the graveyard) with the hope of shaming or blustering her into intercourse. Failing that, there's masturbation, eternally unisex: he can **belt it** or **stroke it (off)**, while she **stirs it up** ('it' being 'the stew').

Nothing unisexed, however, about this final application of 'it': the voicing of male contempt. In this case it returns to that object of fear and loathing, the vagina, although it can be taken for the whole woman. Top of this particular pops is **wouldn't touch it with a (barge-)pole** (which can in turn be **ten** or **forty foot** in length) but among the other things our Lothario will withhold from the unattractive woman are **a dog's prick, a hop-pole, a pair of tongs, a red-hot poker, a pitchfork** and **a rotten stick**. But the penis can raise its disdainful head as well: that **I wouldn't touch it with mine** should go without saying, but **I wouldn't touch it with yours** either.

Right. That's **it**.

J
IS FOR
JUICE
AND
JOHNNY

Jus, French for juice as those who have had the slightest encounter with restaurant cooking – whether in the flesh or via some TV superstar – will be aware, comes from meat. It is flavoursome, wholly un-adulterated by foreign substances, at least at the moment of its creation – from the cooking of the meat – and enhances the dish one eats. It is, some might say, no more than a fancy term for gravy, at least in its simplest form.

However elaborate slang may sometimes opt to be, it's also remarkably happy with the obvious. Thus *jus*, or rather **juice** and **gravy**, have long since been called into play to deal with the liquid products of another form of meat: human flesh, or more specifically human genitals (though its allied meanings take in all areas) – semen and what we shall describe as vaginal secretions.

The earliest discovered example of juice, applied either to the penis or vagina, is found *c.*1665 in one of Lord Rochester's poems: 'While I my passion to persue / Am whole nights taking in / The justy juice of Grapes, take you / The juice of Lusty Men!' Nonetheless – and while citations remain the best way of dating a term, sometimes they just aren't on offer – although the idea of juice as spirit, vitality or energy (and all of them usually sexual) has only been found since the eighteenth century, the odds are that it was these, rather than the sexual versions which came first. Juice, which is also found as **cock juice** or **cunt juice**, is seen as the physical example of that energy, pouring out of the body.

Gravy, first as vaginal secretions (thus **gravy bowl**, the vagina) just follows juice: a broadside of around 1670 tells us that 'I slept with her all night: / I supped upon a cony fat / Whose gravy was delight.' And yes, that is a pun on cony/cunt. Rochester, in his lubricious (and but once performed) play *Sodom* (1684) is as ever to the point: 'You'll find Some of their cunts so stuff'd with gravy thick / That like an Irish bog they'll drown your prick.' Gravy has also meant sweat and blood, most specifically (and disgustingly for those of us who have resisted the wonderful world of intravenous drug use) as the experienced user's description of the mix of blood and heroin solution that is created in a hypodermic syringe before it is re-injected into the vein; it can coagulate while in the syringe and, when this happens, must be heated before the injection. Nice. So much more elegant in the mid-eighteenth century when an **injection** was simply semen at the point of ejaculation. Gravy can be expanded as **beef gravy**, **baby gravy** or **baby bouillon**, which latter have their own synonyms in **baby fluid** and **paste**.

JIZZ AND JAZZ

The idea of spirit and energy is also found in the mid-nineteenth century's **jism** (otherwise **chism**, **gism**, **gissum**, **gizm**, **gizzem**, **gizzum**, **gyzm**, **jiss**, **jissom**, **jiz**, **jizz**, **jizzum**). Its roots are unknown, although one should note the northeastern US dialect *jasm*, energy. Thus, it starts life as energy (hence **jizzless**, apathetic) and by the late nineteenth century means semen. In the southern states, around 1930–40 it actually meant gravy (as does **bull gism** or **bull fuck**, both of which play on the apparent similarity of bull semen to cream gravy; and in a nice circularity **bull gravy** means gravy too). The preferred modern spelling seems to be **jizz**, at least in its compounds: **jizzbag** or **jizzbucket**, either a contraceptive sheath or a general term of abuse; **jizzbags**, the testicles; **jizzrag**, a handkerchief or similar piece of material into which one masturbates; **jizz rocket**, the penis and **jizzwater**, again semen. To **lick someone's jizz** is to be impressed.

Jism − so it is currently believed, though the debates run fast and furious and quite unresolved – has another major role, perhaps its most important, as the most likely ancestor of the word **jazz**. All sorts of theories have been proposed: roots in French, in a West African language, in African–American sex slang and elsewhere have been suggested, and abandoned. The current position links the term to mid-nineteenth century use of jism, meaning spirit or energy; its first use has been traced to players on the 1913 San Francisco Seals baseball club, as reported by one 'Scoop' Gleason in the *San Francisco Bulletin*. As he put it in 1913: 'Everybody has come back to the old town full of the old "jazz" and they promise to knock the fans off their feet with their playing … What is the "jazz"? Why, it's a little of that "old life," the "gin-i-ker," the "pep," otherwise known as the enthusiasm.' So there you are. The progress from baseball to music is uncharted, but examples of the latter usage appear almost contemporaneously. And in time jazz would come to mean sexual intercourse and semen, and offer such sexual terms as **jazz house** or **joint**, a brothel, and the **jazz mag**, which Roger Mellie's admirable *Magna Farta* (2008) terms an 'art pamphlet [or] one handed reading material'.

SPOOCH, SPOOF AND SPUNK

Moving through slang's terms for semen, one finds **spunk**, its origin in Scots *spunk*, a spark, and another of those terms that see sperm as the tangible outpouring (from that 'tap' the **cock**) of the human spirit. It had already meant energy and courage, and indeed a match, before the semen meaning appeared in the mid-nineteenth century. Since then it has become a widely used – perhaps *the* most widely used – term. A **spunk** or **spunk-rat** can mean someone attractive, and as well as meaning brave and plucky **spunky** refers to semen. A **spunk-head** is a general term of abuse, as are **spunk-bag** (also a condom), and **spunk gullet**. The idea of a container also comes into **spunk-pot**, the vagina (thus Rochester *c.*1673: 'To be a Whore, understanding, / A Passive Pot for Fools to spend in'). A **spunk-bubble** is an attractive young woman or nubile teenager and a **spunk bucket** or **spunk dustbin** a promiscuous woman or certainly one who is branded as such. The **spunk-hammer** and the **spunk trumpet** are both the penis. Spunk also offers a number of sound-alikes: **spadge**, **splooge**, **spoo** (also linked to **spew**, to vomit), **spooch**,

spoof, **spuff**, **spoo**, **spratz**, **spuzz** and **spoot**. As verbs they can all mean ejaculate or achieve orgasm.

And, underlining its wide use, it has generated a number of rhymes: **Harry Monk**, **Maria Monk** (from the 1836 blood-and-thunder romance *The Awful Disclosures of Maria Monk*), **pineapple chunk**, **Thelonious Monk** (the jazz pianist Thelonious Monk (1917–82) and **Victoria Monk** (the music-hall star Victoria Monks (1884–1972), best known for her version of 'Won't you come home, Bill Bailey?').

CUM, SCUM AND PEDIGREE CHUM

Pedigree Chum, normally a dog food (and there may be a play on **dog**, an ugly girl here) rhymes with cum. **Cum**, as we know, is no more than pornography's chosen spelling of come, and as a noun its primary meaning is semen. Again, it has generated a number of compound uses. These include **cumchugger**, an enthusiastic fellatrix; **cum chum**, a homosexual male; **cum drum**, a condom with a reservoir for semen; **cum dumpster** or **catcher**, a promiscuous girl; **cum freak**, anyone obsessed with sexual gratification; **cum queen**, a homosexual man who likes semen, whether swallowed during oral sex or ejaculated over his body; and pornographic film-making's **cum shot**, the moment of ejaculation, invariably performed (for the camera) outside the partner's body. Meanwhile, **cum-sucking** is a general insult.

From cum to scum. **Scum** has meant semen since the 1940s, but it is probably found more commonly in compounds – where it doubtless overlaps more with the standard use of the term than in direct sexual references. Thus **scumbag** is used for a contraceptive sheath but, with its variants **joe scumbag**, **scum** and **scum wad**, is more usually a term of general abuse, as are **scumball**, **scumbelly**, **scumbucket** (also an unpleasant, dirty place) **scumdog**, **scumhead**, **scumfuck** and **scumfucker**, **scumpig**,

scumsucker and **scumsnorter**. **Bathtub** and **shower scum** stand for a repellent person, but here the scum may be the standard version.

BACK TO NATURE

The eighteenth century was a particularly fecund time for literary euphemisms when it comes to sex. Double entendres too, the over-riding point being to avoid actually saying the taboo terms even as the poet or playright rammed an unmissable elbow into the reader's or audience's ribs. **Nature** is surely one of the former. It meant the vagina, the penis and, of course, semen. More recently, in US black use, it has meant one's libido or sex-drive (thus **lose one's nature**, lose one's sex-drive), though for that can can go back to John Cleland's *Fanny Hill* (1748–9): 'After playing repeated prizes of pleasure, nature overspent, and satisfy'd, gave us up to the arms of sleep.' All compounds are euphemistic: **nature's duty**, sexual intercourse; **nature's founts**, the female breasts; **nature's** or **Dame Nature's privy sea**, the hymen; **nature's scythe**, the penis; **nature's treasury**, **tufted treasure** or **workshop** all the vagina.

Equally 'natural' is **butter**, a term for semen since the late seventeenth century, and thus **buttery**, semen-filled. **Butter-boat** (a pun on standard English *butter-boat*, a container in which one serves melted butter) stands for the vagina, as does **butterbox**. To **beat** or **churn the butter** is to masturbate, while for a woman to **make butter with her tail** is to have sex. Synonymous is **melted butter**, which also means an attractive woman, especially a mulatto who has a 'yellow' skin tone. And if **marrow** means semen, then a **marrow-pudding** is a penis.

DUCK BUTTER, GORILLA MILK AND SOGGY BISCUITS

Although there is no special link to oral sex in any of them, many terms for semen emphasise its 'food' quality. Hence one finds **batter**, as in **belt one's batter**, to have sex or to masturbate, and **splatter one's batter**, to ejaculate. Others include: **beer**, **bollock yoghourt**, **cocoa** (as in **come one's cocoa**, either to ejaculate or confess), **custard** (hence **clear the custard**, to masturbate) and **love custard**, **dick-drink**, **jimmy** (as in penis) **wine**, **duck butter** (the smell, reminiscent of duck droppings plus the colour of butter), **egg white**, **fruit-juice**, **gorilla milk** and **hot milk** and of course **milk** itself (hence the verb **to milk**, to masturbate someone). Not to mention **dog-water**, **ice-cream** or its attendant **jelly** (which gives **jelly jewellery**, ejaculated semen, covering the face and throat of one's partner, a popular version of which is presumably the **pearl necklace**), **monkey-juice**, **nut-butter** (the **nuts** being the testicles), **sauce** and **soul sauce** (a black man's semen, or, by metonymy, the man himself), **tatty** (i.e. potato) **water**, **spud juice** (which can also be illegally distilled alcohol, based on potatoes) and **spudwater**, both of which are the product of the **love spuds**, the testicles. The **sugar basin** is the vagina, which is filled with **sugar**, thus giving Bessie Smith's song 'Want Some Sugar in My Bowl'.

Food also provides a number of semen-related images. A **candy-maker** is a male homosexual who masturbates (but does not fellate) a partner, then swallows the resultant semen; **cookie-crumbs** (playing on the standard American meaning of *cookie* as biscuit) are semen stains on the trousers, as is a **dicksplash**, which can also be a noxious individual. If **cream** or **whipped cream** are semen, then the **cream jug** is the vagina, and the plural **cream jugs** the female breasts. **Pudding** or **white pudding** is another term for penis (for instance in a poem collected in 1719: 'Margery came in then with an Earthen Pot, / Full of Pudding that was piping hot') and the **pudding-bag**, the vagina; it has also meant intercourse (**have a hot pudding for a woman's supper**) and, finally, semen.

The **nads** (i.e. gonads) are the testicles; thus, semen is **nad-jam**. **Nelly**, Australian slang for cheap wine, can also be the potentially 'drinkable' semen, as is **nectar**, popularly, albeit incorrectly, known as the food of the gods (which was in fact ambrosia): as the **amber nectar**, of course, it advertised

another well-loved Australian drink. **Nectar** can also be found around 1600 as a piece of literary talk, meaning vaginal secretions.

Then, as recalled by generations of schoolboys, there is a charming little game named **soggy biscuit** or in Australia (where Sao is a brandname for a savoury cracker) **soggy Saos**. It is very simple: the participants masturbate and then ejaculate onto a biscuit: the last to reach orgasm must eat the semen-covered dainty.

LOADED GUNS AND JUNGLE JUICE

Moving on from food, the **load** (a burden or weight, in this case in the testicles or stomach) has a variety of meanings in the context of the body or bodily fluids: faeces or a bowel movement; a bout of venereal disease; an ejaculation of semen, hence an orgasm for either sex; a large penis; or a large amount of semen in the testes and thus the intense urge to have sex. A **loaded gun** is the penis before ejaculating its 'load' of semen.

From the gun the logical step is to the **ammo** or **ammunition** which it 'shoots'. Semen can also be **axle grease**, **baff**, **crunt** (the residue in fact of any form of bodily fluid), a **dose**, **face-cream** (thus **face-painting**, the ejaculation of semen over one's female partner's face), **fetch**, **French dip**, **glue**, **goo**, **herbalz**, **jit** (thus **jitbag**, a condom or, indeed, an unpleasant person), **jungle juice** (which also applies to the vagina), **jip**, **joy juice**, **knob snot**, **lather**, **letchwater**, **medicine** (hence **take one's medicine**, to have sex), **mess**, **mettle** (i.e. **mettle of generation**), **milt** or **roe** (both standard terms for fish eggs), **muck**, **ointment**, **paste** (and **man-** or **population paste**), **pecker** (i.e. the penis) **snot**, **pud water**, **scad** (possibly from Cornwall or Devon dialect *scad*, a brief shower of rain), **skeeter**, **snot** (usually a nasal problem), **spangles**, **spence**, **spend**, **spew**, **starch**, **sticky**, **stuff**, **tallow**, **white swallow** (usually in the context of fellatio), **water of life** (otherwise whisky or gin), and **vitamin S** (for semen). **Slime** (hence the unpleasant **slimebag**, **-bucket** or **-ball**) can also mean ejaculate and gives the possibly apocryphal example of post-coital Australian pillow talk: 'Bruce, di ya slime yit?' Still, the ever-inventive Aussies have also likened an orgasm to a **flock** (or **nest**) **of sparrows** (or **geese**, **peacocks** or **swallows**) **flying out of one's backside**, and for that much can be forgiven.

FROM SNOW STORMS TO RAINBOW KISSES

With that in mind, the ejaculation or application of semen calls up a number of practices (and yes, do try these at home). A **double-shot** is two ejaculations of semen during a single bout of intercourse and a **snow storm** a heavy ejaculation. A **sud-up** is the mix of vaginal secretions/semen that follows intercourse, while a **white Russian** (the similarity of white semen to the colour of a white Russian cocktail) refers to the swapping of ejaculated semen from mouth to mouth. A **hot hello** is a trickle of semen from the vagina following intercourse, while **milm** means to smear with semen and **Uncle Albert's beard** refers to semen that has been ejaculated over a partner's face and throat.

To **dream off** (as in **spunk off**, etc.) is to have a 'wet dream', a nocturnal emission. **Irish confetti** refers to semen spilled outside the vagina, the product of the coitus interruptus, as practised by pious Catholics. **Felching** – and I appreciate that this is teaching your grandmother time – is to lick out the semen from the anus of someone who has just enjoyed anal intercourse and then spit it into the partner's mouth, while **melching** involves sucking newly ejaculated semen from the vagina (possibly with the aid of a straw). The etymologies are unknown, though one word expert has suggested a link between **felch** and *filch*, an old cant word for hooking something out of a shop window. **Melch** blends felch with **minj**, itself from Romani *minj*, the vagina. On the topic of swapping fluids, there is also the **rainbow kiss**, a passionate kiss following an orgasm reached through reciprocal oral sex between a man and a menstruating woman, thus involving the mixing of semen and vaginal secretions/blood in the mouth. A **rainbow necker** (from that innocent verb to **neck** or pet) is a person who has oral sex with a women while she is menstruating. A **snowball** is semen that has been ejaculated in a partner's mouth and is then returned via a mouth-to-mouth kiss; it can be a verb as well.

Is there really a Seaman Stains in Captain Pugwash? No matter, slang makes up for him even if it is just a rumour. **Map** can mean a face but in sexual contexts it refers to a semen stain on a sheet. Maps can variously be of **Ireland**, **England** or **Africa** (and France has the same thing with *carte de géographie*). Down Under there's the **mapatasi**, **map of Tasmania** or **map o' Tassie**. Stains can also be **pecker tracks**. **Poontang**, most likely from French *putain*, a whore, means the vagina, but it can also stand for semen, and **poontang juice** comes from the vagina. The vagina can also stain the undies or the sheets, resulting in punning **clitty** (i.e. clitoris) **litter** or a **snail trail**.

FANNY PECULIAR

Slang being the macho lexicon that it is, women traditionally get short shrift. A slight deviation is permitted for vaginal secretions – but after all, what's getting **Little Miss Roundheels** (because of which she keeps tumbling over backwards) so wet and willing but some stud's gross and bloated member? So here we go: **binderjuice**, **come-juice**, **crotch oil**, **bitch butter**, **curds** (yes, as in Little Miss Muffet, but no, forget the link to **muff**), **grease** and **goose-grease**, **drool**, **booty juice** (which mixes in a little sweat and comes from the **booty**, either the buttocks or vagina), and **clam juice**, from **clam**, the vagina. The clam also offers **clam-diving** or **-jousting**, cunnilingus (often lesbian), **clam jungle**, female pubic hair, and **clam spear**, penis; a **clam smacker** is a lesbian and **clubbing the clam**, female masturbation. Other terms include **flap** (i.e. labia) **snot**, **French dip**, **jelly**, **letchwater**, **love juice**, **pussy juice**, **nectar**, **wax** and **fud slush**. **Cooze** (also **coose**, **coosie**, **cooz**, **coozey**, **coozie** and **coozy** – all of which are variants on **cunt**) can refer to a vagina or its secretions or to a woman, usually branded as either promiscuous or unattractive, and the word is thus a term of abuse aimed at a woman, in other words, a cunt.

Although it means nothing more than the buttocks across the Atlantic, **fanny** means the vagina in the UK and the aroused vagina leaks **fanny batter**. The origin of fanny remains unknown, but it may well come from John Cleland's celebrated *Memoirs of a Woman of Pleasure* (1748–9), nicknamed 'Fanny Hill' (which can be 'translated' as 'mount of Venus') after its heroine. *Memoirs* is perhaps unique among porn books: it has no dirty words at all, just a vast range of euphemisms, such as **battering piece** for penis or **centre of attraction** for vagina. Fanny has spawned its own set of terms, among them **fanny-artful** or **-fair**, the vagina, **fanny flap**, the labia, **fanny magnet**, a successful womaniser, **fanny nosher**, a lesbian, **fanny nudger**, a vibrator, and **fanny rag**, a sanitary towel, which can also be a **fanny rat** (a description sometimes applied also to the penis or a pubic louse). A **fanny hat**, otherwise a **cunt hat**, is a trilby – the crease in its centre supposedly equating with the **crack**, **slice** or **central cut** (another Cleland-ism).

A **season breast** is one that has been 'seasoned' – that is, smeared with vaginal secretions. To **queef**, incidentally, is to release a 'vaginal fart' (noisy rather than malodorous), while **punta** and **wolf-pussy** both refer to the unpleasant smell of an unwashed vagina.

RAINCOATS AND RUBBER BOOTS

Semen gets all over the place, and most dangerously – at least in slangworld – all the way to the female eggs. The pope may rail against it, but on the whole the condom is a central part of sexual life. And thanks to all those **damp** vaginas, a number of terms describing condoms play on an image of wetness and protecting oneself therefrom. Among them are **raincoat** or **caterpillar's raincoat** (playing on the shape of the penis?), **dick mac** (and **dick sack**), **diving suit** or **wet suit**, **dunker** or **dunkie** (**dunk** meaning to dip), **overcoat** (also **Dunlop** or **one-piece overcoat**), **jacket**, **sweater**, **boot** or **rubber boot**, **glove** and **willy-welly**. As well as being a reference to a winter tread tyre, as used in the 'wet', Australia's **winter tread** is a pun on **tread**, to have intercourse. **Head gasket** (i.e. the head of the penis) and **washer**, meanwhile, evoke engineering.

Protection also underpins **safe** and **safety**, **armour** (thus **fight in armour**, to have sex using a condom), **cheater** (one is cheating conception), **insurance policy** and **lifesaver** (indeed it does). Not that everyone seeks that protection. An **apache**, intercourse without a condom, plays on the Apache Indian style of riding bareback, which leads to **bareback**, usually found in gay contexts. This gives **barebacking** or **bareback riding**, having unprotected sex, and **bareback rider**, a man who has sex without a condom. AIDS can be the **bug**, and a **bug-chaser**, however perverse, is one who refuses to indulge in safe sex, and may be seen as pursuing, consciously or otherwise, that devastating illness. The adjective **raw** is used of condom-free sex, and **raw dog** is the noun.

JOHNNY, JIMMY, REGGIE AND RONNIE

And since we are at J it would be foolish to overlook **johnny**, or **rubber johnny**, still a popular term after 50 years or so of use. Alternatives are **john**, **joey**, **jo-bag** and perhaps **jolly-bag** (although a **jolly** can simply mean intercourse). **Jimmy**, a term for penis that has come out of rap music, gives **jimmy cap** and **jimmy protector**. Whether **Reggie and Ronnie**, the late Kray Brothers, would appreciate their role as rhyming slang for johnny is unknown, but there it is. For those of a nervous disposition there is **johnny-jibber**, the loss of erection that may be experienced when attempting to put on a condom.

Other terms include **blob**, **body bag** and **balloon**, which also refers to a condom that is used to carry heroin, cocaine or any other powdered narcotic; a **balloon-knot bandit** is a male homosexual. To these may be added **party balloon** or **party hat** (otherwise the flashing light on top of a police car), **helmet**, **lubie** (from standard English *lubrication*), **fantastic plastic**, **flunky** and its rhyming equivalent **wise monkey**, **franger**, **frikkie** (from South Africa), **frogskin**, **love envelope**, **nongy** (apparently a mispronunciation), **pro** (i.e. prophylactic), **tonkie** and **rib-tickler**. And of course there are the French, with **French letter**, **French cap** (an alternative to the better-known **Dutch cap**), **French safe** and, best-known, **French tickler**, a contraceptive sheath with extra protrusions for added stimulation. As ever, a **frog** is another way of saying French. An **f.e.** is a **French envelope**. The **doings** (also the male genitals) and **necessaries** merely state the need for contraception. The term **how's-yer-father** is rather more obtuse: coined in a music-hall sketch performed by the comedian Harry Tate (1872–1940) and popularised by the services during the Second World War, it is probably best-known in the phrase **a bit of how's-yer-father**, meaning sexual intercourse, but of late it has also meant condom.

THE SPORTING LIFE

A contraceptive sheath may sometimes be referred to as **sporting equipment**. **Sporting**, ever since the early nineteenth century, has had a number of secondary meanings based on the idea of sexual intercourse as **sport**, an idea first conceived in the early sixteenth century. The **sporting life** is the hedonistic one; while **sporting goods** or a **dealer in sporting goods** is a male homosexual prostitute and a **sporting house**, **crib**, **mansion**, **resort** or **room** are all brothels or gambling dens; a **sporting lady**, **girl**, **woman** or **sportswoman** works in the former.

Finally, and perhaps the most intriguing name for a condom: **Mrs Phillips' purse** or **ware**, for which one turns back to 1796 and the contemporary lexicographer Francis Grose for an explanation:

> 'These machines were long prepared and sold by a matron of the name of Phillips, at the Green Canister, in Half-moon Street, in the Strand. That good lady, having acquired a fortune, retired from business, but learning that the town was not well served by her successors, she, out of a patriotic zeal for the public welfare, returned to her occupation; out of which she gave notice by divers hand-bills, in circulation in the year 1776.'

Whether she was related to Mrs Phillips, that brothel-keeper who, in the mid-nineteenth century, ran a house at 11 Upper Belgrave Place, is alas unknown.

K

IS FOR

KHAZI

> *The Khasi of Kalabar:* May the benevolence of the
>   god Shivoo bring blessings on your house.
> *Sir Sidney Ruff-Diamond:* And on yours.
> *The Khasi of Kalabar:* And may his wisdom bring
>   success in all your undertakings.
> *Sir Sidney Ruff-Diamond:* And in yours.
> *The Khasi of Kalabar:* And may his radiance light
>   up your life.
> *Sir Sidney Ruff-Diamond:* And up yours.
>   *Carry On Up the Khyber* (1968)

The letter is K, the word is **khazi** and our text today brings light to bear upon the slang vocabulary's many terms for lavatory, or as they say in those areas of society unblessed by the late Mitford sisters, the toilet.

As befits so vital an amenity, the khazi is but one of a number of allied spellings: **carsey, carsi, cawsy, karzi, karzie, karzy, kazi** and **kharzi**, which show, among other things, yet another example of what happens when one attempts to set down on paper that which usually appears but between the lips.

Based on Italian *casa*, a house, it arrived via Polari, the language of the stage (and latterly the camper end of homosexuality) in the mid-nineteenth century. It is one of a number of available definitions: others include a brothel, a thieves' den, a pub and simply a house. And the khazi, figuratively, can describe any messy or otherwise unappealing place. *Casa* is also the root of the earlier **case** (from the seventeenth century), which again offers us a selection of sheltering roofs: a house, a shop or warehouse, a brothel (or **case-house**, owned by a **case-keeper** and wherein works the **case-fro** or **case-vrow** – from German *Frau*), a 'thieves' kitchen' and, of course, a lavatory. To **crack a case** is to break into a house (quite the opposite of Plod's variation) while to **go case** or **case-o** (or **have a case**) **with** is to live with someone or, in an era that pre-dated the modern call-girl, to work as a genteel prostitute from a flat, rather than walking the streets.

THE METAMORPHOSIS
OF AJAX

But back to the khazi and its many coevals. Although bog, crapper and dunny (at least Down Under) have come to take precendence, one of the oldest recorded terms for a lavatory seems to be **ajax**. This term, with no apparent link to any aspect of defecation, was popularised by the Elizabathan courtier Sir John Harington (c.1561–1612) in his pamphlet *The Metamorphosis of Ajax* (1596), a light-hearted plea for the introduction of the water-closet. Perhaps a little too light-hearted – such was its supposed coarseness that a less than amused Queen Elizabeth I temporarily banned its author from court. Nor does it seem that Sir John was the first to use the word: after all, Shakespeare's *Love's Labour's Lost* is dated a year earlier, and there we find – the bard being as admirably devoted to puns as ever – 'Your lion, that holds his poll-axe sitting upon a close-stool [itself a primitive WC], will be given to Ajax.' The greater likelihood is that Harington too was punning: on 'a jakes', which piece of toilet talk has been recorded as available since at least 1533. **Jakes** (also **jacque's** – a hit at the French or just sixteenth-century spelling? – **jake** and **jaxe**) has given **jacks** (still popular in Ireland), and the **jake-** or **jack-house**. The **jakes-farmer** or **-barreler** was he who emptied the privies. But such an etymology wasn't at all what Harington himself wanted, and he declared otherwise. Still unable to resist the pun, he conjured up the image of a constipated old fellow, astride the pot, straining with all his might and crying 'Age aches, age aches.' Maybe Gloriana was right – though coarseness be damned.

Abandoning Merrie England to its own devices, one moves on to **bog**, **bogs** or, originally, **boghouse**, a creation – at least as a word – of the mid-seventeenth century where it is listed in the first of a succession of slang dictionaries as a synonym for privy. It has always been, as the original OED put it, 'a low word, scarcely found in literature, however common in coarse colloquial language'. And elsewhere too. There is no mystery to the etymology: one need but picture one. That's right: boggy. And as a well-used term, bog has created its own small group of compounds: the **bog-blocker**, a non-specific term that denotes anything particularly unpleasant (the image is of some obstruction, probably faecal, blocking a lavatory); the **bogbrush**, with which one cleans the bog (a **bog brush upside down** is a cropped, spiky haircut, supposedly resembling a lavatory brush); **bogroll** and **bog bumf**, lavatory paper; **bog queen**, a gay man who frequents public toilets for sex; a **bogshop**, an outside privy; and **bog wash**, a youthful initiation rite whereby the victim has their head pushed into a lavatory pan which is then flushed (the 1968 movie *If . . .* , set in an English public school, may provide the sole on-screen portrayal – it costs serious money to get that kind of character-building).

CRAPPER'S CASTLE

After the bog, crap. **Crap** itself means excrement and its roots lie in the Dutch, *krappen*, to pluck off, cut off or separate, and the Old French *crappe*, waste or rejected matter, siftings, particularly 'the grain trodden under feet in the barn, and mingled with the straw and dust' (OED). The ultimate root is medieval Latin *crappa, crapinum*, the smaller chaff. Its earliest, seventeenth-century, use referred to money and can thus be seen as linked to one slang definition of **dirt** as cash (and a further etymology brings in the French *crape*, dirt). The excrement meaning arrived in the mid-nineteenth century. The first lavatorial uses for crap are obviously contemporary, and are found as **crapping-ken** or **-casa** (i.e. 'shitting house') and **crapping castle**, that vital part of the Englishman's home. The odd one out, chronologically, is **croppenken**, and it throws all the rest into confusion. Its first use is in 1674, included in Richard Head's explication of seventeenth-century lowlife, *The Canting Academy*, as '*Croppinken* A Privy or Bog house.'

Croppen itself is based on dialect *croppen*, a tail, and ultimately from standard *crop*, to cut off – and thence back to the origins of crap.

Crap is the unequivocal root of **craphouse**, a lavatory, any unpleasant, dirty place, and in US show business, a small, unfashionable venue. **Craphouse luck** is unexpectedly good luck, while the **craphouse rat**, condemned through the usual prejudices, stands as a byword for cunning or dirtiness.

And while I can only apologise in advance to the world's popular etymologists for what follows, crap is also the root of **crapper**, a lavatory. Rather, like it or not, than Mr Thomas Crapper (1836–1910), a doubtless admirable plumber whose manhole covers adorn Westminster Abbey to this day, but who, despite much theorising, was not even the inventor of the flushing water closet. He popularised it – vastly, and we should all be grateful for his addition of the floating ballcock (one of his nine patents) – but the crapper, as in the basis of his fortunes (he even boasted a royal warrant, from Edward VII, though sadly – fittingly? – the firm went into liquidation in 1969) comes from crap.

And just to confound matters, crapper meaning lavatory did not enter the vocabulary until after it had been used in US campus slang, in 1900, to describe an unpleasant person. Its application, in the 1920s, to US criminals served to extend the put-down to prisons themselves. Not until 1927 do we find a reference to what has become the usual meaning. Since then, more developments: the crapper can be the anus or buttocks, and in the sense of talking crap, a braggart or a liar. A **crapper dick** was a plainclothes policeman, who specialised – until such entrapment was finally outlawed – in hanging around public lavatories in the hope of entrapping gay men having sex. The same name was used for extortionists who posed as policemen to blackmail homosexuals. **In the crapper** means finished, failed, rejected, abandoned or rendered useless; a New Zealand variation is **in crapper's ditch**.

DUNNY HA-HA

And while we're in the antipodes, on to the **dunny**. Or, long before we reach Australia's adaptation, the **dunnaken**, **dunegan**, **dunnakin**, **dunnick**, **dunnikan**, **dunniken**, **dunyken**, **donicker**, **donigan** and **donagher**, all of which comes from the old word *danna*, dung, and *ken*, a house. Yes, it's another **shithouse**. It gives the American underworld **donegan** or **dunnigan worker**, a thief who hangs around public lavatories, hoping to steal from discarded coats or take parcels or anything else that has foolishly been put down. But its real gift is the dunny or **dunnee**, a term that is first recorded, in a fine example of Australia's pervasive multiculturalism, in Xavier Herbert's *Capricornia* (1938): 'Chineeman him no-more jiggel – him no-more lat belonga dunny', though more pleasing (not to mention understandable) is a 1948 example: 'You wasn't here when the dunny blew up.' Along with dunny, there's the **dunny cart**, a vehicle used to remove excrement; the **dunny man**, who drives it; **dunny roll**, lavatory paper; the **dunny-brush**, which like the bog brush is also used as a term of abuse; the **dunny budgie**, a fly that can be found in the privy (the budgie referring to its size and noisiness – the Lucky Country, eh?); and the cunning **dunny rat**, a target of predictable calumny. To **flap like a dunny door in a high wind** is to act in a panicky, nervous manner, in contrast to **bang like a shithouse door in a gale**, a male term of ultimate sexual approval, implying great feminine allure.

The **loo**, considered quintessentially middle-class and even squeamish, has a number of possible origins: French *l'eau*, water, or *bordalou*, a portable commode resembling a sauce boat and carried by eighteenth-century ladies in their muff; standard English *leeward*, the side of a ship turned away from the wind and as such the side over which one would urinate or defecate; or an abbreviation of or pun on Waterloo (whether the station or the battle it commemorates). Socially the opposite, and perhaps the most recent popular term, is **shitter**, from, of course, **shit** (see under **S is for Shit**, p.204). As well as a lavatory it can represent the anus or any form of disgusting place, e.g. a prison's punishment cell; one who defecates in public; or, as a thief, one who likes to excrete inside the places he robs. In coprophiliac sex (if you don't know you sure won't need to ask), it is one who defecates on their partner.

FROM FRANK ZAPPA'S TO ROSIE O'GRADY'S

Having laid out the primary lavatories, it seems suitable to take time to run down the rhyming slang that they have accrued. Shitter gives **banana fritter**, and both the country and western star **Tex** (1905–74) and his wife, the movie actress **Thelma Ritter** (that they can also rhyme with bitter (beer) is probably no compensation). The Muppet Show's **Kermit the Frog** presumably has no objections to rhyming with bog, nor, logically, could Star Trek's **captain's log**. The boxer **Gene Tunney** (1898–1978) rhymes with dunny, as does the phrase, here transmuted into a noun, the **don't be funny**. The late **Frank Zappa** rhymes with crapper, while the tennis champion **Ilie Nastase** offers khazi and **Mrs Chant** rhymes with 'my aunt', to visit whom is to go to the loo. Mrs Ormiston Chant (1848–1923) was a well-known moralist, and this was doubtless one of her earthly rewards. Last of the proper names is the mystifying, at least to Brit ears, **Angus Armanasco**. This one, memorialising the Aussie racehorse trainer Angus Armanasco (1907–2005) rhymes with **brasco**. Brasco? It's 'where the brass knobs go'. Boom! Boom!

More rhymes can be found in **house of wax** (and **wax** itself can mean excrement); the **jacks**; **rag and bone** (the throne); **Rosie O'Grady's**, the ladies' (lavatory); **savoury rissole**, a 'pisshole'; **snake's hiss**, a 'piss' but also a lavatory; **lemon and dash**, in which one has either a wash or a 'slash'; the **family tree** (rhymes on lava-tor-ee); and **one and two**, the loo.

TEAROOMS, COTTAGES AND THRONES

The idea of a **throne**, i.e. lavatory bowl, gives another aspect of **that place where the queen goes on foot** and the centrality, at least of the public lavatory, to certain areas of gay life. The throne, or the **king's throne** or **throne room**, is the WC, while **on the throne** means defecating. A **pretender to the throne** refers both to a heterosexual who poses as gay for the purposes of avoiding the draft or to a vice squad policeman who poses as gay to entrap real homosexuals. Thus, pursuing the regal imagery, to **abdicate** (the throne) is for the reigning 'monarch' – in this case a queen? – to leave a public lavatory in which he is soliciting to avoid interrogation by its attendant or worse still a policeman. To be **dethroned** is for a gay man to be ejected from the public lavatory where he is looking for sex.

The public bogs that provide such thrones have their own names, the most important of which is **cottage**. This was categorised by J. Redding Ware in his *Passing English of the Victorian Era* (1909) as a usage of 'fast youths', in which he attributed it to 'the published particulars of an eccentrically worded will in which the testator left a large fortune to be laid out in building "cottages of convenience"'. It may even be true, and so far the OED has yet to help us. As a public convenience, or indeed anywhere gay men meet (other than actual bars), it gives **cottage queen** or **cruiser**, a male homosexual who solicits in public conveniences, and **cottaging**, frequenting such gathering places. Almost as well-known – though perhaps no longer – as cottage was **tearoom**, which may have been based on **tea**, meaning urine (the **tea-voider** had meant a chamberpot many years earlier), but was more likely just a camp image of a load of queens sitting (or rather standing) around as at a tea-party. The tearoom hosted **tearoom queens** and **tearoom cruisers**, who searched for **tearoom trade**, a term that was both generic for the world of sexual assignations, pick-ups and consummation practised in public lavatories and for the men who enjoy being fellated there.

Synonyms include **cafeteria** (you can get 'something to eat'), **carousel** (one goes round and round looking for sex), **fairy house** or **joint** and **fairy's phonebooth**, **service station**, **lollipop** (the sucking), and **zipper club**, based on the lowering of the zipper of one's fly in order to enjoy quick, spontaneous oral sex, i.e. a **zipper dinner**. To visit a cottage is to **go on a milk run** – **milk** being semen. Finally, South Africa's **slangpark**. An apparently odd word – do they just *talk* dirty to each other? – until one appreciates that *slang*, in Dutch, means snake (in German it can be a watch–chain) and that for South African gay men, the word stands for penis. Thus the 'snake-park'. Simple, is it not?

MAKING LOVE TO THE LAV

And the lavatory has another vital function: as a repository for vomit, at least in the world of the US campus. In every case the image is the same: the commode-hugging drunken sufferer, prostrate upon their knees, head deep in the toilet bowl, gastro-intestinal functions working at full tilt – albeit in reverse. Thus we have **worship at the white altar**, to vomit, **drive the (porcelain) bus**, and **make love to the lav** or to **the loo**. One **speaks** or **talks on the big** or **great white telephone** and may address oneself to **God** or more usefully to **ralph**, an onomatopoeic term that – go on, say it – sounds just like an upchuck. And while the bowl is probably not made of porcelain (though one cannot speak for such as the Beckhams), one can also pay one's respects to the **porcelain god** or **goddess**, as well the **enamel god**. Terms include **kiss**, **bow to**, **hug**, **make love to**, **pray to** and **worship the porcelain god**, and in all cases **goddess**. That big white telephone can also be a **porcelain telephone**.

PRIVY PARADISE

Other than *garde-robes*, a form of castle storeroom which harboured some kind of seat above a long and hollow drop (and where one also stashed one's clothes), the earliest lavatories, the boghouse included, were external structures, or privies, and it is among these that are found some of the first names for any kind of lavatory. One of them is probably the oldest of all such recorded terms, slang or otherwise, and dates from the eleventh century: the **gong-house**, a word that is based on Anglo-Saxon *gang*, the act of walking, and which as such is both euphemistic and, however remotely, an ancestor of the child's plaint, 'I've got to go'. The **gong farmer** was a cleaner-out of privies, a nightsoil man.

Other early terms include the **coffee-house** or **-shop**, both looking to the 'coffee-coloured' contents of the cesspit; **spice island**, which played on its stench; the **necessary house** or **(house of) office**; the **chapel** or **office of ease**; the **house of easement**; the **convenient** or **convenience** (one that has lasted); and **my uncle's**, although that phrase was far more commonly associated with a pawnbroker's. A **wedding** (perhaps based on standard English *weeding*) was the emptying of a privy, while to **go backwards**, either from the position of the anus on the body or the privy behind the house, was to visit the bog. A **smokeshell** was the steam that arose from its still warm contents. Perhaps the most

interesting is **cuzjohn**, as used in the 1734–5 editions of Harvard College's regulations: 'No freshman shall mingo against the college wall or go into the fellow's cuzjohn.' **John** is presumably its abbreviation. The word **mingo**, to piss, is a direct borrowing from the synonymous Latin. **Jericho** is otherwise a figurative place of retirement, banishment or concealment, i.e. 'let [him] go to jericho', while **jerry**, a chamberpot, is based on standard English *jereboam*, a double magnum of wine, and may be extended as **jerry-come-tumble**, a lavatory, and **jerry-go-nimble**, diarrhoea. **Egypt**, another synonym for 'elsewhere' (hence **Bumfuck, Egypt** – the epitome of 'far away') is a natural qualifier. Well-known in America, but not elsewhere, is the **Chic Sale**, named for 'the champion privy builder of Sangamon Co., Ill.', and best known for his book *The Specialist* (1929). The **throttling pit** is the place – what else? – where one **chokes a darkie**.

Privy (from Old French *privé*, intimate, personal) itself plays a role in slang: the punning **privy council** is an outhouse, and a **privy-queen** is a gay man looking for sex in or around public lavatories. The **privy counsel**, however, is the vagina, otherwise the **privy paradise**, **privy hole** and indeed **privy**. (Whether these smear the vagina as 'dirty', or whether they point up its role as a 'private part' or indicate its place 'at the front' of the body are all open to suggestion.) A last round-up offers **California house**, **backy**, **dumpty-doo** and **dumpy** (variations on dunnee), **hoosegow** (from Spanish *juzgado* and far more usually meaning a jail) and, bringing us back to the world of *Carry On*, **kybo**, which abbreviates **Khyber Pass**, the arse. The **library** refers to the catalogues that were hung in the privy as toilet paper. And a little piece of history: the **Cockney's luxury**: breakfast in bed and using the pot, rather than leaving the warm house for a trip to the outdoor privy. The **po** usually means a chamberpot, from the 'affected' euphemism *pot de chambre*, but the phrase **after you with the po, Jane** referred not to a shared potty, but to the need to take turns in using an outdoor privy; in time it would apply equally to the indoor facilities.

LET EVERYONE PISS ON LYING DICK TWISS

The chamberpot, a miniature, portable lavatory if you will, was once a normal piece of bedroom furniture, the **gazunder** (i.e. the bed) as one nickname had it. Space precludes the listing of every name, but some are worth a little exploration.

Probably the earliest is the **jordan**, found in the fourteenth century. Some have tried to link it to jordan-bottle, but more likely was the synonymous standard use of *jordan*, a pot or vessel formerly used by physicians and alchemists. Such pots might often have held urine for analysis. The **looking glass** carried a similar image – both one's reflection in the urine, as well, possibly, as the attention paid by contemporary physicians to the urine itself. Thus the eighteenth-century riddle: 'Q. Why is a Chamber-Pot call'd a Looking-Glass? A. Because many rarely see their Faces in any other.' The **pisspot** (or **pee-pot**, **piss-barrel**, **pissing-pot**) had its brief moment of fame in 1710 when there appeared in Clapton near Hackney, then a village near London, a house (perhaps a tavern) known as Pisspot Hall. As Francis Grose explains, it was 'built by a potter chiefly out of the profits of chamberpots, in the bottom of which the portrait of Dr Sacheverell, preacher, was depicted'. Dr Henry Sacheverell (*c.*1674–1724) was a High Church and high Tory cleric, who preached two sermons in 1709 that resulted in his impeachment on charges of seditious libel. He was condemned, but received so light a punishment as to claim victory. His supporters were as vehement as the unknown potter. The Rector of Whitechapel commissioned an altarpiece in which the figure of Judas Iscariot was represented by that of the Dean of Peterborough, one of the Doctor's most virulent critics. A similarly 'biographical' chamberpot was the **twiss**. In this case the victim was one Richard Twiss (1747–1821), an English writer who had authored a highly critical 'Tour in Ireland'. To take their revenge the Irish produced a chamberpot

135

with a picture of Richard Twiss inside it, beneath which was inscribed the rhyme 'Let everyone piss / On lying Dick Twiss.' Finally, there is the late seventeenth-century's **Oliver's skull**, a reference to the late Oliver Cromwell, of far from blessed memory.

Across the Atlantic the mid-nineteenth century name was, among others, the **badger**, giving rise to a practical joke – the **badger fight** or **pulling the badger** – whereby a full pot was emptied over some unfortunate's head; this was known as **christening** them. Thigh-slapping stuff, to be sure. Nineteenth-century Britain offers **jemima**, which doubled as the serving maid and the chamberpot – underlining her duties in removing it, and the twentieth century's **charley** or **charley whitehouse**, i.e. from the whiteness of the **shitpot**. **It** (otherwise the genitals or sex) was a euphemism, as was **Sir John** (otherwise a parson or a penis). The **stinkpot**, also the vagina, was not. **Chamber music** represents the sound of urine hitting the pot, and the urinating penis is seen in **member mug**, **master can** and **jockum gage**. One last contender: the **remedy critch**, which is based on standard English *remedy*, meaning 'ease', and *critch*, an earthenware vessel, ultimately from *cratch*, a stable hayrack and thus a *crèche*: the term is used as such in early descriptions of Christ's birth.

L

IS FOR

LING

Then the girl shoved her hand 'neath her
clothes in a shot,
And rubbed it about on a certain sweet
spot;
Then, blushing so sweetly, as you may suppose,
She put it her hand up to the fishmonger's nose.
Tolderol, &c.
The fishmonger smelt it, and cried with delight,
'I know what you want, by the smell, now, all
right,
'Twas a good thought of yours, recollection to
bring;
I'll tell you directly – you wanted some ling.'

'The Maid & The Fishmonger' (1837)

The ling, states the late but eternally great Jane Grigson in her *Fish Cookery*, 'is somewhat tasteless … eatable and good for soups, but they don't have the merits of cod.' Sorry girls, but the guru has spoken and cod, or should one say **cods**, rule. Or so they do in that man-manufactured utopia that is slang and its stereotypes. For the ling, otherwise this 'Monday fish' as Mrs Grigson dismisses it, is just one of that most sensitive of slang's subsets: the vagina equated to a fish. And just in case you're struggling as to labia/fins, clitoris/tail or some such connection, let us be clear: the vagina resembles a fish because like a fish it stinks.

So first on the slab is the **ling**. Initially a woman, albeit considered as a sexual object (ain't they all?), and thus Shakespeare in *All's Well That Ends Well* (c.1602): 'Our old ling and our Isbels o' th' country are nothing like your old ling and your Isbels o' th' court.' And almost immediately afterwards, woman considered as her vagina in Mennis and Smith's 'Description of three Beauties' (1656): 'Mopsa with her puddle Dock, / Her Compound or Electuary, / Made of old Ling, or Caviary.' **Puddle dock** – when the vagina doesn't stink it's wet, just like a fish – is a little bonus. Almost simultaneously ling described the female sexual odour, which by the 1920s lost its sexuality and meant simply a stench. **Ling-grappling**, like some bizarre fairground attraction – staged no doubt in a pit of mud – meant sexual intercourse.

The **cod**, ling's culinary conqueror, is not, of course the vagina. Standard English *cod* means a bag, which gave the early sixteenth-century cod, a scrotum, and thence slang's cod, the penis and plural **cods**, the testicles (the *scrotum* remained standard English). The **cod-piece**, otherwise that flap on the breeches which covered the male genitals and was worn until *c.*1600, meant the penis; only the **cod-trench** meant the vagina. It stank too.

GONE FISHING

Before moving on to other species, let us pause for the generic: **fish**, and again, let us resist illusion: the link is based on genital odour. That's it – not shiny eye, nor colourful scales, nor yet sinuous movements. Coined in the mid-sixteenth century, when it wasn't just the over-ripe language of the market's fish-women that caused Londoners to shy away from Billingsgate, slang's fish meant both the vagina and the woman. Thus things stayed for three centuries, at which point promiscuous women, usually prostitutes, joined the party, and, a century later, the gay world took it up, variously using fish to describe a heterosexual woman, a gay man who masturbates while performing oral intercourse, an effeminate male homosexual, any form of sexual intercourse, a 'feminine' lesbian and semen. A new inmate at a US prison is also a fish.

The odour continued to wash over a variety of compounds, often coined by less than admiring gay men. **Fish-cunt** and **fish-fanny** – who'd have possibly imagined – meant a woman; a **fish dinner** was sexual intercourse with a woman and thus the woman herself; and a **fish market** was the vagina, a brothel, or, on campus, a women's dormitory. If the **fishmonger** (also a womaniser) was a madam or a bawd, then the **fishmonger's daughter** was a prostitute. A **fish supper** is sexual intercourse, especially in the context of a conjugal right, and may relate to the older **warm the old man's** or **husband's supper**: to stand in front of the fire with one's skirt lifted. The **fishpond** and **fish tank** represent the vagina, as does **bit of fish** (also intercourse); to **have a bit of fish** (**on a fork**) is to have sexual intercourse, as is to **slip someone the fish** (although here it is the penis that has the aquatic life). A **fish queen**, another gay term, is any man, irrespective of sexual choice, who enjoys **eating** or **chewing (the) fish**, i.e. cunnilingus. A **loose fish**, possibly from the whaling jargon loose fish, meaning a whale that is fair game for anybody who can catch it, is either a promiscuous woman or an all-out whore. To **go fish** is for an effeminate gay man to take the 'feminine', passive role during sex, for a 'masculine' homosexual or lesbian to give cunnilingus or for a gay man to become coy or flirtatious, i.e. to react like a teenage girl. To **go fishing** is to go out looking for a sexual partner. Last of all, the insult **fish fingers!** refers not to Captain Birdseye but implies that someone has placed his finger(s) in a woman's vagina and then failed to wash them – his fingers smell accordingly.

OLD TROUT AND HOT TUNA

Thus established, it's down to variety: if **milt** (fish roe) stands for semen, then to **double one's milt** is to ejaculate twice without withdrawing and the object of the ejaculation the **milt market** or vagina. The Caribbean's **salting**, i.e. 'salt thing', or salt food, refers to dishes cooked with salt fish or meat; one of which in slang terms is the vagina. The **scate** (i.e. skate) can stand for both the vagina or a prostitute, while the **snapper**, another vagina, is in addition a bout of first-rate sex or a very attractive girl (with whom one has had it). Similarly aggressive is the **snapping-turtle** (**puss**), coined by Terry Southern in *Candy* (1958): 'Then I hit him with my snapping-turtle just as he was getting his big soulful Hebe nuts off.' The reference is not merely to the vagina, but to the use of the muscles therein to intensify the copulatory experience. The **tench** is a fish, but it already has another role in slang: a prison; the tench as vagina could equally play on either origin. The **trout**, however, is unequivocally piscine: the trout itself is the vagina, an **old trout** an old woman and to **have a trout in the well** is Irish for being pregnant. The trout also plays a central part in the exotic **grope for trout in a peculiar river**, a synonym for intercourse probably invented by (and used by no one other than) Shakespeare, and found in *Measure for Measure* (1603).

The **tuna** is yet another variation on the fish/vagina theme, and can be extended to **tuna taco**, a woman's genitals, especially in the context of cunnilingus. The tuna can also be a girlfriend, or in gay use, a homosexual sailor who will only take the passive role in fellatio – a cry of **hot tuna!** indicates that one has just seen a sexy man. Still at sea, **seafood** (once Prohibition-era smuggled whisky, often brought into the States by boat) refers to sailors as the object of gay lust, and hence the **seafood queen** is one who prefers sailors for sex. Back to the fishy vagina, seafood can also signify cunnilingus, or the woman with whom one enjoys it. A **sea pussy** is a homosexual sailor, while to **part the red sea** is to masturbate a woman.

141

CLAM-JOUSTING

To turn from fish to crustacea, which, if nothing else, frequent the sea and which – slang not being the best of taxonomers – bear the same fishy image when it comes to the female **damp**. In fairness, the **clam** (and its cousin the **bearded clam**, which for the purposes of intercourse can be **speared** or **split**) gains its admission to the lexicon by way of its bivalvic opening and shutting. Thus its first meaning was the mouth; the vagina comes a little later, and can also be used for the whole woman. More recently we have had **clam chowder**, **jam** or **juice**, all being vaginal secretions; **clam-diving**, cunnilingus; **clam jousting**, lesbian sex (presumably rubbing two clams together); the **clam jungle**, the female genitals and pubic hair; **clam smacker**, a lesbian and the odd man out **clam spear**, the penis. To **club the clam** is for a woman to masturbate. The **whelk** or **periwinkle** as vagina takes us back to the fish connection, although the cod-aggressive **I'll have your whelk** may refer to something else again.

A lobster is pink, at least subsequent to its immersion in the boiling pot, and in this case it is the colour that confers the role: the penis, at least in Caucasian contexts, can be seen as pink and thus a **lobster**. The **lobster-pot** is naturally the vagina, although it can also be a gay sailor who subjects himself to anal intercourse.

Finally the **oyster**, which once more alludes to the opening/shutting side of life, although slang would surely never miss out on an allusion, even subconscious, to the perils of such a bivalve gone bad and thus make the usual link of the female genitals to a threat. Still, movement is predominant, hence Thomas D'Urfey in 1719: 'And now she has learnt the pleasing Game / … She daily ventures at the same, / And shuts and opens like an Oyster.' Following the pattern already established, the oyster can represent the basic triumvirate: the vagina, the promiscuous woman and the full-on whore. In addition its slippery consistency gives us semen, or a gob of phlegm. A pair of **oysters** are, naturally, the testicles and compounds offer the **oyster** (i.e. semen) **catcher**, the vagina (and here, perhaps not deliberately, one has a hint of the substantial list of woman = bird terms, since the standard oyster-catcher bears feathers, not fins), to **catch an oyster**, to have sex, and to **inhale the oyster**, to fellate. **Oyster-faced** refers to the creature's 'beard' and means unshaven. For connoisseurs of late-Victorian porn, both *The Oyster* and its 'senior partner' *The Pearl*, will be immediately recognisable as the titles of popular 'journals of facetiae and voluptuous reading' and home to such one-handed thrillers as 'Lady Pokingham, or They All Do It' and 'Sub-Umbra, or, Sport among the She-Noodles'.

FOUNTAINS OF LOVE

No water, no fish, and thus the vagina has embraced a number of watery terms that underline its state when excited. On the whole, references to sex prefer to pass over any adjacent excretory functions, but **pisser** can mean vagina – as well as penis. Other terms include **sluice**, **duckpond**, **damp** (another Terry Southern coinage), **watercourse**, **-box**, **-gap** and **–mill**, **fountain of love**, **living fountain**, **wayside fountain** and **pump**. The most interesting is **stream's town**, a term that is found in connection with the eighteenth-century phrase a **Tipperary fortune**, referring to a woman who has no actual fortune other than her own body and defined by Grose in 1785 as: 'Two town lands [i.e. the breasts], stream's town [the genital area] and ballinocack [the anus, from Irish *baille*, a town and of course **cack**]'.

M IS FOR MOTHERFUCKER AND MIAOW

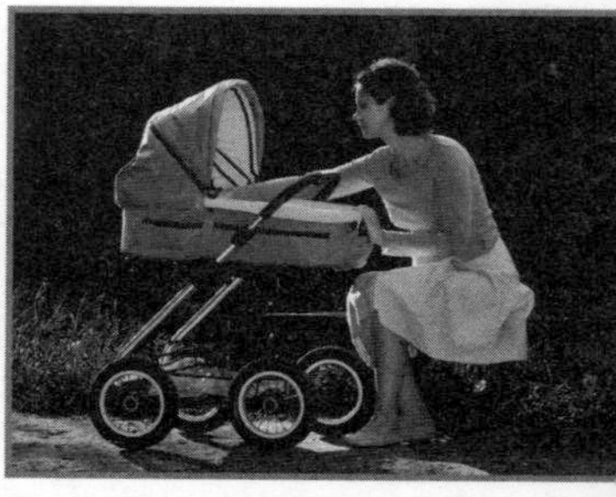

I t's hard to say, well, not so much hard as constricting, but there is no way round this. Following, as we are, at least so far as is feasible, the Carlin canon, M is for **motherfucker**. The oedipal polysyllable. Of course there are plenty of other M's that might qualify. Some might get an outing below and masturbation alone opens a whole can of worms. And as for menstruation … But M, one cannot escape it, is for motherfucker.

Incest, from Latin *incestus* meaning 'unchaste or impure', is pretty much on the social no-no list. It's a form of child abuse, like it or not, and with concomitant effects on the victim, and it's mainly a father–daughter thing. Nonetheless the mother–son stuff is popular, if mainly in porn, where 'Goodness, Billy, you've gotten to be a really *big* boy. Just let me …' is a remark almost universally followed by 'Oh gee, Mom … '. Yet **motherfucker** and **motherfucking**, while open to neutral use, are on the whole not used congratulatorily, especially when they refer literally to … fucking your mother. A **bad** or **mean motherfucker** may in context be an admirable individual, but such praise is not based, one can rest assured, on a person's domestic arrangements. Nor, before we look further at the primary term, is mother always the object. **Father-fucker** can both be a gay synonym, and is used in the same ways, including that of a positive epithet. And a **granny-jazzer**, while essentially euphemising the root term, seems pretty unequivocally to refer to one's grandmother (**jazz** being a still-popular alternative to fuck, and offering such kindred terms as **jazz mag**, for a 'men's magazine'). And while these are Hindi rather than English, **banchoot** and **betechoot** mean literally sister- or daughter-fucker, from *ban*, sister, or *betee*, daughter, plus *choad*, a male copulator. (Despite the apparent similarity, it is unlikely that **choad**, meaning penis, is related, being most likely based on Najavo *chodis*, penis.) Such terms were included in the celebrated dictionary of raj jargon, *Hobson-Jobson*, in 1886, but with a proviso concerning 'Terms of abuse, which we would hesitate to print if their odious meaning were not known "to the general". If it were known to the Englishmen who sometimes use the words, we believe there are few who would not shrink from such brutality.' Motherfucking, it would seem, was beyond the pale.

DEM SWEET MOTHAFUCKAS

It is presumably a reflection of the power of the incest taboo – especially those precious moments with mama that give a whole new meaning to the phrase 'hand-reared' – that motherfucker and its derivatives remain by most calculations the 'dirtiest' of all 'dirty' words. For that reason alone it is also one of the hardest to date. The term can be found in 1929 in Rufus Perryman's song 'The Dirty Dozen': 'Now you's a jumpin' motherfucker, cheap cocksucker, / Goin' out in the alley doin' this, that an' the other.' But there's no doubt that the term was in use long before – R.S. Gold, in his *Jazz Lexicon* (1964), claims its existence in the black community at least as far back as 1900. And although it has moved out into the wider world, carried there no doubt on the ever-widening waves of rap's popularity, it remains most widely used within black populations. Essentially a negative, the ultimate in insults, it can variously stand for anything one dislikes, an infuriating or surprising state of affairs, or in contrast a black-to-black term of affection or a compliment, e.g. 'Jimi Hendrix was a bad motherfucker on guitar.' It can also mean nothing more than 'thing', no judgement implied. It can be a synonym for **damn**, e.g. 'I don't give a motherfucker', an indefinite standard of comparison, e.g. 'crazy as a motherfucker', or a large or outstanding example and a place. It offers phrases such as the intensifying expletive **for a motherfucker**, thus 'he has guns for a motherfucker', meaning he has a great many guns, and the declarations **I'll be a dirty motherfucker** or **I'm a motherfucker**.

The possible uses have been well summed up by an interviewee included in Edith Folb's study of American black talk, *Runnin' Down Some Lines* (1980):

> 'You jus' be sayin' dat any way come to your mind. Like you got some o' dem sweet mothafuckas. They righteously together brothers, got they game uptight, they on dey J.O.B.! Right on! Got dem lowlife thugs. They mean mothas. Don't be messin' wid 'em. Blow you away in a minute! Johnny he my ace, now he a bad mothafucka. He together. Strong rap to d' young ladies – and he go down wi'chu right now! We tight. Gots dem little ol' punks. Think they together, be talkin' out d' side dey neck! Jive mothafucka don't hold no air! See like da's one o' dem slangs got all differn' kin'a meaning. Don't be callin' young lady dat. Dude use dat talk 'bout other dude.'

MOTHERFRIGGING MOTHERFUGGERS

Given its taboo status, motherfucker has engendered a wide range of what can be termed semi- or quasi-euphemistic synonyms. They are, one might suggest, the best testimony to the word's power. The simple abbreviation **mother**, tops the list, along with **motherfugger**, employing the barely masked euphemism **fug**, coined by Norman Mailer for his novel *The Naked and the Dead* (1948).

With no other rationale but the vaguely alphabetical, here are some of the leading contenders (I offer both the -er and -ing forms): **mother-bugger, mother-feryer, mother-flicker, mother-flunker, mother-fouler, motherfrigger, mother-fuyer, mother-grabber** (also **father-grabber**), **motherhead, mother-hopper** and **mother-hubba**, plus its variants **mother hubbard,**

mutha hubbard and **mother hubber** – and hence John Lennon's assurance in 'Gimme Some Hope' that that 'No short-haired, yellow-bellied, son of tricky dicky / Is gonna mother hubbard soft soap me.' Along with which come **mother-hugger**, **mother-humper**, **mother-jiver**, **mother-jumper**, **mother-lover** (a euphemism's euphemism), **mother-plugger**, **mother-raper**, **mother-rubba** or **mother-rubber**, **mother-eating**, **mother-feeling**, **mother-flunking**, **mother-fouling**, **motherfrigging**, **motherfreying**, **mother-grabbing**, **mother-hopping**, **mother-humping**, **mother-jiving**, **mother-loving**, **mammy-loving**, **motherlumping**, **mother-ramming**, **mother-sucking**, **mother-hugging**, **mother-raping** (the term of choice in Chester Himes's Harlem stories of detectives Grave Digger Jones and Coffin Ed Johnson) and the exclamation **mothersomething**!

Mammy or mama can substitute for mother, thus offering **mama-huncher** or **-hunching**, **mammy-dodger** and **-dodging** and **mammy-dugger**, **mammy-jammer** (also **mamma-**, **mama-**, **-jabber**, **mammie-**, **mammy-jammy**), plus **mammy-jamming** and the rest. The same goes for **mammy-tapper** and **-tapping**.

Merely silly are **fuckermother** and **futhermucker**, but there are a number of synonyms that are maybe less than immediately obvious. These include **Mary Frances** (a very Irish version), **maw-dicker** and **mo dicker** (both using dick, to have sex), **mickey-fickey** and **micky-ficky** (playing on motherfucker and **ficky-ficky**, the clichéd invitation to sex offered to horny holiday-makers), **mofo**, **mofuck** and the simple **m.f.** Others are **mothereff**, **motheren** and **motheroo**; the sacrilegious (and one would prefer to assume unlikely) **mother superior**; **muddy funster**; **mudfucker** (a reference, perhaps to Lenny Bruce's dictum: bereft of a human partner, a guy will 'fuck anything, even mud'); and **muhfuh** and **muhfukuh** (both phonetic rendering of black pronunciations). The variations of censorship in Anglo-Saxon countries have led to a variety of attempts by film-makers to mask the brute reality, the best of which is probably director Alex Cox's gloriously (and doubtless deliberately) inapposite use of **melon-farmer** when he redubbed his film *Repo Man* (1984) for the anodyne restrictions of the small screen. The term **meidnaaier**, Afrikaans for maid-fucker, is not a synonym: it refers to one who has intercourse with black women.

Shorn of any extension, **motherfuck** comes in both noun and verb forms. The former is a highly derogatory term for a person or an object; it can also appear as a more 'extreme' synonym of **damn** ('I don't give a motherfuck') and **hell** ('get the motherfuck out', 'what the motherfuck'). The verb is another stand-in, used as a general curse, as in 'motherfuck the pigs!' (the police that is, not the generally blameless porkers). As an adjective, **motherfucking** (with such alternatives as **m-fugging**, **mother-fugging**, **muthafucken** and indeed **sisterfucking** as well as those listed above) is a general intensifier and may also be used as an infix, to accentuate or denigrate the word thus altered, e.g. **emanci-motherfucking-pation**. Finally comes **motherfucking A!**, like its peer **fucking-A!** an exclamation used to denote astonishment or dismay; and in positive senses acceptance, praise, recognition.

THE CAT'S MIAOW

But M does have alternative constructions, and one is miaow. Not slang as such, but it shows the way: after such sordid wanderings, let us return then to the domestic hearth: to our **cat**, our **puss** and our **pussy**.

The origins of the standard word *cat* are lost in time. Cats were domesticated in ancient Egypt or even earlier, and every recorded language seems to number some form of feline cat/kat/kot/gat root in its most basic vocabulary (even if the ancient Greeks preferred *ailuros*). But beyond that? No news to date. In slang terms, in the fifteenth century it denoted a prostitute; by Shakespeare's era it embraced any woman, especially a spiteful and malicious one – thus an **old cat**, an unpleasant, gossiping old woman. Turning itself on its head, it has also meant an attractive girl, or a girlfriend (pretty or otherwise). A cat can be a lesbian. All these suggest the cat's stereotypically 'feminine' characteristics. Its fur inevitably leads to the use of cat as another term for the female pubic hair, and from there it can mean a lady's muff (and a **muff**, of course, takes us back to that **fur**, which itself …). The female genitals may also be associated with a **black cat with its throat cut** or a **cat's head cut open**.

The slang cat comes with a selection of compounds. New Zealand's **cat bar** recalls the era when pubs offered a ladies' only or ladies and escorts' bar; those who frequented them might be a **cat party**: women only. Whether the guests include a **cat-lapper**, a (lesbian) cunnilinguist, who can say. A **cat fight** involves two (or more) women, while a **cat-scrap** describes one of the participants. A **cat flat, -shop, -nest** or, most popularly, **cathouse** is a brothel, while a **cat-lamb** formerly meant an ageing, worn-out prostitute. In her prime, a cat-lamb may have been a **cat o'mountain**, a spirited whore (and a direct steal from the standard use, meaning a panther or cougar). She might have experienced the **cat-wagon**, which meant both the police wagon that took whores to jail after a raid, or a travelling brothel. This latter was found in many US rural areas before the anti-'white slavery' legislation of 1910: the women travelled and worked from a horse-drawn covered wagon, following the cattle trails or visiting cowboys out on the range. Around the same time, and in rather smarter circumstances, one could have encountered a **cat on a testy dodge**, a genteel female beggar who asked for money at people's houses, often backing her request with a (fake) testimonial from a charity. There is one cat, however, who is not a woman: defined as the penis, it comes from the synonymous Italian *cazzo*, although there may be a wink in the direction of the lecherous tomcat. **Catfood**, in this context, means sexual intercourse and **skin the cat** means to enjoy it.

PLAYING PUSSY

The informal puss, followed by puss(y)cat and pussy, all appeared around the same time: the sixteenth century. The word is linked to the Dutch *poes*, German regional *puus*, Danish *pus*, Irish *puisin*, and so on. These all appear as 'call-names' ('come here! puss! puss!'), although there is a further sense of *poes* as a large soft mass – but the evidence suggests that this came after, rather than before the cat. And **poes**, for Afrikaans speakers, has its own role, as slang for the vagina, with compounds **poesboekkie**, a porn book or magazine; **poesface, -head**, or **-licker**, a trio of insults; and **poesplaas**, a place where the cunts are figurative rather than factual: a reformatory. As for **puss**, it was first used (originally borrowed from dialect) to describe a hare; later it acquired invariably 'feminine' senses, variously signifying a (young) woman, a prostitute (or madam), the vagina, the 'female' of a lesbian couple, and, in gay circles, the anus (from its 'vaginal' role in sodomy) or an underage boy.

It is **pussy** which was and remains the 'star' of the show (or 'Poosy' as Sean Connery immortally apostrophised Honor Blackman in *Goldfinger*). Like puss it meant a woman – the assumption being of her sexual availability – before it focused on her vagina, and thus, metonymically, became sexual intercourse. Thence it used the various feline stereotypes. The 'softness' of the cat gives one who is a 'pussy', i.e. gentle or kind; a male homosexual or at least a man who is judged to be or teased as being so (thus **pussified**, effeminate); a coward or weakling (one who is **pussy-ass**), again with an implication of homosexuality; and cowardice itself. The 'furriness' offers the female pubic hair, a rabbit, a fur garment (hence the underworld's **pussy-hoisting**, stealing furs, **pussy mob**, a gang of fur thieves and **pussy-shop**, a furrier's), while the 'cattishness' gives an old woman, usually a spinster, who is inquisitive and meddling. And simple synonymy offers the cat-o'-nine-tails (also the **puss**).

THE PUSSY GAME

Even as slang terms for sexuality go, pussy is pretty impressive. The list is substantial: the **pussy eater**, **-kisser**, **-licker** and **-sucker** are cunnilinguists (as well, in context, as toadies and sycophants), and **pussy-kissing** and so on represent the actual act. A girl may have a **p.e.e.p.**: a perfectly excellent eating pussy. A **pussyboy** is strictly a passive male homosexual, but of late it has become a general insult, implying cowardice or homosexuality. Such **pussies** are of course **pussy-whipped** (or **hen-whipped**, **p.w.'ed** or **p-whipped**), though in this case the object of the chastisement is a heterosexual husband; to offer a second definition: being besottedly in love, implies, perhaps, a slight improvement in his status. The **pussy hole** is the vagina; **pussy juice**, vaginal secretions; the **pussy glommer**, a hand; and **pussyhair** either the pubic variety or, like a **cunt hair**, an infinitesimal amount; and like cunt, **pussyhole** can be a simple insult. So too is **pussyclaat**, **pussyclaht** or **pussyclot**, a sanitary towel (from standard English *cloth*).

If **pussy-bait** is money then a **pussy magnet** is an irresistible male – who may indeed be rich. The **pussy-bully** is a dedicated womaniser, while the **pussy-struck pussy bandit** or **pussy-hound** is a man who is obsessed with sex and seduction. With money definitely in mind we enter the world of commercial sex, the **pussy game**. Here they are, the **pussy posse** (or **pussy patrol**) checking out the **pussy parlors** (strip-clubs) and the sellers of **pussy pictures** (porno snaps) and ogling the girls in **pussy printers** (ultra-tight short-shorts) or **pussy pelmets** (micro-mini-skirts) as they queue for their monthly check-up with the **pussy prober** (the gynaecologist).

A **pussy pusher**, meanwhile, is a heterosexual; a **pussy queer** or **pussy queen** is a lesbian, who may or may not sport a **pussy tickler**, a moustache. The **pussy bumper** is similarly clad in sensible shoes, but the term can apply to male heterosexuals and effeminate gays as well. From there we get **bump pussies**, to have lesbian sex, although, camping it up, gay men can use it too and it can also refer to any situation where the two gay partners find themselves too sexually similar (both passive, both active) to have satisfactory sex.

For a woman to **feed her pussy** is to have sexual intercourse; she can also **give up** (**some pussy**) or **throw some P**. For once we find an image of a woman taking the active role; the man, after all, has to **get some pussy** – and it may not always be on offer. She can also **peddle, pop, sling** or **sell** her pussy – work as a whore – or merely **fan her pussy**, flaunt herself sexually. Faced with all this overt sexuality, man's best riposte is to **fuck up someone's pussy**, to interfere with a rival or a companion's efforts at seducing a woman. And if that fails, look out, you don't want to **play pussy and get fucked**, in other words to act weakly and to suffer as a result. Anyway, quite unimpressed, she will probably **poke her pussy**, play with herself. Still, never let us say that our chaps don't come back fighting. Once a stereotype (see under **L is for Ling**, p.137) always a stereotype: pussy stinks, and so does **pussy in a can**, the sardines sold a US prison commissary.

N IS FOR

NANCY

'**A** Third would be telling what a forward Baggage her Daughter *Nancy* was; for tho' she was but just turn'd of her Seventh Year, yet the young Jade had the Confidence to task her Father Where Girls carry'd their Maidenheads that they were so apt to loose 'em?'

N. Ward, *Compleat & Humorous Account of Remarkable Clubs* (1709)

Daughter? Up to a point Lord Copper, as they say, and which as connoisseurs of Evelyn Waugh can tell you, means up to no point at all. Ned Ward's catalogue of clubs in the book mentioned above covers a variety of what, at least in his time, were considered the less than orthodox, and this remark comes from his study of the Mollies' Club, a gathering of male homosexuals. Nother **mother** nor **daughter** were what they seemed, only what they wished, at least within the easy privacy of closed doors, to appear. Thus too **molly** itself, which was one of the first of the list of female proper names recorded as a nickname for the generic gay man, and was the most popular synonym for homosexual for many years (a year earlier, in his *London Terræfilius*, Ward himself had expounded on one examplar who 'behaves himself more like a Catamite, an Eunuch, or one of those Ridiculous Imitators of the Female Sex, call'd Mollies, than like a Son of Adam'). The term had originally been a slang synonym for the buttocks, and there is little doubt that those who began using it as a derogatory nickname were fully aware of that. And, as intimated in Ward's researches, among these re-gendered proper names was **Nancy**.

TALKING MISS NANCY

It was, apparently, a chance sighting: Nancy seems to have slipped from sight until the twentieth century, but as a noun, often varied as **nance**, **nancy-boy** or **nan-boy**, as the derivatives

nanciness, **nancitude**, **nancifully** and **nancified**, and as a verb, usually as **nance about**, it returned in force. **My nancy!**, however, seems to have no gender overtones, meaning merely 'go to hell!' Other versions include **Nanette**, adding a somewhat unnecessary feminine diminutive, **Natalie** and **Natalia**. **Nancy Dawson** is actually based on a legendary flesh-and-blood prostitute (she died in 1767), about whom a sailor's hornpipe was written; the collectors of First World War forces' slang, Fraser and Gibbons, cite her as 'a celebrated former hornpipe dancer of Covent Garden and Drury Lane Theatres', but by the end of the nineteenth century 'she' meant an effeminate young man.

Miss Nancy, adding the female salutation to the well-established name, was one of the primary names for a gay man from the early nineteenth century till at least the 1940s. It began life suggesting effeminacy, though it is possible that full-out homosexuality was yet to come on board. Maybe no-one wished to say so. The word gives such derivatives as **Miss-Nancyfied** and **Miss Nancyish**, effeminate, and **Miss-Nancyism**, effeminacy. To **talk Miss Nancy** was to speak in an effeminate manner. Miss Nancy was not the only gay 'miss' in the world of camp: **Miss Fitch**, which rhymes with **bitch**, is both an unpleasant woman and a 'feminine' male homosexual; **Miss Jane** is effeminate; **Miss Morales**, Latin American; **Miss Man**, the police; **Miss Peach**, an informer; **Miss Xylophone**, particularly thin; and **Miss Flash**, a user of amphetamines. Perhaps best-known is **Miss Thing** (or **Miss One**, **Miss It** or **Miss Thang**), a term used to greet or describe another gay man and also a figurative description of the inner femininity that comes with being gay or which makes one gay – and with which, when necessary, one can confer, whether for advice, complaints or other barings of the breast.

HAIRY MARY, MARJORIE AND MEG RYAN

Not so opaque as such 1930s terms as **so** or **that way**, or **gay** itself, which long predated the popularisation that accompanied the rise of the Gay Liberation Front of the late 1960s and beyond, the use of female names to identify the **girl-boys**, remained ever useful. Gay Lib may have seen off the greatest excess of camp (and with them the more exaggerated items of vocabulary – at least among those whose wrists were henceforth determinedly and very publicly stiffened), but in its prime the style was ubiquitous. Of them all the most widespread was the most basic of women's names (with or without a touch of Catholic Mariolatry – now we could all be our Lady): **Mary**. The name had been a generic for some time. In the casual brutality that underlines colonial heriarchies, it was used in the Antipodes to offer an undifferentiated name for a Native Australian woman, otherwise known (when not simply as a **coon**) as a **gin** (from Dharuk *diyin*, woman, although also – quite coincidentally – it also, of course, abbreviates Aborigine). In turn gin gives such compounds as **gin-banger, -stealer, -masher** and **-shepherd**, all denoting a white man who enjoys a bit of **black velvet**. In Ireland the name, sometimes extended to **mary ann** or **mary jane**, was applied to a female servant. In South Africa it could be bestowed upon any black woman, almost always a servant too, as well as on any Indian woman, usually a fruit or vegetable hawker (she was also known as **coolie mary**, **coolie** being another term – unflattering of course – for an Indian; it comes from a variety of Indian languages in all of which the term means 'a man for hire' and thus a (menial) labourer).

The gay use of Mary originated in the 1920s (alongside the approximate alternative **Marjorie**) and would persist as the most popular camp proper name, typically in the phrase (aped in a less politically correct era by an infinity of comedians) 'Get you Mary!'. In addition are **hairy Mary**, used by the camp sorority to tease a masculine homosexual, and **St Mary**, which may refer to the basic term but is in fact Australian rhyming slang and means **fairy**, a homosexual male. (More rhyming slang can be found in **Meg Ryan**, which rhymes with **iron**, as in **iron hoof**, a **poof**.)

As previously noted, Mary can be extended to **Mary-ann**, and the name was already being used to mean a gay man in the mid-nineteenth century. It could also mean a heterosexual girlfriend (in Australia) or a dressmaker's dummy. Other gay senses include that of a young boy used as a catamite in prison and, with a deliberately tortured pronunciation, a US Mar-ine. The name **Mary Worthless,** to describe an ageing, unattractive male homosexual, plays on the American strip cartoon *Mary Worth* (starring a self-appointed agony aunt, which apparently followed on from an earlier similarly named strip featuring an old apple-seller who doled out humble wisdom to her customers), launched in 1938. However, a more recent link may well be to a running skit, also titled *Mary Worthless*, on US TV's *Carol Burnett Show* (1967–78), in which the star, suitably made up and costumed, introduced herself with the words, 'Hello. I'm Mary Worthless, and I'm a do-gooder', before handing out advice – whether people wanted it or not.

OTHER FRIENDS OF DOROTHY

From Mary the list is endless. **Abigail** began life a lady's maid, best-known when used as such a character in Francis Beaumont and John Fletcher's play *The Scornful Lady* (1610), although 'she' in turn was presumably named after the expression 'thine handmaid' used in the Bible by Abigail the Carmelitess (1 Samuel 25:24). By the 1950s, the lady's maid was something of the past, but her new role, as an ageing, conservative homosexual, was certainly not.

Ada, another term that can signify the buttocks, can mean a German homosexual (in South Africa) or any gay man who cannot find a sexual partner (could there be a stereotype that links the two latter meanings?). **Adele Adder**, an assonant female proper name backed by the image of the stereotypically untrustworthy snake, is vindictive or bitchy. **Aggie** is variously a gay sailor or gossip, while **Agatha** is the one who gossips. **Agnes** is usually employed, as is Mary, as a term of address. **Annie**, otherwise the anus, is a gay man. An **aunt** or **auntie** is an older man, thus, **Aunt Mathilda** and **Aunt Mame**, named after an eponymous 1958 movie starring Rosalind Russell as an eccentric, rich aunt. Movieland also provides the generic **friend of Dorothy**, the Dorothy in question being she of Oz, or more properly the actress and gay icon who portrayed her in the 1938 hit movie *The Wizard of Oz*: Judy Garland.

HELLO, DOLLY!

Barbie is best-known as the name of a blue-eyed, blonde-haired designer-labelled plastic doll, created in 1959 for little girls and apparently a role-model for some of their elder sisters, some of whom find a lack of female genitals, whether in the doll or apparently their own bodies, no bar to adopting the name. Perhaps unsurprisingly it tends to describe a transvestite. Barbie's plastic consort **Ken** is used to describe 'a painstakingly fashionably dressed and groomed male' and on the US campus, where the terms originates, he apparently swings both ways.

Doll, which made its debut in the 1500s, meaning prostitute, is one of those terms that can happily accommodate both aspects of the polymorphously perverse, as can **dolly** (which may merely extend it, but may equally find its roots in Italian *dolce*, sweet). In New Zealand's women's prisons, borrowing from the conventional gay use, it describes the younger lover of a 'butch' lesbian. The **Dolly Sisters** was a camp synonym for a pair of policemen; their originals were the popular singers Janszieka (1893–1941) and Roszika (1893–1970) Deutsch, better known as Jenny and Rosie Dolly. A **doll-** or **dolly-boy** is a young man, sometimes on the game; the latter term evolved from the **dolly-girl** or **-bird**, that mini-skirted staple of London's 'Swinging Sixties', an attractive young woman (typically a secretary or shopgirl) in her late teens or early twenties as found in such centres of 'swinging London' as Carnaby Street or the King's Road.

FROM BESSIE TO JESSIE

To continue down the alphabet, **Belle**, from the French meaning a beautiful woman, is an equally beautiful young man; **Bessie**, which also means a blackjack or club, is a term of address (could it be something phallic?), while **Beulah**, playing on what is seen as an 'old' name, a black gay man. Still in the black world is **Charlene**, which can found to describe a white woman, especially one who is in a position of authority over blacks, and as a popular camp nickname for a homosexual man. The reference is to **Mr Charlie**, a less than complimentary nickname for a white man, again as part of the power structure (his non-gay female counterpart is **Miss Ann**). **Effie** conveniently crosses the proper name with the word 'effeminate', while **Esther** is (and at least in biblical terms was) a 'Jewish queen', as is **Golda**, another 'typical' Jewish name; **Ethel** is simply a more general useful name. **Fern**, which may have some play on botany's maidenhair fern, can be variously the female genitals and pubic hair, the buttocks or a gay man.

Once more on Mary's pattern, **Georgette** can be a camp term of address, as are **Gertrude** and **Gertie** (though in South Africa it means, albeit in gay parlance, a heterosexual woman). Gertie has also meant a promiscuous woman and a prostitute. (The name, perhaps, was seen as 'working-class', with all that that implied to middle-class fantasists.) **Geraldine** is older, i.e. over 40. **Gina la Salsa** ('saucy Gina') was an effeminate Italian homosexual (though the salsa ought to imply someone Spanish or Puerto Rican). In South Africa, the simple use of an initial gives **Ida**, **Indiana**, **Ira**, **Irene** and **Ivy**, all of whom are Indian gays. **Jane** can work for women, girlfriends and, indeed, a woman's lavatory. It can also represent the embodiment of one's feminine side, although the better-known image (other than Miss Thing, above) is **beads**, defined by Bruce Rodgers as 'one's inner awareness of being homosexual, a metaphorical string of beads worn by all male homosexuals'. This in turn has given **drop one's beads**, meaning accidentally to reveal one's homosexuality by a slip of the tongue or other blunder; **rattle one's beads**, to complain; **read someone's beads**, to chastise or berate; and several other phrases.

While **Jessie** can fall into the category of 'typical' Jewish names (although the spelling should be Jesse) it, and **jessie-boy**, has been one of the most widely used of derogative terms for any gay man. For whatever reason, it is synonymous with perceived weakness, and as such can be applied to a weakling of any gender, being extended, at least in the traditional ideas-fearful UK, to intellectuals. A **woman-jessie** is a weak man who physically abuses women.

FAGS AND FAGGOTS

France's national heroine **Joan of Arc** joins the list, punning on the classic American anti-gay put-downs **faggot** and **fag**. In her case the faggots were those piled around her prior to her burning, but the roots of faggot itself remain unproven. One, somewhat fanciful, version suggests that a faggot was used in the burning of heretics, and thus became transferred to the name of an embroidered patch (like the pink triangles of the Nazi concentration camps) worn by unburned heretics; homosexuals are certainly considered as 'heretics'. More feasible is the descent from the eighteenth-century use of faggot as a pejorative for a woman (and thus playing on homosexual effeminacy), especially in the derogative form of a 'baggage', which stems from the faggots that one had to haul to the fire.

Fag may be linked independently to the British public school fag, a junior boy performing menial tasks and possibly (Tom Brown, avert your eyes!) conducting homosexual affairs with the seniors. Bruce Rodgers, the collector of gay slang, acknowledges all these and suggests a link to fag, meaning cigarette, because cigarettes were considered effeminate by 'cigar-smoking he-men.' Finally, there is the Yiddish *feygele*, meaning little bird (thus the synonym **birdie**).

FROM JOE THE GRINDER TO SUZY WANG

Who knows quite who decides which names are 'typically' feminine, but **Jocelyn** (sometimes **Jozlin**) is one of them and earns its place here. **Gussie**, from Augustus, and **Cecil** (need one bother to lisp it?) are others, though in their cases the names are male (if not apparently 'masculine'). **Bruce**, another candidate for a derisive 'th', joins them, however infuriating this may be to Australians, not to mention Scots devotees of Robert the. **Martha**, however, though undeniably female, is seen as butch and describes a gay tough-guy. **Maud**, conversely, is back among the 'oldies' and attaches to one seen as dowdy or overweight. **Mavis** is effeminate. **Jody** is a prisoner's younger lover, and is presumably seen as another 'feminine' name. That said, as an elision of 'Joe the Grinder', his usual role – as used derisively by US troops, prisoners and other isolated men – is that of the lover who takes the 'girl you've left behind' and thus any variety of male civilian. As the Second World War US Army chant has it: 'Ain't no use in going home, / Jody's got your girl and gone. / Gonna get a three-day pass, / Just to kick old Jody's ass.'

And then there's **Nellie**. Or **Nelly** and **Nell**. The assumption is the female name, and as such it's up there with Jessie in popularity, but one shouldn't overlook the potential of rhyming slang nellie duff, a **puff** or **poof**. An alternative rhyming slang root might lie in Nellie Dean, a **queen** (and the name of a once-popular song first sung in 1907 by music hall star Gertie Gitana (Gertrude Astbury, 1887–1957), 'The Staffordshire Cinderella' – London still boasts a pub name, honouring her and her 'signature' hit). Meaning an overtly effeminate gay man, it has been used as a term of address, a general term for a fool and, on US campuses, a lesbian. It gives **nelly-assed**, effeminate, and **nelly out**, to act effeminately. One could also be a **nelly mary**.

As well-known and as old as Nellie is **Pansy**, which may have enjoyed a brief American flourish as an admirable person c.1900 (on the pattern of the earlier **lily**) but, with **panz** or the reduplication **pansy-wansy**, it had almost immediately become a gay man and, some would doubtless have claimed logically, a contemptible cowardly person. One could be **pansified**, effeminate, and **pansy**, act in an overtly 'gay' manner; to **pansy up** meant either to titivate oneself in an effeminate manner or to flirt.

Like Esther, **Sheba** was another queen, generally black (as was her original, much pursued by King David); so too is **Sheena**, in her case reigning like her cartoon inspiration, over the jungle. **Sally**, more properly abbreviating Salvation, as in Army, was once also a gay whore, as defined in US prisons (the pious meaning very likely not forgotten). **Suzie Wang** doubly punned on the movie *The World of Suzie Wong* and **wang**, the penis; for a while, and very camp, it meant an Oriental homosexual. Finally, another working boy, **Susan Saliva**, who, as they say with reference to his fellatio-on-demand, 'lives by his spits'.

WOMEN IN SENSIBLE SHOES

It's a long way from nancy, and the alphabetically inflexible may even suggest that we're a few letters askew as well, but slang makes its own rules and who are we to gainsay them? So let us note some more of the ways in which gay language has aggregated a few more feminine words to its armoury.

First has to be the simplest: **woman**. Setting aside that splendid euphemism, the **woman in comfortable** (or **sensible**) **shoes**, i.e. a lesbian, woman itself has a small lexicon of effeminacy, all based on the canard of the 'weaker sex'. Thus the term has meant a tramp's young and gay companion – otherwise known as a **gonsel**, which despite its 'mistranslation' in the movie *The Maltese Falcon* (where it describes the young, inadequate hoodlum 'Elmer' as a 'gunman') actually comes from German *gänslein*, a little goose. Woman is also used in US prisons for a prisoner's male lover, although their homosexuality may only exist for the length of the sentence. In parts of the West Indies it means any homosexual, old or young, otherwise known as a **woman-man**.

Femme means woman in French and nothing French is ever far from gay vocabulary. It may be, as an epigram of 1577 suggested, that there are 'three ills that mischief men ... The fem, the flud, the fire', but at that stage the 'fem' was the heterosexual variety. By the 1930s, at least as recorded, 'she' was an effeminate gay man too, and within a decade the term had been extended to cover 'feminine' lesbians, especially the 'female' partner of a couple.

KEEPING IT IN THE FAMILY

If Mary was the camp world's favourite given name, then **mother**, once a procuress (hence such real-life brothel-keepers as the late seventeenth century's 'Mother Damnable of Kentish Town' who was 'So fam'd, both far and near far' and such fictional sisters as Mother Cunny, Mother Snatch-Sucker, Mother Knab-cony – literally, 'snatch-sucker' again – and Mother Midnight) was its primary term of self-description. 'Your mother … ' meant oneself and began innumerable sentences. More specifically, mother was one who introduced a younger man into the homosexual world, or simply meant any gay man. **Mother Ga-ga** (from **gaga**, eccentric) was a fussy, gossipy, interfering older homosexual and **Mother Parker** a tough, older one. **Mother-love** has meant both a homosexual man having sex with a heterosexual woman and sexual intercourse between two homosexual men of the same 'type', i.e. passive and passive or active and active. A **mother superior**, while logically an older, experienced and sophisticated homosexual, was once also a police sergeant.

After mother, **daughter**, a homosexual brought into the gay world by a homosexual friend. And thence to sister. Like Mary, **sister** can be a consciously camp term address, and like mother it can be self-referential: 'your sister'. A sister was once the platonic gay friend of another gay man; it was similarly used by lesbians. A **sister-act** describes any gay couple, as well as a homosexual man having sex with a heterosexual woman. The **sisters** are police, usually when working as a patrolling pair. **Grandma** is logically an old(er) homosexual; hence **grandpa**, an ageing lesbian.

While **sissy**, one of the most widely used of terms to pour scorn on gay men, is synonymous with standard English's *sissy*, a coward, both terms are ultimately based on *sister*, presumably a weak one. Otherwise found as **ciss**, **cissie**, **cissy**, **sis**, **siss** and

sissie, it has meant a weakling, an effeminate man or boy (since the 1910s) and was specifically extended to homosexuality a decade later. It exists in a number of compounds. The weakling and/or effeminate gay man can be a **sissy-boy** or **sissy's ass**, a **sissy-pants** (on the model of smartiepants), **sissy-britches** or **sissy soft sucker**. In ostensibly gender-free uses, the **sissy-bar** is a metal loop fixed behind the seat of a cycle or motorcycle. A **sissy cure** was, among 1950s narcotics users, tapering off a narcotic addiction rather than stopping immediately (with the concomitant withdrawal pains). In the same era a **sissy rod** was a weapon fitted with a silencer.

And thus to royal families. While it isn't quite on the level of **queen** (see under **Q is for Quean**, p.183), **duchess** comes a reasonable second. Certainly at the same court. The ageing affected gay man is thus named; in camper days the **grand-duchess** referred to a heterosexual woman who occupied pride of place in a homosexual male coterie as well as to an experienced, older, sophisticated homosexual man.

FILLIES AND COWS

And finally, some animals. **Filly**, as in 'a cracking little', has been a staple of a certain brand of (ex-) military man for some time. Whether his tastes would extend to the gay use, where again it describes an effeminate boy or indeed a 'passive' lesbian, must be left to the imagination. Its standard meaning is, of course, a young mare (though an older **mare** has no gay connotations, it's simply one more way of being rude to woman). Last of all, a **cow** can be another form of **limp wrister**, while to be **cow-crazy** is, from a gay point of view, to be bizarrely besotted with women, in other words **straight**.

O

IS FOR

ONAN

Our lesson for today: Genesis chapter 38, verses 1–10:

1 And it came to pass at that time, that Judah went down from his brethren, and turned in to a certain Adullamite, whose name was Hirah.

2 And Judah saw there a daughter of a certain Canaanite, whose name was Shuah; and he took her, and went in unto her.

3 And she conceived, and bear a son; and he called his name Er.

4 And she conceived again, and bear a son; and she called his name Onan …

6 And Judah took a wife for Er his firstborn, whose name was Tamar.

7 And Er, Judah's firstborn, was wicked in the sight of the lord; and the lord slew him.

8 And Judah said unto Onan, Go in unto thy brother's wife, and marry her, and raise up seed to thy brother.

9 And Onan knew that the seed should not be his; and it came to pass, when he went in unto his brother's wife, that he spilled it on the ground, lest that he should give seed to his brother.

10 And the thing which he did displeased the lord: wherefore he slew him also.

And that, my chickabiddies, is how we got AIDS. Not to mention over-population, and its attendant poverty, starvation and, coming to your life very soon, worldwide food riots and the wars that will follow. And yea, a great darkness did *surely* cover the land.

Of course, the wretched Church fathers weren't talking about contraception – just coitus interruptus (which is odd, since as we know, this can only be carried out on minor railway stations (see p.313), which were also some way in the future) – but what mattered is simple and all-encompassing: no ejaculation without procreation. Which means – you, boy with the hairy palms, pay attention – no masturbation, a word that is believed to link a pair of Latin ones; *manus*, the hand, and *stupare*, to defile, plus a smidgeon of *turbare*, to disturb, and is thus a direct ancestor of the moralists' favourite: self-abuse.

WANKERS, BANKERS AND HANDLE CRANKERS

There are many, many terms for self-abuse – and enough of the mealy mouth: let's call it **wanking** – and you can tackle a selection of those below. But first, the masturbator, the filthy, self-polluting, godless, weak-limbed and wet-brained **wanker**. Wank – or **whank** as the Americans persist in calling it (on the same lines as they can't manage **bonk**, for fuck, but seem determined to respell it **boink**, although this is not wholly foolish: all the earliest citations seem to offer 'h' too) – is officially registered as 'etymology unknown'. But it certainly seems to fit the eighteenth-century Scots dialect *whank*, to beat or thrash, given the preponderance of violence, for once aimed at oneself rather than at some unfortunate woman (with whom one is 'making love'), that backs up this particular mini-lexicon. There is also the Yorkshire/Lancashire dialect word *wanker*, a simpleton, but that may have followed wank. Having said that, the records of wank are slim: the first instance occurs in the 1940s; since then it has picked up additional uses: a general derogative description of a lazy, incompetent, unpleasant person; an undesirable situation or thing; and that which is wanked, i.e. the penis. To **go like a wanker's elbow** is to be extremely busy and the **wanker's doom** (coined in the 1940s RAF) is a figuratively unpleasant fate. Wanker gives a predictable range of rhyming slang; **Allied Irish, Swiss** or **merchant banker, handle cranker** (or simply **cranker**), **ham shanker, monkey spanker, oil tanker** and **Sri Lanka**. A **yanker** certainly rhymes, but may simply depend on yank, to pull.

And if wank is the auto-erotic activity of choice in the UK, then across the Atlantic the word is **jerk**. Or **jerk off**. Again it seems to have appeared around the Second World War, perhaps a decade earlier. Jerk or jerk off, or their variants **jack** or **jack off** thus give a pair of nouns: the **jerk-off** and the **jack-off**. The synonym **jag-off** is possibly no more than a mis-transcription. Jerk also underpins **jerkwad** and **jerker**, a wanker to be sure, but one who likes to save his one-hand action for his visits to strip clubs, porn movies and the exciting like.

VIRTUOSI OF THE SKIN FLUTE

As suggested, the vast majority of slang terms for a masturbator are based on some form of violence. Among them are **beat-nuts**, **boffer**, **flogger**, **duff-** and **dummy-flogger**, **fist fucker** and **fuck-fist** (in this case the fist is the fuckee, not the fucker), **frigger**, **frigster** and **frigstress**, **meatbeater**, **salami slapper** (that same salami that one **hides** when an accommodating partner is available), **rod walloper** (and simple **walloper**), **plankspanker**, **whacker** and **dickwhacker**. The apostle Peter doubtless railed as keenly as any against the lonely art; it is fitting that he should be memorialised as a **peter-beater** or **peter-puller**. Other terms using **peter** as the penis include **peter-eater** or **-puffer**, a male homosexual fellator or a heterosexual fellatrix; **peter-meter**, a notional means of measuring the size of a penis, or the excitement it is experiencing (the original peter-meter was popularised by *Screw* magazine in the late 1960s, when it was used as part of reviews to assess the degree to which a pornographic film or book was arousing); **peter-pitching**, (of a man) sexually active; and **peter-pusher**, a fucker. And like the peter the phallic **pud** can also be pulled, hence the **pud-puller** or **pud-whacker**.

Otherwise the words concentrate on the penis – as do the above, but the difference is that the violence is downplayed.

Thus we find **bone-stroker** or **stroker**, **butt-chuckler** (from standard English *chuck*, to throw or toss), **gristle gripper** (he grips the **gristle-hammer**), **knob-jockey**, **knob shiner**, **pickle-lugger**, **taffy-tugger**, **tapdancer** (though he or she usually masturbates someone else), **tosser** and **toss-arse**, **tugger**, **yankee**, **wire-puller** and the somewhat literary **virtuoso of the skin flute**. A **doodle** is a penis, thus a **doodle-case**, both a masturbator and the vagina; the **doodle-dandler** or **-dasher** both maintain the good work. The **milk woman** is a female masturbator, although the **milker** returns to the macho side of the street; a **pencil squeezer** is not just a masturbator, but of a pencil-sized penis. The **seed beast** can't keep his hands off it, while the **hank freak** has his own special (not to mention crusty) hankie.

Finally the word **Nescafé**, for once escaping its role as ersatz coffee, and taking on that of a hand gesture used to indicate one's contempt. The gesture is based on the shaking of a jar of coffee, imitating that of male masturbation, and thus means wanker. It is underpinned by the rhyming slang **Gareth Hunt** (the star of the Nescafé adverts who actually shook the coffee) who rhymes, of course, with **cunt**.

DO-IT-YOURSELF

Now, having promised that words meaning 'to masturbate' will be tackled, far be it from me and all that. However, given the context, it is time for what one might call a bit of do-it-yourself. So. Take the two columns on the following page. Choose one word from the verbs, follow it by 'a', 'one's', 'the' or another preposition of your choice and finish off the mixture with one of the nouns. That's it really. You know what they say: it's like riding a bicycle, you never forget.

VERBS

adjust
bash
beat
belt
biff
blast
bleed
bloat
blow
bludgeon
boff
bop
bounce
buck
buff
choke
churn
clobber
consult
crack
crank
cream
defrost
diddle
do
feel
fist
flap
flog
gallop
grease
grip
hump
juice

lather
loose
lube
mangle
massage
milk
oil
please
polish
pound
pull
pummel
pump
punch
punish
ride
rub
shake
shine
slap
smack
spank
strain
strangle
stroke
strum
tickle
torture
varnish
wax
whack
whittle
wrestle
yank

NOUNS

bacon
bald-headed
  bandit
banana
beef weasel
bishop
bull
butter
candle
cheese
chicken
dog
dong
donkey
doodle
dummy
emperor
finless
  dolphin
flounder
frankfurter
fruit
German
  helmet
goat
goose
gopher
gorilla
ham javelin
hog
little brother
lizard
love
  truncheon

maggot
meat
midget
mole
monkey
monster
moose
mule
munchkin
mutton
one-eyed
  dragon
one-eyed
  monster
one-eyed
  worm
pelican
percy
pony
pope
pumpkin
purple-
  helmeted
  warrior
python
salami
tentacle
trouser snake
tube
turkey
weed
weenie
wood
worm

P
IS FOR
PRICK
AND
PISS

Prick does not appear on George Carlin's list (see Introduction, p.8) – the penis is represented by cock (see under **C is for Cunt**, p.37) – but it would be an error to class it among those words that have somehow bypassed the censor's eye. Its ultimate etymology is simple enough, standard English *prick*, a pointed weapon or implement, which the OED explains is linked to such words as West Frisian *prik*, prick, small hole, puncture, puncture mark, Dutch *prik* (feminine), iron tip of a weapon, goad, pointed instrument, small stick, penis, small roll of tobacco, and Old Danish *prich*, *preck*, *prikke*, dot, mark, small hole, minute particle, small detail, centre of target, bullseye and others.

In 1540, prick could denote 'a pert, forward, saucy boy or youth; a conceited young fellow' and the term is defined as 'humorous or contemptuous', but not indecent; it might have referred simply to the lad's 'sharpness'. The earliest non-standard sense, a woman's term of endearment for a man, is only indirectly linked to the penis, i.e. he possesses one, but the OED's first citation suggests that the term was already at least punning. Taken from a 1540 translation of the play *The Comedye of Acolastus*, it offers the following: '*Aco.* Wylt thou gold ... any pieces of golde? *Lais.* This chayne my lyttell prycke ... I wolde fayne haue this chayne (of golde) my pretye pryncockes, or my ballocke stones.' Setting aside the appearance of 'ballocke stones' (still standard at that date), the 'lyttell prycke' is noted as a translation of Latin *mea mentula*, literally 'my penis'. Add to that the appearance of 'pryncockes' (literally 'prime cock'), a sexual interpretation is not merely possible but highly likely. Or at least the most obvious of puns. Six decades later John Florio put the two together again: '*Pinchino*, a pillicock, a primcock, a prick, a prettie lad, a gull, a noddie.'

There is possibly some ambiguity about the first appearance of prick as a penis, in the *Manifest Detection of Diceplay* (*c.*1555), one of the basic texts of slang collection. 'To turne his pricke vpward, and cast a weauers knot on both his thumbs behind him.' Turn his prick upward? Well, it's all down to context. Fortunately the ever-informative Florio comes to our rescue in '*Pinco*, a prick, a pillicock, a pintle, a dildoe ... *Scazzata*: a thrust, a push, a foyne, or the serving to a woman of a man's pricke.' No opacity there. And anyway, six years earlier we find 'The pissing Boye lift vp his prick' in a translation of R. Dallington's *Hypnerotomachia*. Only one question remains; although the OED, up to and including its current 2008 revision, labels the term quite unequivocally 'coarse slang', one must ask (as did Eric Partridge) how this could be so: the 'pissing Boye' sounds coarse to many modern ears, but piss was still standard, and it is likely that prick too, like so many of its 'dirty' peers, still had a century or two to go before it was exiled to the wastelands whence only the slang lexicographers – and indeed users – would rescue it.

Since then it has accrued some extra meanings: a fool or incompetent (a transference typical of many terms that begin by meaning no more than the penis), a hypodermic syringe, and in figurative use any form of aggression or attack. It may also be employed as a nickname for anything phallic, e.g. a flagpole.

ALL PRICK AND BREECHES

As in the case of **dick** and **dickhead**, prick has many compound forms. **Prick-cheese** is smegma; **prick-chinking** is sexual intercourse; **prick-pride** is an erect penis (of which one may be proud but which is also 'proud', i.e. projecting out of the body); and to **go on a pricknic** is to fellate, with the fellator or fellatrix being a **prick-sucker**. **Prick-arsed** or **-nosed** is a term of abuse, while a **prick peddler** (like a **dick peddler**) is a male whore. The **prick holder**, **prick-purse**, **prick-scourer**, **prick-skinner** and **prick-hole** are the vagina, all denoting its primary role in slang: somewhere to put the penis or, as at least some Victorians put it, 'where Uncle's doodle goes'. A **prick office**, meanwhile, was a mid-seventeenth-century term, either a brothel staffed by heterosexual male prostitutes or a group of regular brothel patrons. The sense of fool gives us **prickface**, **prickhead** (though that can also mean a bald-headed man) and **pricky**, obnoxious. To **act the prick** is to behave foolishly, to 'mess about', as is to **prick around**.

The prick-as-penis provides a number of images: **all prick and breeches** or **all prick and no pence** signify a braggart or fake, one who is 'all talk and no action'. **All prick and ribs like a drover's** or **shearer's** or **swaggie's dog** denotes one who

like the rural hound is both lean and eager. To represent **a spare prick at a wedding** or **a spare dick on a honeymoon** (often preceded by **standing around like** …) is to be absolutely useless (the assumption being that only the bridegroom's will be required). **May your prick and purse** (or **the two Ps**) **never fail you** was a popular eighteenth-century toast (others include **tight cunts and easy boots!** or **best!**, i.e. 'the best cunt in Christendom'). A promiscuous woman has had **more pricks than a second-hand dartboard**, **a pin-cushion**, or **a primus**, while Australia's **put some flick in one's prick** refers to something that will supposedly increase one's potency. To **go prick scouring** was to have sexual intercourse, as is **prick the master-vein** and the more recent **pour the prick**. To **prick-lick** is to fellate, while to **get on someone's prick** is to infuriate them. To **pull one's prick** is to masturbate, but also to promote oneself or to tease or to deceive a third party.

PISSING ABOUT

The simplest origin of **piss**, for which the verb came first, is that it echoes the act that's being performed. The word seems to have emerged across Europe around the same time, and there is no proven example to show that one use particularly led to another, but it does appear that for English purposes the Normans brought it across the Channel, and the word was cut down from Old French *pisser*. Its first recorded use was *c.*1300 and the word was standard, or at least acceptable, till around the seventeenth century. Henceforth, yet again, the word was amongst those considered 'coarse' and as such removed from polite discourse. Since then as well as urinate (into a urinal or on oneself or one's clothes) it has meant to issue vaginal secretions, to exude liquid other than urine and, in phrases such as **piss down**, to rain heavily. In figurative senses it can mean to complain or whinge, to deride, attack or disdain. The early nineteenth-century **piss-quick** was gin mixed with marmalade and topped up with boiling water, one of the many hot alcoholic drinks popular at the time; the name comes either from the colour or the fact that it apparently increased one's desire to **pee**. A person who was considered **as good as ever pissed** was as good as there has ever been, while **I'll be pissed** implies impossibility. To **piss blood** is to work extremely hard, to worry excessively, to make a great fuss or to suffer a great deal. To **piss bones**, **children**, or **hard** meant, *c.*1900, to go into labour, to give birth.

Three senses inform the bulk of phrases using piss: to waste (whether effort, time or money), to fear and to deal with a person (usually negatively). **Piss around**, **about**, **away** and **piss-ball about** all suggest wasting time; to **piss up a rope** is to be engaged in a futile exercise and to **piss in(to) the wind** (given the futility thereof) is to waste both efforts or time. The concept of **pissing (money) against the wall** dates from the fifteenth century; it first referred specifically to wasting one's money on drink and thence progressed to wasting it on anything. As to fear, the primary form is **piss in one's pants**, itself a development of **piss in one's breeches** and a synonym for **piss oneself**. A **piss-breeches** (or **piss-bag** or **-bucket**) is a contemptible person. To these one might add **piss one's tallow**, which means both to sweat (through fear?) and, of a man, to be sufficiently sexually excited as to ejaculate (without actual intercourse), a use that comes from the standard *piss one's grease*, or *tallow*, which refers to a deer which becomes lean in rutting-time.

PISSING IN THE SAME POT

The bulk of phrases, however, concentrate on human relations, and the use piss should leave one in little doubt as to the nature of such relations. It's all nasty. To **make someone piss** is to annoy, to infuriate or to disgust as well as to beat up or to defeat. To **piss all over**, **piss on** (and **piss on someone's parade** – a hugely popular phrase, yet almost invariably bowdlerised as 'rain' or 'pour') are all to defeat. The transitive **piss-parade** is to shatter illusions or to ruin an otherwise satisfactory situation. The declaration that one **wouldn't piss on someone if they were on fire** states the speaker's absolute contempt or loathing for the person thus decried; for one to **look like he wouldn't piss if his pants were on fire**, is to appear, and likely be, quite stupid. To **piss all over someone** (or **in someone's ear**) **and tell them it's raining**, or to **piss up someone's leg** is to deceive them, though to **piss down someone's back**, **piss in someone's pocket** or **in the same pot** mean to flatter, to curry favour, to be extremely close to someone, or to ingratiate oneself.

Further phrases offer **piss and moan** or **piss up a storm** – both mean to complain, whinge or make a major fuss; the latter can also mean to urinate for a (relatively) long time. To **piss in** or **piss it** or **piss through** all mean to accomplish with a minimum of effort. To **piss in a quill** meant to agree on a plan; this odd phrase is based on the narrowness of a quill and the need to bend the flow of urine to achieve the feat. To **piss on a nettle** was to be annoyed, uneasy, tetchy and thus gave **on**

nettles, anxious, uneasy. To **piss on ice** on the other hand was a 1920s US term that meant to live well, specifically in the context of visiting an upmarket restaurant – where blocks of ice are placed in the urinals. To **piss when one cannot whistle** is a late eighteenth-century term that means to be hanged: it indicates the loss of bowel control that results from **dancing the Paddington frisk** (in pre-drop days the victim's friends would often tug on his legs to speed the action of the rope – an act that obviously required even greater selflessness than it immediately indicates). The rope, of course, rendered whistling quite out of the question. Finally, there is the dismissive **think it's just to piss through**, the teasing remark of one who knows (or claims to know) about **the other** (i.e. sex) to one who does not.

Piss also provides a useful selection of dismissive exclamations. Aside from the simple **piss off!**, there are such embellishments as **go (and) piss up a rope!, a flagpole!, a pipe!, a shutter!** or **your leg!**. One may also **piss around a pretzel!**

A PIECE OF PISS

Like its verb, the noun piss refers to urine (and the act of urination) and vaginal fluid. In addition it deals with drink, whether as a neutral synonym or, and often in combinations, any sort of weak or otherwise unpalatable drink, whether alcoholic or non-alcoholic – in Scotland the word is often found as **pish**. Figuratively, and written with **the**, like so many obscenities it can work as a general intensifier; as well as signifying the essence, the 'daylights'. It can also stand for rubbish, nonsense, anything or anyone unappealing, worthless and finally (often alongside vinegar, which one is also full of) high spirits.

Urine first. In the days of wigs – for men that is – one that had turned an unpleasant yellow was **piss-burned**. Around the same time one might, for lack of many things better, encounter the **piss prophet** or **pisspot-peeper**, a physician who makes all their diagnoses on the basis of inspecting the patient's urine, which arrived via his **pisspipe** or penis. **Pisspot** of course was a chamberpot, as **pisshouse** was (and remains) a lavatory, as well as being generic for any unpleasant place and specifically a police station. The **piss-kitchen**, however, was not a place but the kitchen maid who worked (and we assume pissed) there. A **pisscan** was a US prison, although American jails had long since moved beyond the grim latrinal arrangements of the UK's older establishments – perhaps it was just figurative. Wholly real are **piss-flaps** or **-flappers**, the labia, and the **piss freak**, one whose sexual satisfaction derives from being urinated on. A man who has a **piss hard-on** or a **piss-horn** will be **piss-proud**; in all cases this refers to his morning erection, although to be **piss-scared** (or **scared pissless**) is a less appealing situation. The **piss stop**, punning on the Grand Prix pit stop, or **piss call**, describes any stop taken during a journey in order to urinate. A **piss test** is a urine test, usually taken in prison to seek out traces of drugs. A **puddle of piss** is unpleasant, whether a person or thing, while a **piece of piss**, an RAF coinage, can be something that is either very easy, or quite loathsome.

A **piss-factory** is a pub and, although it may well serve piss, the image is of urinals. Similarly a **piss-cutter**, a drunken spree or binge, is better known as a measure of quality: a generally obnoxious or, equally feasible, an admirable or exceptional person or thing; it can also describe a serious set-to. And piss, logically, underpins a number of drink-related terms. All of these, with the exception of **snake's piss**, which refers to the sort of alcohol that, when you've had enough (that euphemistic synonym for 'too much'), is likely to lead to violence (note **snakebite**, much loved by bikers), are invariably weak or even deliberately diluted. Although some of the species cited would usually be thought of as seriously macho, or at least not the sort you'd want to stroke, the emphasis is always on **piss**, weak drink. Thus one finds **buffalo piss**, **bull piss**, **cat's piss**, **dog's piss**, **gnat's piss**, **horse piss**, **monkey piss** and **shark's piss**. Other than the snake's contribution, only **panther piss**, strong home-brewed or cheap liquor, otherwise known as **panther sweat** (not to mention **monkey-swill** or **rat-track whiskey**) puts a bit of hair on the chest. The **piss artist**, of course, is a heavy drinker keen to **hit the piss** (he can be admired – or not), and out **on the piss** alongside him at the bar are the **pisshead** and **piss-tank**. A New Zealander who **would drink the piss from a brewer's horse** is a dedicated drinker. **Piss and punk** refers, in US prisons, to bread and water (why punk means bread no-one appears to know). An Irish **can of piss**, however, is an unpleasant person.

TAKING THE PISS

The piss means the daylights, or the essence, and it tends to be something that slang feels must be removed. A variety of synonymous terms include **beat the piss out of, mangle the piss out of, pound, kick, knock, whip** and **whop the piss out of**. The piss concerned can also be **living** or **holy**. To **rip the piss out of** is to tease aggressively, as is **take the piss** (**out of**) or **piss-take** which variously means to attack verbally, to sneer or jeer at, or, of a situation, to appear ludicrous – thus the phrase **don't take the piss**, i.e. 'you must be joking.' More recently it has meant to act absurdly, to play the fool and, of a man, to have sexual intercourse.

Piss can also be used as a (usually) negative intensifier. Thus **piss-easy**, very easy (as is **a piss in the hand**); or **piss-making**, infuriating ('enough to make you piss') – though a **piss-maker** is an alcoholic. Other examples include **piss-ache, piss-awful, piss-poor** or **-rotten** – all meaning appalling, unpleasant, distasteful; **piss-poor** can simply mean very poor. To be **piss-sick** is to be utterly contemptuous and **piss-ugly**, very plain indeed. **Piss-elegant**, conversely, is the picture of smooth. **Piss-willie** or **piss-fart** refer to an insignificant person and **piss-in-the-face** to a despicable one, while a **piss-walloper** is impressive even if they might **feel their own piss**, i.e. become intoxicated with their self-importance.

To finish off piss, a selection of phrases. **All piss and wind** (also **all piss and wind like the barber's cat**; **all wind and piss**; and **all piddle and wind like the barber's cat, full of shit and sticks**) refers to a loudmouth or a braggart or their empty talk. It can also describe a very thin person, who may otherwise be referred to as a **long** (**thin**) **streak of piss** or **pelican shit**. One who is **like a snob's cat – all piss and tantrums** is of no value (the snob being a cobbler, and the predecessor of today's social elitist). A fool lacks **enough sense to pour piss out of a boot**, and when one feels nothing but contempt, one **wouldn't give someone the steam on one's piss**. Finally, **piss over teakettle** means head–over–heels.

Q IS FOR

QUEAN
QUEEN QUEER
AND
QUIM

Once upon a time, close by the **throne** where she gaily struck **camp** (unless was forced, by those spoilsports **Lily Law** and **Hilda Handcuffs**, to **abdicate**), lived ... the Queen of the Fairies. No Titania he, but as the stereotype bizarrely has it, more of a Bruce. That said, he could also be **Tondelayo** (a Black queen), **Bathsheba** (a queen who liked the baths), or **Esther** (if he was Jewish). In all cases he could be **screaming**. And his best friends called him **Mary**.

The use of **queen** to mean a homosexual, usually an older man (and otherwise known as the less regal **auntie**), is over a century old. And despite the general outlawry of camp by the **butch** advances of gay liberation, it remains as popular as ever, whether used by itself, or in a whole cottage of combinations. But before queen, and probably its root, is **quean**, a term which emerged in the eleventh century to mean a woman and which lasted as a perfectly neutral term until around 1500, when it fell from grace, becoming an 'impudent' (OED), promiscuous female, possibly an actual prostitute. As Palsgrave's prototype English-to-French dictionary put it in 1530: 'Queane, garse, paillarde' – respectively, modern French *garce*, a trollop, and one who, as the modern *Trésor de langue française* defines it, 'loves the pleasures of the flesh and joyous life'. Although the writer Robert Nares suggested it came from Anglo-Saxon *cwean*, a barren cow, the OED prefers a variety of north European terms, meaning (old) woman; underpinned by Dutch *quene* and *kween*, both meaning hussy.

The efforts of Havelock Ellis and his *Sexual Inversion* (1897) notwithstanding, early twentieth-century gay sexology was still essentially mucky foreign stuff in the hands of such as Krafft-Ebing (*Psychopathia Sexualis*, 1886) and unsurprisingly the first record of a gay quean comes in 1910, in the *Jahrbuch für Sexuelle Zwischenstufen* (Almanac of Sexual Terminology, in which Krafft-Ebing himself had published his theories of homosexuality in 1901), where the terms **bitch** or quean are both defined as '*mehr oder minder schmeichelhafte Bezeichnungen für homosexuelle Männer*' ('in varying degrees, flattering [i.e. euphemistic] names for homosexual men'). By 1935 the term had arrived in US prisons as a synonym for 'pervert' and elsewhere via the Australian verb **quean up**, to dress carefully, though not invariably effeminately. Quean would continue, but really only in the way that **cum** otherwise unnecessarily substitutes for **come**, to underline its sexual meanings.

QUEEN OF ALL THE FAIRIES

Queen, which, as well as its regal meaning, had started life as a variety of heterosexual females (a pretty girl, a wife, a mother), had already taken over. Its first modern appearance was recorded in 1919, when a gay man admitted, throwing in a few synonyms for good measure, that 'I never told anyone that I was a queen or a cocksucker or a pogue.' The image of effeminacy that underlies it is much older. Thus, in 1729, the author of *Hell on Earth* observed: 'It would be a pretty Scene to behold them in their Clubs and Cabals, how they assume the Air and affect the Name of Madam or Miss, Betty or Molly, with a chuck under the Chin, and O you bold Pullet I'll break your Eggs, and then frisk and walk away to make room for another, who then accosts the affected Lady, with Where have you been you saucy Queen? If I catch you Strolling and Caterwauling, I'll beat the Milk out of your Breasts I will so.' But the use is of the 'female' word in a consciously male context.

In gay senses, queen can mean an attractive, effeminate young US prison homosexual, much sought after and fought over, and in Australian jails a transsexual. It can lend itself to such puns as **Queen for a day** (from the once popular US TV show), **Queen Mother** and **Queen of All the Fairies**. It can be used, ironically, of heterosexuals. **Queens' Row**, a nod to the 1941 film *King's Row*, starring Ronald Reagan, is a section of a US prison where homosexual inmates have their cells and, more specifically, the pick-up area of the Public Gardens in Boston, Massachusetts. Sadly the phrase **where the queen goes on foot** (or **where the queen sends nobody**) refers to a real monarch and one can also note Sir Thomas Urquhart's 1653 definition of the Spanish *cagar*, to shit, as 'to do that which the king himself can't get another to do for him'.

FROM DRAG QUEENS TO DRAMA QUEENS

But it is as a combining form, in this case indicating a variety of homosexual interests or practices, that queen is most widely found. The earliest reference, although the use is doubtless much older, comes in 1949 in the wonderfully entitled *Gaedicker's Sodom-on-the-Hudson* (a tip of the hat to the short story writer O. Henry's naming, *c.*1900, of New York as Baghdad-on-the-Hudson), a tome compiled by one 'Swasarnt Nerf' (who that same year had also edited *The Gay Girl's Guide*). Wrote Swasarnt: 'There is something of a rendezvous for the Wall Street queens in the Federal Hall Museum.' This was but the tip of a magnificent iceberg. Perhaps the best-known was and remains **drag queen**: an effeminate homosexual who prefers to dress as a woman, sometimes as a professional female impersonator. The drag refers to that of 'her' garments along the floor (the term had already been employed in the theatre and music hall for 'straight' female impersonators).

In 1965 the *Guild Dictionary of Homosexual Terms* contained the following list:

> '**eyeball queen**: A homosexual who derives more pleasure just from looking than from anything else; **green queen**: A homosexual who gets gratification from having sexual intercourse near the trees and bushes of parks. The dangerous aspect of this activity adds to his pleasure; and **snowflake queen**:

A male homosexual who likes to have semen from orgasm by masturbation sprinkled over him while lying down; it is not unusual to open the mouth to try to catch a few drops.'

In 1972 Bruce Rodgers's *Queens' Vernacular* listed, among many others:

'**alley queen** one who enjoys and seeks out sex in alleyways; **auntie-queen** young man who seeks the companionship of older men; **levis queen** homosexual with a jeans fetish; **buy queen** a homosexual man who has a desperate compulsion to buy furnishings for the home; **coffin queen** one who finds the usual business of death ... erotic; **dalmation** [*sic*] **queen** (from the *dalmatian* dog = the mascot of the firehouse) any fireman and **dangle queen**: one who likes watching what he's doing sexually in a mirror.'

And that was far from the end of it. Elsewhere the list includes the **catalogue queen**, a homosexual man who uses physique and body-building magazines as masturbatory pornography; the **cuff-link** queen, **cuff-link faggot** or **finger-bowl faggot**, a wealthy (older) male homosexual; and the **Easter queen** (which plays on the Easter bunny, i.e. he 'comes quick as a rabbit'), a premature ejaculator. A **fish queen** is variously any man, homo- or heterosexual, who enjoys cunnilingus, a male homosexual who openly associates with women, with the supposed aim of appearing to be bisexual or simply a heterosexual man. US prison slang extends the use of fish queen to describe a gay inmate who has newly arrived at the prison (the term **fish** meaning new, naïve). The **fladge queen** enjoys being flagellated; the **Gucci queen** is an affected, fashion-conscious older homosexual; and the **hormone queen** is a male transvestite who takes oestrogen and is presumably en route to turning into what the Fifties termed a **Copenhagen capon** (acknowledging the pioneering sex change operation performed in Denmark in 1952 for Christine, formerly George Jorgensen). The **opera queen** enjoys verbally abusing his partners; the **talcum queen** is a black homosexual who prefers white partners; the **tearoom queen** (or **cruiser**) hangs around public lavatories for sex, as does the **bog queen**; and the **toe-jam queen** is a gay foot-fetishist. The **Xerox queen** requires every sexual partner to resemble his predecessor; the **belly queen** likes flat six-packed bellies; the **slap queen** is caked in make-up (you *slap* it on; the term is originally theatrical); and the **cleavage queen** … is heterosexual. Perhaps best-known, and certainly the one that's crossed the border from camp usage to the mainstream, is **drama queen**, anyone considered to be creating an excessive fuss or 'making a mountain out of a molehill'.

QUEER BUSINESS

Homo-, as one is constantly reminded, is as old as any other of the sexualities, but the language whereby it has been described, at least as regards slang, is relatively modern, rarely extended back much before the late nineteenth century. Some terms, such as **betty**, **molly** and other female names allotted to gay men, might be found over a century earlier (see under **N is for Nancy**, p.154), but the core names, usually pejorative, come later. Like queen, **queer**, whether as a noun or adjective comes on-stream in the early twentieth century. Rooted in German *quer*, meaning oblique or skewed, queer had played a role in criminal slang since the 1500s. (An alternative etymology, no doubt acknowledging the dialectal origins of some criminal terms, suggests Welsh *chwired*, craft, deceit or cunning.) A wide range of objects and people had been labelled queer, meaning either bad – the antonym of the underworld's all-purpose positive, **rum** – or fake or counterfeit, especially of money, jewellery, official papers and so on. Other uses include ill, out of sorts, mad, in difficulties and, of machinery, out of order.

The use as a pejorative description of homosexuals does not emerge until *c.*1915. It can also be found, less often, to describe 'straight' individuals who opt for unconventional sexual practices. And, again like queen, its initial record is to be found in an academic journal, in this case the *Journal of Historical Sexuality* (1914): 'Fourteen young men were invited ... with the premise that they would have the opportunity of meeting some of the prominent 'queers,' ... and the further attraction that some "chickens" as the new recruits in the vice are called, would be available.' (**Chicken**, which had meant an underage girl since the 1820s, was not new: in the gay context it was at least 20 years old.) And despite the inroads of 1960s gay liberation into such abuse, queer persists. Along with such synonyms as **queerie**, **queery** and **queervert**, it remains far from correct, politically or otherwise, but as in the case of what some would see as the even more opprobrious **nigger**, it has been reclaimed by some militant gay men as an affirmative.

Among its compounds one finds **queerbait**, the gay world's **jailbait** (though that can cross gender boundaries), an effeminate young boy who attracts, or is supposed to attract, older male homosexuals; as a verb it means to seek out a homosexual encounter for money. A **queer-basher** is one who specialises in beating up (and usually robbing) male homosexuals, hence his occupation: **queer-bashing**; **queer-rolling** and **queer-roller** mean exactly the same. However, the **queer shover** is but a passer of counterfeit money and to **push** or **shove the queer** is simply to circulate counterfeit cash or notes.

QUIMS, QUAINTS AND QUIFFS

Like so many ostensibly heterosexual words, **quim**, the vagina, can be found in a gay sense, used to mean a 'girl's' anus, but on the whole the word remains on the straight side of the tracks. The apparent etymology suggests a play on Celtic *cwm*, a valley, but the OED squashes that as 'unlikely on both semantic and phonological grounds'. Gordon Williams, writing in 1994 in his *Dictionary* of sixteenth- and seventeenth-century sexual language, adds the long-obsolete word *queme* (OED spelling *queem* and hence *queemness*, pleasure), 'which not only means pleasure, but in the sense of joining or fitting closely, or slipping in'. It may also be variation of the older vagina-synonym **quaint**. Ultimately and logically the link is a semi-euphemistic one to **cunt**.

The unadorned word means vagina, and a woman or women collectively, viewed in a sexual context. As noted, the gay uses turn it into an anus, and in US prisons a quim is a heterosexual inmate subjected to homosexual rape. Thereafter the compounds and phrases are strictly heterosexual. **Quim bush** and **quim whiskers** both refer to the female pubic hair, **quim nuts** to the labia, especially when notably large and pendant, and **quimstake** (or **quim-stick** or **quimwedge**) to the penis, which can be **quimfill**, i.e. fully embedded in the vagina. To **quimwedge** or **go quim-wedging** is to have sexual intercourse, as is **having a bit of quimsy**. A **quim-sticker** is a womaniser; he **goes quim-sticking**. Finally, **quimling** is manipulation of a woman's body in an attempt to produce orgasm, generally regarded as genital manipulation by the tongue, but not limited to such.

Perhaps the earliest synonym of all for cunt is **quaint**, with its own alternatives **quainter**, **quent** and **queynte**, which appears in the late fourteenth century in Chaucer's bawdy *Miller's Tale* (1386), where 'prively he caughte hire by the queynte'. Other q– terms for the vagina include **quiff** or **quoiff**, which may give the exotic **queef**, a vaginal fart, emitted during intercourse and usually noisy rather than malodorous. Quiff can also be a generic for all women and, like similar terms, be extended into gay use as a male homosexual. **Quimsby** extends quim, while **quiver** is a literal translation of Latin *vagina*. And **quoniam** is probably a simple q– term but may also be one of those Latinate euphemisms for the genitals, in this case meaning literally 'whereas'.

R IS FOR RAM

All these **poles** and **holes**, all this **riding** of that poor over-worked **beast with two backs**, it takes it out of a bloke. Or some blokes anyway (and for them, just see under **N is for Nancy**, p.154). But for real men, **horsecocked studs hung like a jack donkey** (or a **schwantz like a baby's arm with an apple in its fist**), it's all part of the day's play. 'God, he was an animal!' bemoans his unfortunate prey, and even if the animal on her mind is the octopus ('hands all over the place') he thinks something a little more … macho, and with that in mind, and with a tip of the hat to slang's primary preoccupation, the glorification of things and people male at the expense – well, look at the stuff, Equal Opportunities Commission it ain't – of those female, R is for ram.

Like the images that follow there isn't anything special to offer about the **ram** except that it has this … image. And it's an image that has attached itself to our sexual predator since the early seventeenth century. The initial image is of the penis, the **battering ram**, thus in Fletcher's play *The False One* (1623) '[he] studies her fortifications, and her breaches, And how he may advance his ram to batter the Bullwork of her chastitie.' But where else does the **battering piece** get its own image? The ram as ladykiller begins as an adjective, **rammish**, which leaves us in no doubt as to its meaning. Another early play, Middleton's *Phoenix* (1604) offers: 'What a fortunate elder brother is he, whose father being a rammish plowman, himself a perfumed gentleman, spending … the sweat of his father's body in monthly physic for his pretty queasy harlot.' Not that rammishness was a men-only attribute; a 1660 number of the *Wandering Whore* lists 'Honor Brooks the rammish Scotch whore' as well as one Ursula who 'had half a crown for showing her Twit-twat there, and half a crown for stroaking the marrow out of a mans Gristle.' What became of them, these whores of yesteryear, those juicy **bits** turned to ageing **drippers** and **artichokes**: gone to the Lock Hospital – at very best.

Still, that wouldn't worry our ram, whose thrusting penis was quickly extended to stand for his whole lusty self, dedicated to **tupping** his **ewes**. And when he aged, it was simple: he became an **old ram**, though his young contemporaries, especially the girls, tended to use the term with something of a sneer. Thus it was, until the 1980s, when a ram became an act of sexual intercourse, and to be **ram-shackled** meant being subjected to anal intercourse, usually by a person with a large penis.

STUDS AND STUDETTES

The ram plays his role at one end of the field, the **stud** at the other. The stud, a stallion or mare kept for breeding, entered slang in the later nineteenth century, meaning a man, not invariably but usually sexually successful. By the 1920s it meant simply any man, even, presumably, a eunuch, and a decade later was taken up by the US black lexicon, in which it implied sophistication, but again not special sexual ability. Reading the examples it is often hard to distinguish one from the other – maybe the writers/speakers were equally indistinct – but the differences did and do exist, and the sexual aspect is certainly the foremost. Other studs include a masculine lesbian, a male homosexual, a half-caste aboriginal woman used for sexual pleasure (and otherwise called a **stud gin**), a male prostitute catering to either sex, a 'masculine' jail homosexual (who usually reverts to heterosexuality on release), the penis and, finally, a physically strong or athletically powerful man or woman. And a **village ram** is the rural equivalent of the **town stallion** or **bull**. The standard English word *twigger*, referring to a ewe that is a prolific breeder, incidentally, produced **twigger**, as applied to a promiscuous woman.

A **studette** is a sexually and socially successful, physically attractive woman, while **studola** (a play on the 1950s playola, a form of record business corruption) is a concentration of winning womanisers and **studly** describes one who displays the characteristics of a sexually successful man. A **stud broad** is a 'butch' lesbian and a **stud dog** or **horse**, another male sexual predator, the latter being popular as a term of address. A **studhunk** (and isn't a **hunk** already sufficiently macho?) is another ladykiller, while a **stud hustler** is a gay male prostitute (playing the 'man's' role) and a **stud-muffin** (from **muffin**, US campus-speak for an admirable individual) is an exceptionally successful and attractive person; it can even be used of an animal. To **stud up** is for a gay man to attempt that process so devoutly wished by his moral judges, going 'back' to being straight.

BANTAMS, BUCKS AND BUCKERS

After that the zoo comes thick and fast (and see also **Z is for Zoo**, p.295). Just don't look for the petting corner – although one does find the **bantam**, usually a small variety of domestic fowl, whose eligibility is presumably based on his **cocky** strutting. First, Bambi's father: the **buck**, and after him the **stag**. The buck is a he-goat or male deer, and in the seventeenth–eighteenth centuries it was also a bold, daring person of either sex, with our roistering lady's man turning up around 1670. Nonetheless his earliest incarnation – a reference of course to his **horns** – was as a cuckold. He could also be a fool; thus these lines from John Taylor's *An Armado* in 1627, a wonderful recitation of contemporary terms for sucker, all of which, like the buck, come from the animal kingdom: 'Traps for vermin, Grinnes for wild Guls, Baytes for tame Fooles, Sprindges for Woodcockes, Pursenets for Connies, Toyles for mad Buckes, Pennes for Geese, Hookes for Gudgeons, Snares for Buzzards, Bridles for old Jades, Curbes for Colts, Pitfals for Bulfinches and Hempen-slips for Asses.'

Two uses of buck have survived (other than in the ever-popular historical use: the hero of a novelistic bodice-ripper) and neither are especially complimentary. The first is also unequivocally racist: a black person, all too often extended to buck nigger, not merely black but sexy too (and also capable of ripping the odd bodice on his day). The other comes from modern Liverpool, where a buck (and bucker or buckess) is a tearaway, a young, aggressive criminal. Most recently the term has come to mean an extremely attractive person of either sex.

The predatory buck appears in a number of combinations: buckish, meaning dashing, roistering; a buck party or buck's night, a party for men only; and buck nun, a bachelor (but *nun*? It must be some kind of fantasy of celibate bachelordom). A buck of the first head was a celebrated debauchee, whose excesses outpaced those of his peers, while an old buck or a buck fitch (from standard English *buck-fitch*, a male polecat) was an ageing lecher or an old roué (who could also be a snuffler or fumbler). The punning freeman of bucks is an adulterer, with the emphasis on buck, a cuckold.

STAGS AND STALLIONS

Alongside the buck stands the stag ('the male of a deer, esp. of the red deer; spec. a hart or male deer of the fifth year' according to the OED). While the stag is strictly an unaccompanied man at a dance or similar gathering (hence to go stag, to attend a social event without a female partner) or any form of party or similar entertainment attended only by men, it is unlikely that such men are postulant monks. The compounds make that clear: a stag line was the collection of numbers of unescorted men at a dance, standing in line eyeing the women; it can also be a gathering of gay male prostitutes in a park or similarly well-known area. The stag month was the first month that follows childbirth: at such times, and in what some might consider better days, a man's infidelities were considered acceptable. His wife, the new mother, was a stag widow. The stag movie (or stag, stag film, stag flick or stag show) is a pornographic film (supposedly enjoyed only by men). The stag night or stag party, generally any social event from which women are excluded, is specifically the traditionally uproarious eve-of-wedding party held by a groom and his male cronies. A **stag dance**, however, was an event found in such single-sex societies as mining camps: a men-only dance, performed in bar-rooms or taverns. Finally the question **stag or shag?**, will you be coming, usually to a party, alone or with a female companion?

The equestrian world gives **stallion**, which has been applied not merely to sexual athletes, but to female courtesans and kept women (though this may come from French *estalon*, a decoy, an enticement, or from stale, the lowest class of prostitute); to a heterosexual male prostitute or kept man; to a pimp; to the penis; to a tall, good-looking black woman, possibly highly sexed; to a female prostitute; and to a 'masculine' lesbian with a large clitoris. The **thoroughbred** is similarly multi-purpose. The womanising image, of the 1960s and beyond, was predated by those of an admirable or dependable person, and a dealer who sells pure or high quality narcotics. Further meanings of thoroughbred include a sophisticated hustler; a successful, trustworthy villain; and a prostitute with style, sophistication and knowledge, generally considered among the élite of her profession. Not that this image was that new: John Cleland, a connoisseur of women of the town, wrote in *Fanny Hill* of 'that hackney'd, thorough-bred Phoebe, to whom all modes and devices of pleasure were known'. There is also **horse** or **hoss**, but surely not he of TV's ranching Cartwrights. The hobby horse, meanwhile, is not strictly an animal, being made of wood, but in the early seventeenth century a **hobby horse man** was a womaniser or an adulterer: it was all down to 'riding'.

ALLEY CATS, BILLY GOATS AND LOUNGE LIZARDS

The **cat**, at least as used originally in the jazz world, where it may possibly have come from **alligator**, a jazz fan, gives **the cat that cracks the whip**, a playboy. Other furry friends include the **alley cat** (who can equally well be female), a **tomcat** (originally a female whore) and a **tough cat**. The **fox** and the **mink** provide alternative synonyms. The **billy-goat** or **goat**, usually an **old goat**, is a lecher (as supposedly is the animal) and **goatish** means lecherous. A **tush-hog**, once US campus slang for a person who is sophisticated with money, is an aggressive sexual athlete; a **hogger** can be an Irish street-corner idler or, on campus, a fat, homely young woman. And yes, it can mean penis.

All those previously listed can be seen as up-front in their attentions. The **lizard**, stereotypically, is less honest as regards his motives: since the 1910s he's been a smooth and highly plausible fortune-hunter or womaniser, typically (in the time-honoured tradition of Agatha Christie red herrings) working his charms in hotels or (once upon a time) ocean liners. His preferred area of operations is, of course, the lounge, and the **lounge** (sometimes **sofa**) **lizard**, **louse**, **snake** or **serpent** has long since been a social phenomenon – although a sub-definition refers to a poor or miserly man who would rather court a woman in her own house than take her out on the town. The **parlor lizard**, or **parlor athlete**, **ornament**, **rat** or **snake**, is wholly synonymous.

One cannot leave the **lizard** without noting his allied role, for the penis (for which see under **Z is for Zoo**, p.296). Still in the lounge or thereabouts was the **poodle-faker** (based on the role of a poodle as a fashionable pet between the wars), who was one who cultivated women's society, whether for sexual conquests or social advancement. The **cake-eater** was much the same: a self-indulgent or effeminate young man who attended smart tea parties and charmed old ladies. By extension he was any wealthy young playboy.

FANNY RATS AND CHEESEMEN

As should be clear from the ram and lizard, the womaniser and his penis can often be denoted by the same slang word or at least related. Hence the **axe**, the **poker**, the **pistol**, the **beard-** or **rump-splitter** and the **dangler** (like the penis he 'hangs around') who was also a well-known eighteenth-century character: one who follows women in the street but never actually speaks to them (the stalker is not a modern invention). Using the penis underlines another group: the **sticksman**, the **fanny rat** (he gets up there 'like a rat up a drain'), the **button** (i.e. vagina) **worker**, the **dorkbinder** and the **swordsman** – a very old image, e.g. a ballad included in Thomas D'Urfey's *Pills to Purge Melancholy* (1719–20): 'Brave Carpet Knights in Cupid's Fights, their milk-white Rapiers drew.'

A **woodsman** is one who has **wood**, i.e. an erect penis. **Jock** or **jockum** means penis, and the **jocker** was a late nineteenth-century term for a tramp who travels with a younger partner, who works for him and possibly acts as his catamite. From there it came to be a predatory homosexual (especially in the context of prison) who forces his attentions on younger/weaker men or boys; the most recent meaning is of a lecher. To **dick around** is to waste time, but it also means to chase girls. Somewhat ambiguous is the **cheeseman**: on the one hand it implies a socially inept person, on the other a sexual superstar. The question remains as to whether the root is **cheesy**, i.e. tacky, or such penis-related phenomena as **cheese tube**, the urethra, and **cheesy head**, a penis that has not been cleansed of smegma. Neither exactly flatter any **Handsome Harry, Lusty Lawrence** nor **Good-time Charlie**.

THE THRILL OF THE CHASE

Chasing, of course, is what it's all about. The animals with whom the sexual predator has been equated may not do much in the way of hunting (after all, those super-macho stags and bucks are actually herbivores), but he certainly does. Not for nothing is he known as a **meatmonger** or **fond of meat**, as well as a **sheep-biter** or a **mutton-fancier**. Nor is poultry safe: the **chicken** is an underage girl or boy, and the **chicken-hawk, -butcher, -man, -chaser, -freak, -fancier** or **inspector** is one who hunts them down. **Chicken-eyes** is a synonym (on the pattern of **short-eyes**, a prison term for a paedophile). Other chicken-based terms include **chicken dinner**, an attractive young boy or girl, and **chicken rustler**, a male homosexual who has been placed in charge of underage boys, e.g. a scoutmaster or choirmaster. Still in the henhouse is the **pullet-squeezer**, one who prefers the youngest partners, i.e. pullets or young chickens.

Other womanisers include the **fishmonger** (for the link of fish to women and their genitals see under **L is for Ling**, p.137), the **ho jockey** or **whore chaser**, the **linen-** or **leg-lifter**, the **mouse-hunter**, the **striker**, the **smock-** or **petticoat-hunter** and the **tail-chaser**. **Moll** and **dollymop** both mean a girl, and he who pursues them is a **moll-hunter**, **molrower** or **dolly-mopper**. (Dollymop is itself another example of the woman as fish: it combines **dolly** with standard English *mop*, a young whiting or gurnard, thus a young woman. In this context one might note the old German slang *Backfisch*, a teenage girl, literally a 'fish for baking'.)

The hunter likes to see himself as a sportsman (oh yeah? since when, other than in Gary Larsen's cartoon utopias, did the animals carry guns?) and **sportsman** is another term for a seducer. As Ned Ward put it in the *London Spy* (1699), referring to the prostitutes available at the Bedlam (properly Bethlehem) Hospital, "Tis a new Whetstone's Park [a well-known 'ho stroll' to the north of Lincoln's Inn Fields] where a Sports–man, at any Hour in the Day, may meet with Game for his purpose.' The **sportsman's gap** is the vagina. Allied terms include **gunner, sharpshooter, rifleman** and **hotshot**.

FLESH HOUNDS AND FANNY-HOPPERS

And the aim of this hunting, chasing and shooting? The body and its possession. So first, still in the world of field sports, a trio of hounds: the **poon-** or **gash-hound** (**poontang** and **gash** both meaning vagina) and the **flesh hound** (or **flesh-fly**). The **bum**, both the buttocks and the vagina, gives **bum-fighter, bum-ranger, bum-tickler, bum-worker, bum-shaver** and **bum-faker** (from **fake**, to make). The **bust-maker** refers to the standard English *bust*, the female breasts, i.e. the increased size of those of a pregnant woman. Similar is the **figure-maker**, although **figure-waltzing** described the writhings of one who was being publicly whipped as a judicial punishment (**taking air and exercise** as the old lags used to laugh it off). With bum comes **arse**, and thus **arse-bandit** (otherwise a gay man), **arse-hound** and **arse-man** (who also finds the girl's rear end to be her most alluring part. Another word for the posterior (and the vagina) is **crumpet**, perhaps because the shapes are apparently the same (or it could be the 'softness'), and thus the **crumpet-man** joins this group. Resemblance also underpins **hog's eye man**, though the **hog's eye** itself is the urethral hole in the penis. The **flower-fancier** prostrates himself before his beloved's **flower** – at least until he can 'pluck' it, an image that also gives **orchid-crusher**, i.e. the equation of the delicate flower with girlhood.

Less complimentary, but typical of slang terms for the vagina, is **gulley**, otherwise **gutter**, and a **gulley-raker**, which can elsewhere mean a cattle whip or a cattle thief, means both the penis and a womaniser. And although the logical root of **holemonger** and **holer** is hole, one shouldn't overlook the thirteenth- to fifteenth-century *holour*, a fornicator or whore-monger, and, as such, applied to men only. And does anything really change? 'When your man come home evil, tell you you are getting old … That's a true sign he's got someone else bakin' his jelly roll,' sang Ida Cox in her 1928 song 'Fogyism' and the **jellyroll**, properly a variety of an American sweet, is the vagina. A **jellyroller** is one who is obsessed by its conquest.

Tit-kisser and **fanny-hopper** both show that in the playboy's eyes every female part is up for grabs, though **pooner** (again from poontang) and **junta**, rhyming on 'cunter', take us back to the basics. The **pieman**, unsurprisingly, likes to 'eat'. A **mutton-cove** or **-fancier**, or a **muttoner**, is presumably just as 'hungry', although his 'utensil' is his **mutton-gun** or **-dagger**, **mutton** itself being one of the earliest slang terms for a woman (as in **mutton in long coats** or a **piece of mutton**). The OED suggests 'food for lust', but it's probably simply an old sheep as opposed to a young lamb.

KEISTER BUNNIES AND WHISKER-SPLITTERS

Last among the 'body parts' is the **keister** (or **keaster**, **keester**, **keyster**, **kiester** or **kister**), all of which come from the German *kiste*, a box, and which in German slang means the rump. An admirable and useful word, meaning variously a safe, the anus and anal sex, a burglar's bag of tools and a salesman's sample bag, it has sadly never crossed the Atlantic, but had it managed to we too would rejoice in the **keister-bandit**, both a heterosexual playboy and an aggressive prison gay man. Among other keister terms, albeit unrelated to seduction, are the **keister-stash** or **-plant** (any slim, hollow item, e.g. a biro tube, that can be placed in the anus and used to transport money, drugs and the like); **keister bunny**, a person who uses such an anus-based hiding place to run contraband; and **keister-stab**, to have anal intercourse.

Attached to the body is the **hair**, in this context naturally pubic, which is equally the source of male desire (and can mean a woman in its own right). Womanisers can be **hair-mongers**, and for a man to **put down some hair** is to have sexual intercourse. The **fleece-hunter** or **-monger** plays a similar role, as does the **whisker-splitter**. **Hare-finder** may play on the standard term meaning one whose job is to find hares; on the other hand it sounds very much like a pun, which the **bird's-nester** surely is. Finally the **tuft-hunter**, a piece of Oxford University slang meaning a social climber or toady – from the golden 'tufts' that adorned the mortar-boards of nineteenth-century aristocratic undergraduates as opposed to the black ones of the hoi polloi – can be used of one who pursues a more prosaic, but certainly more alluring, 'tuft'.

CHARVERING DONNAS AND FEATHER-BED SOLDIERS

And once he's in there, the **lover-boy** earns himself a few terms roughly based on the sheer fact of fucking. The **chauvering cove** comes from **charver** (also **chaffer** or **chauver**), to have intercourse, which most likely comes from the Italian *chiavare* (slang for fuck) and *chiappare* (catch, seize). Thus, a **charvering donna** or **moll** is a whore, while the 'seize' aspect of the word is found in **chauvering omee** (from Italian *uomo*, a man), a policeman. The act itself underpins **nugging cove**, from the sixteenth-century **nug**, to have sex, itself from dialect *nug*, to jog with the elbow, to strike, or even possibly Latin *nugae*, trifles. The **shag** in **shag artist** (which literally means shake) can be found as early as Francis Grose's dictionary of 1788: 'He is but bad shag, he is no able woman's man.' It also offers **shag-pad**, where a seducer takes his victim, and **shag-wagon**, in which he conveys or even fucks her, unless they opt for his **shag-pit**, the bed.

Bed action gives **bed-presser** and missionary-position sex **belly bumper**. The **feather-bed jig** is sexual intercourse, and a **feather-bed soldier** is a lecher (as well as a soldier who tries his best to avoid any demanding tasks). To **clip** and to **do** both mean to have intercourse; thus the **clipper** and **doer** are sexual success stories. **On the lash** is one of the latest terms for a hedonistic existence – thus the mythical **Count Lasher**, whose alternative title could be Don Juan. Lash also gives **Lash LaRue**, which reflects on the US entertainer Lash LaRue 'King of the Bullwhip'. A **dasher** is 'fast', whether a man or woman, but a **fast worker** still tends to refer to men only, **sex machines** who work **as fast as greased titties**.

One final term demands inclusion: the **butter-and-egg man** was a widely known 1920s character, a prosperous farmer or small-town leading citizen who comes to the big city (New York by choice) and poses embarrassingly as a playboy. The term was popularised by the nightclub owner Marie Louise 'Texas' Guinan (1884–1933), otherwise celebrated for her invariable greeting, 'Hello sucker!' Columnist Walter Winchell attributed the term to master of ceremonies Harry Richman, while the original 'butter-and-egg man' was supposedly 'Uncle Sam' Balcon, a New York provisioner. The term was first broadcast further afield by Louis Armstrong's song 'The Butter-and-Egg Man' (1924) and then by George S. Kaufman's similarly named play of 1925.

S is the big one. Ask any dictionary maker. Editing, checking, correcting, the long trek from A–Z (actually making the list of words is not so simple, one does not say, 'Right, I'll do all the A words first' – never happens; you don't think so? trust me, I'm a lexicographer) is like some (seemingly) endless trek across the terrain.

Of course it does end, A will always, eventually, reach Z, but there are, as it were ups and downs. A, a gentle meadow, then the near vertical climb to the massive chunk that is B, a slow descent through C and D (and 25 per cent of the book is done in just four letters) and on one goes; tiny E is all downhill (though not in French, where they have all those e-acutes – but what are they but S disguised), F, G, H, and M have their moments, and the air definitely starts to thin again at P, but S, S is the Everest, the big one. Two whole volumes in the hardcopy OED. More words and phrases in my own slang database than there were in the entire alphabet of my first one, in 1984. All of which suggests that *S is for...* offers a potentially vast choice. But inevitably, irresistably, and with the content of this book in mind, one is drawn to a single, would you believe four-letter word. Yes. S is for **shit**.

Its etymology is simple. As a good 'Anglo-Saxon' word, it comes from Anglo-Saxon *scite*, and is linked to a variety of similar terms from northern European – Teutonic – languages, all meaning dung. The variation *shite* appears to have an extra root in Anglo-Saxon *scitte*, meaning diarhoea. The OED traces it to 1308, when it was part of the standard vocabulary. By 1699, when London's indefatigable Ned Ward, going to places that others might prefer to avoid, noted 'The mixtures of Scents that arose from Mundungus – Tobacco, foul Sweaty Toes, Dirty Shirts, the Sh–t Tub, stinking Breaths and uncleanly Carcasses', the day of the discreet hyphen had arrived, and shit had been exiled from respectability. The hyphen would not start to be dropped until the late nineteenth century, and that usually in porn, equally indefatigable, but this time as regards sex. *My Secret Life*'s 'Walter', mounting yet another servant girl, tells us that 'I could see … a smear of shit on her chemise.' As to respectability? That all depends. Like **arse** or its own synonym **crap**, shit lives on the margins: technically an outlaw, it seems to gain an increasing welcome, or at least a blind eye. And in compounds such as **bullshit** it finds no door policy at all.

SHIT, SHITE AND SHITS

Shit is not, as it were, alone; it has a close relation in **shite**. That said, shit means almost exactly the same, whether literally – excrement – or in the abstract – rubbish, nonsense, an unpleasant person, something useless, second-rate, inferior or disgusting, or 'the daylights'. Many of the shit-terms can be given an extra 'e' without in any way diminishing their force or meaning. There are some, however, that seem to be occasions (and often Irish), nonetheless, when the five-rather than the four-letter word stands alone. Thus a **shitehawk**, a worthless person; to **break one's shite**, to collapse in laughter; to **have one's shite**, to be due to suffer, usually as an indication of rejection; **sure as shite on your shoe**, certainly, and its opposite, **you will in your shite!** no chance! no possible way! A **shite-shifter**, literally a mover of excrement, is an Irish term of abuse; **shite and onions!** a less than appetising exclamation; and **shite-rags** (sixteenth century) 'an idle lazie fellow'. Equally old is **shitefire**, a literal translation of the Spanish *cacafuego*, and as such a term of abuse applied to a hot-headed person. (The *Cacafuego* was the nickname – for its heavy armament – of a Spanish treasure ship captured in 1579 by Francis Drake, an exploit – some call it piracy, others 'rule Britannia' – that earned him his knighthood.) The **shite-poke**, literally a 'shit-bag', is a dialect term for the bittern (from its habit of defecating when frightened) and is perhaps a distant relation of another 'dirty bird', the **windfucker**, or kestrel, itself related to the northern dialect *fuckwind*, defined simply as 'a kind of hawk'.

To turn now to the meanings and uses of the word. The obvious one is excrement, as encountered in a lump, pile or **turd**.

But as an act of defecation, one must wait until the 1920s for the first recorded (though surely not the first spoken) instance of **go for**, **have** or **take a shit**. And in 1931 George Orwell (still Eric Blair) must have confused the reader of a letter in which, fresh from his tramping experiences, he offers 'Pony: a shit'. The word, since **pony** is rhyming slang (**pony and trap**) and represents an abbreviation as it ought, should have been **crap**.

Again prefaced by 'the', and this time in the plural, **the shits** can be diarrhoea, terror, fear or anything objectionable or unpleasant, as well as a bad temper. They are found in such phrases as **get the shits with**, to become annoyed (with someone) and **give someone the shits**, to annoy, to infuriate someone, and to **go the shits**, to sulk.

TALKING SHIT

From hereon in, it's pretty much all figurative and abstract. Setting aside the basic verb, below, shit proves yet again that the 'dirty' words, that wretched gang of miscreants, much despised by those who claim their use denotes 'a small vocabulary', can actually come up with nuances and variations that most of the staid foundations of the language would never even dare attempt. Indeed, even among its peers, shit seems more than usually capable of variety. I am no shrink, and shudder away far more fastidiously from attempting any kind of psychological assessment than I do from wading through what some might dismiss as a linguistic bog, but I have heard that shit can signify rather more than just … shit. So let us attempt to scale this mini-mountain. My apologies if at times my information seems to degenerate into a list: it remains the best way to show what's on offer. Nor will you find everything here: there's just too much. But we must try.

The first description of an individual as **a shit**, often modified as **little**, **dumb**, **stupid** or other form of contempt, arrives in 1870 in a limerick of which the punchlines ran 'Just to chaff him a bit / She said, 'You old shit, / I can buy a dildo for a sovereign.'

Since then it can be used neutrally, or to describe a boastful or pretentious person, or, as **the shit** – and of things as well as people – as the best, the ideal or the ultimate. Many abstract uses are negative. It can mean an unpleasant or difficult situation, especially when one finds oneself **in (the) shit**. And there are other, neutral uses, most coined since the 1930s, since when it may refer to any thing (material or otherwise), irrespective of its actual quality. It may also be used as a general abstract term for a thing, a situation, an opinion or idea, the precise meaning varying as to the context, e.g. **I don't like this shit**, I don't like what's happening. Conversely, it can suggest nothing – as in to **not mean shit**, not matter or not mean anything, and **not worth shit**, not worth anything. It can refer to abuse or offensive and contemptuous treatment, e.g. to **take a lot of shit**, **don't take any shit**, and in a wholly abstract non-judgemental sense one's possessions, one's actions, one's life. It can also mean the essence, the daylights, as in a variety of phrases based on – **the shit out of**. It can be a form of communication, usually negative: nonsense, rubbish, lies, prevarications, often in the phrase **talk shit**, and while it can mean influence – one can **pull shit** – such influence is probably less than positive.

SHIT, EH!

Far more concrete is a group of terms based on drugs. The original refers to opium-based narcotics, specifically heroin, and occasionally morphine. The pleasure/guilt equation needs no further comment. Extended to cannabis, the root is more likely the colour of hashish: brown, although the guilt seems to return when dealing cocaine, especially as crack. 'Money is like muck, not good except it be spread' declared Sir Francis Bacon around 1600: the image has persisted and shit, another form of muck, means money. Similar links can be found in a number of underworld and prison uses where shit is found variously as gunfire, prison food, tobacco, a weapon, a prison riot and as a criminal him- or herself. It can also, in its most recent form, describe HIV or AIDS.

The last simple noun use is again prefaced by 'the'. In **who the shit are you?**, **let's get the shit out of here** and the like, shit serves as an obscene intensifier that lies somewhere between the stronger **fuck** and the milder **hell**. And it works as an intensifier just as well without the need for 'the': **would I shit! did she shit! Shitless**, meanwhile, represents a state of abject terror ('scared shitless') while the less-common **shitted** means the same. **Shit-all**, like **fuck-all**, **sod-all** or **bugger-all**, means zero.

Shit! is of course one of the most useful of exclamations; it can be expanded, possibly redundantly, as **shitfuck!** and as **shitfire!**, **shit and piss!**, **shit on toast!**, **shitty!**, **shithot!** (the adjective shithot meaning excellent), **shit and derision!**, **shit me!**, **shit on you!**, **shit and fall back on it!**, **shit the bed!** and even **oh, shit!** which mixes surprise with undertones of dismay. **Shit, eh!** is an Australian exclamation of moderate astonishment or irony.

To return to nouns, the list of compounds is daunting, but they show just how wondrously available is the word for anyone who needs it. A **shitbag**, the stomach, is also a colostomy bag as well as (and equally as **shitebag**) a repellent person, as is a **shitball**, **shitbum** or **shit-ass**, and, adjectivally, **shit-ass**, **shitaceous** and **shit-arse** all mean very bad. So too is a **shitbird**, though here the 'shit' can refer to narcotic drugs, and if so, a **shitbird** is a junkie. The literal **shitbox** is the anus, as well as a portable latrine, a run-down vehicle and anything seen as bad or inferior. **Shit-breeched** was a seventeenth-century term of abuse, while **shit-catchers** (and **poop-catchers**) are the breeches themselves. A **shitcan** is a refuse lorry, originally dedicated to emptying cesspits (what the sixteenth century termed **gold-finding**, from the colour; today's collector is a **shit-shark**) although the **Shit Bucket** represented the initials of South Africa's Special Branch. A shitcan might also be a lavatory, prison punishment cells and a near-derelict but just drivable second-hand car or motor-bike, one step from the junkyard (so too is a **shitwagon**).

As a verb shit means to do someone a wrong, to stop, to abandon a course of action, to toss away; to dismiss from a job or to denigrate. **Shit-canned** (or **shit-bound**) means in a bad way or bad situation. Other terms for the anus include **shit-chute**, **shitpan** and, the best-known, **shithole**. They can equally refer to an unpleasant, filthy place.

STIRRERS, STABBERS AND STOPPERS

Shit lends itself to a range of insults, all expressing disdain or disgust: **shitheel**, **shit-cunt**, **shitface** (while **shit-faced** means drunk, drugged and, of course, unpleasant), **shit-features**, **shithead** (also a junkie), **shit-lover** (literally, a coprophile), **shitstain**, **shitwad**, **shit-weasel**, **shitpot** (as well as a chamberpot or a lavatory or any unpleasant place or inferior object) and **shit-sniffer**. A disgusting place can be a **shitheap**, **shitfarm**, **shit-pit** (or **-pen** and also a lavatory), **shit-jacket** and above all **shithouse**, which can mean a jail or a repellent person as well as the usual unpleasant place and (outside) loo. The word is mainly antipodean and offers such phrases as **feel like a haunted shithouse**, to have a bad hangover; **out on its own like a country shithouse**, unique, unrivalled; **a shithouse full**, a very large number or amount; and **to the shithouse (with)**!, to pieces, 'to hell'. The **shithouse mouse** is a useless person, but his cousin the **shithouse rat** plays a greater role. This admirable creature – why exactly are rats so reviled: would *you* stay on a sinking ship? – offers a variety of comparisons: **lucky**, **cunning**, **crazy**, **ugly** or **shifty**, all 'as a shithouse rat'. To have **eyes like a shithouse rat** is to have eyes that may seem shifty, but are undeniably acute. Meanwhile a **shit factory** is the buttocks, **shitpaper** or **shit tickets**, toilet paper, **shit-squirting** or **shit-sucking**, dirty or disgusting.

Other shit-based people include the **shit-disturber** or **-stirrer**, who are malicious gossips (hence the verb **shit-stir**).

The **shit-eater** represents slyness, duplicity and toadying, while his **shit-eating**, **cat-eating-shit** or **crud-eating grin** is a smug, self-satisfied smile. The **shitman** gossips too, although he can be no more than a junior figure in a given hierarchy – he **catches the bosses' shit** and if he's on the **shit list** (a list of people one considers distasteful, untrustworthy and otherwise unacceptable) he performs the **shit detail** or **shit-work**, the lousy, dirty jobs. His alternative career path is the **shit-licker**, a toady, but that can also describe a homosexual, a term echoed in **shit-hunter**, **shit-packer**, **shit-stabber** (literally, the penis) or **shit-puncher** (and its synonym the **dung-puncher**). A **shithook** is a foolish, clumsy or unpleasant, aggressive individual whose shit-hooks are their hands (however, fans of Vietnam movies will be familiar with the Shithook, the large CH-47 'Chinook' helicopter). A **shit-shoe** or **shit-shod** has trodden in excrement, and to be **shit-coloured** was a derogative term once applied to a light-skinned black who tried to pass as white. Equally unpleasant is **shit-skin**, a black person.

No shit other than the figurative is involved in a **shit-fight**, a bitterly contested struggle, e.g. a sporting encounter; a **shitpull**, a struggle; a **shitfit**, an emotional outburst; or a **shitstorm**, a very confused or frightening situation. The constipatory **shit-stopper** promotes the image of an event so dramatic or surprising that it suspends one's normal bodily processes, while a **shit sandwich** is either a humbling experience or, more literally, homosexual anal intercourse.

SHITSACKS, SHICK-SHACKS AND SHIT-STICKS

Among the stranger combinations is **shitsack**, which has meant a fool or unpleasant person since the eighteenth century, but its earlier use is as a religious non-conformist and was euphemised as **shick-shack** (also **shig-shag**; **sic-sac**; **shuck-shack**; **shiff-shack**, etc.). The image sprang from its original use as a term of abuse for people who were found not wearing the customary oak-apple or sprig of oak before noon on Royal-Oak Day (29 May, commemorating Charles II's hiding in an oak tree). Such people, no friends of the king, would most likely be non-conformists or Puritans. That day became known in dialect as *Shick-sack Day* and the oak-apple or sprig of oak became known as *shick-shack*. If you wore your oak sprig after noon you became a shick-shack, a fool. As a (**sad**) **sack of shit** it was bowdlerised to make the title of a popular US cartoon strip, 'Sad Sack'.

A **shit-stick** is a contemptible person, the penis (especially when used for anal intercourse) and, in prison, a billy-club. **Shit stompers** are both cowboy boots and cowboys; **Shitville** is one of those generics (like Australia's **beyond the rabbit-proof fence** or America's **West Bumfuck**) that denote a very out-of-the-way, rural place. Still geographic are **shit street** and **shit creek**, where one finds oneself **without a paddle**. A **shitload** (or **crapload**) is a great deal, a **shitsworth** is very little.

The idea of shit as something unpleasant, literal or otherwise, plays its part. **Ain't shit**, whether used of a person, thing or idea, means useless, worthless or of absolutely no value. A **bucket, crock** or **puddle of shit** signify much the same. **And shit** is an all-purpose ending for a sentence, a coarser alternative of 'you know'. **Shit-for-brains** (and **ick-for-brains, poop-for-brains, shite-for-brains**) describes an idiot. **Shit for nothing** (or **shit for the catfish, shit-for-wage**) is third-rate, of very poor quality and a **shit of a thing** something unacceptable or unpleasant. **In a shit** means to be angry, while **in the shit** is to be facing problems, as is, for no perceptible reason, **up the Dutch shit**. To be **up in someone's shit** is to be interfering or 'poking one's nose in' and **up the shit** is used of large quantities. The apology **my shit** means my mistake (a rougher-edged version of **my bad**). **Shit on a string** is something extremely hard or impossible to do, while **shit on a shingle** or **SOS** means primarily minced beef on toast but equally serves as an exclamation of astonishment. **Shit on a stick** can be variously a tough guy, an important person (also **shit on wheels**) or a repellent one.

DOING SHIT

If shit exists so substantially in compound nouns, then who is to gainsay its wide appearance in verbs. Again, it's so very useful. There are the verbs that are either literal or figurative evocations of shit as shit, i.e. excrement: **do**, **have** or **take a shit**, to defecate (though if one adds **on**, one implies creating problems for, or abusing, another); **eat shit**, to abase oneself; **get one's shit blown away** or **backwards**, to be killed; **get one's shit hard**, to make one excited; and **get up in someone's shit**, to get angry with someone else. To **go like shit off a stick** is to move very fast, of a person or vehicle; while to **have a shit**, when not meaning defecate, means (in South Africa and Australia) to become enraged. To have **shit in one's blood** is to be a coward, while to have **shit** (or **dirt**) **on one's liver** (the equivalent of standard English *liverish*, testy) is to be in a bad temper (hence, **shitty-livered**, tetchy). To **have someone's shit on a stick** is to place them at an extreme disadvantage; to **lose one's shit**, to experience something frightening or shocking; and to **push shit uphill**, either to work, talk or act unsuccessfully against the odds or, abandoning the abstract, to have anal intercourse. To **put the shit** or **shits up** is to terrify and to **think one's shit smells like ice-cream** is to behave affectedly and in an arrogant manner.

After which comes a group of verbs where shit equates with trouble or ill-treatment. One can **catch shit**, be scolded or told off, get into trouble or suffer physical harm; **drop (the) shit on**, give someone a difficult time or otherwise persecute them; and **fall** or **get in the shit** (or indeed **crap**), find oneself in difficulties (although it can also mean simply to become involved in a situation). To **give someone shit** or **land them in the shit** is to cause trouble for someone; the former also means to nag or criticise, as does **put (the) shit on**, which can also mean to take advantage, to trick, to deceive; those who **take** or **suck shit** accept the abuse. To **hit some shit** is to encounter problems. To **kick up**, **raise** or **start shit** is to go out of one's way to cause trouble, while **shovel**, **stir** and **sling the shit** suggest malicious conversation. To **put shit in someone's game** is to set out to undermine their plans.

KNOWING ONE'S SHIT

Shit, as noted, can also mean the 'essence', usually in the context of violence. Variations on that theme include **beat**, **kick**, **knock**, **slap** and **thump** (**seven kinds of**) **shit out of**. The shit can also be the 'living shit' and one can **scare** it out of someone. Equally negative, but unmoved by violence, are further phrases in which shit denotes bad feelings, experiences or health. Thus, to **feel like shit** (or **feel shit** or **shitty**) is to feel very bad, whether emotionally or physically and **look like shit** is a 'visual' synonym; to **go to shit** is to decline or to collapse, while to **go from sugar to shit**, of a place and its standards, is to decline severely. To **take the shit with the sugar** is to accept that one must have both bad and good experiences. To **treat like shit** is to treat in a very unpleasant manner, deservedly or not. Then comes shit as a lie. A **line of shit** (from **line**, a deceptive style) is nonsensical, if persuasive chatter; to **cut the shit** (often as an exclamation) is to stop talking nonsense, while **pop shit** is to boast or 'mouth off', **shoot the shit** is to 'tell the tale', and the multi-purpose **talk shit** variously means to seduce, to 'chat someone up', to talk nonsense, to criticise someone behind their back, to boast, to brag, to talk aggressively or to challenge verbally, and to talk slang (and thus the lying or nonsensical **shit-talker**). Even more abstract than a lie, shit can mean 'a thing'. Thus to **know one's shit** is to be very competent, and to **cut shit** is to impress, to influence or to make a difference (though it can also mean to act eccentrically). To **get off someone's shit** is to stop bothering them, usually in the demand 'get off my shit', leave me alone. To **get one's shit together** is variously to calm down, to plan sensibly or to be competent, while to **have one's shit together** (or **down**, or **in one bag**) is to be in full control of a situation. To **pull shit** is to do something devious, underhand or treacherous, while to **play that shit** means to act in a particular way, usually as in the negative **I don't play that shit**, I don't do that. A pair of unaligned uses are to **hit one's shit up**, which means to inscribe one's name and gang affiliation on a wall, and to **get shit of**, which entails getting rid of something or someone.

Shit works as a comparative, and not always pessimistically. **As shit** is a general intensifer, e.g. mad as shit, good as shit; **for shit** means either whatsoever, at all, in any way or very badly. **From shit to Shinnecock** means 'of any sort whatsoever' or across the entire spectrum. A slim person can be **so thin you can smell shit through them**. To **stick as close as shit to a blanket** is to stick very close (**like shit on a shoe**). **Soft as shit and twice as nasty** sums up anyone the speaker dislikes, while **sure as shit** (also **sure as shit and taxes**, **sure as shit rolls downhill from a privy** and the adverbial **shitesure**) implies absolute certainty – albeit of something unpleasant. By itself, **like shit** can mean very fast, enthusiastically, badly or very bad, very much; it also works as a sarcastic retort of dismissal. To **move like shit off a shovel** (or **like steam on piss**) is to do something promptly, immediately or fast; speed similarly underpins **like shit** (or **crap**) **through a goose** or **a tin horn**. The somewhat tautological **like stink on shit** (or **funk on a skunk**, **stank on shit** or **stink on glue**) means very close or extremely intimate, though the imagery hardly tends to affection.

ALL OVER THE PLACE LIKE A MAD WOMAN'S SHIT

Shit also lends itself to a number of proverbial phrases, most of which are based on the shit = excrement meaning. To **act like one's shit don't stink** (also **act like one's shit don't smell**, **act like shit wouldn't melt in one's mouth**, **think one's shit don't stink**, or **think that one's shit smells like ice-cream**) is to behave affectedly and in an arrogant manner. **All over the place like a mad woman's shit** (and the phrase can equally refer to the chaos of her **breakfast**, **knitting** or **lunchbox**) is to be confused and/or extremely messy. Those who **bet a pound to a pinch of shit** (or **poop**) are absolutely confident, whether in an actual bet or merely a point of view; to **break one's shit string** (instead of excrement, there is blood) is to have violent anal intercourse. **Don't get your shit hot** is a warning against over-excitement. **He wouldn't say 'shit' even if he had a mouth full of it** is used of an especially mealy-mouthed, hypocritical person. **I could use her shit for toothpaste** (also **I'd crawl three miles over broken glass to use her shit for toothpaste**) is a hugely exaggerated phrase implying the extent of one's infatuation (and hearts and flowers it ain't). Similarly, **I'm so hungry I could eat a shit sandwich – only I don't like bread** implies the intensity of one's starvation. **You don't know whether you want a shit or a haircut** indicates that a person is very stupid, while **you're all about – like shit in a field** is a sarcastic way of saying you're a useful, alert, efficient person – *not!* **Ten pounds of shit in a five pound bag** (a unit of measure also known as a **blivet**) describes anything considered ugly, especially someone obese or overweight.

SHIT HAPPENS

Shit in the abstract, meaning 'thing' or 'stuff' (usually undesirable) lies behind the following. **Same shit, different day** (also **s.s.d.d.**, and **same shit, different toilet**), life goes on as normal, with no surprises, good or bad; **shit comes in piles**, 'sorrows come not in single spies but in battalions' as Claudius says in Shakespeare's *Hamlet*. Then there's **shit happens**, an all-purpose statement of resignation in the face of life's vicissitudes, i.e. these things happen, a phrase famously bowdlerised by Donald Rumsfeld as 'things happen' when referring to what he doubtless also saw as 'collateral damage' (that ever-useful euphemism for civilian deaths) in Iraq. Perhaps best-known of all is that moment **when the shit hits the fan** (jokily euphemised as the **doo–doo**, **eggs**, **omelette** or **ca-ca hits the fan**, as well as **the excrement** or **solids hit(s) the air conditioning**), i.e. when difficulties start to happen (especially when such problems have been expected).

As might be expected, given shit's fundamental meaning, the word serves as the base of a selection of negatives, among them **not a shit show**, no chance, and **not fit to shovel shit**, of a person, absolutely worthless or incompetent. Others indicate gross stupidity, e.g. **not know whether to shit or go blind** (or **whether to pee or go blind** or **shit or buy gas**), **not know a sparrow's shit** (about), **not know from shit**, **not know shit from apple butter, beans, clay, salami** or **tunafish. Not to know shit from Shinola** refers to a US shoe-cleaning product and **not say shit about Shinola** is to say nothing. That which is **not worth a shit** (or **shit** or **two shits**) is worthless and/or useless.

Lastly, in this catalogue of noun uses, come the exclamations: **for shit's sake!**, indicating one's (mild) annoyance; **go plait your shit!**, go away; **I'll be dipped in shit!**, I'm very shocked; **no shit!**, really?, honestly! or, sarcastically, 'surprise, surprise!'. America's **shit howdy!** is relatively weak, while New Zealand's **shit oh dear!** (or **shit oh dearie!**) expresses one's sorrow or regret. **Shitlaw!** (a mix of the basic shit! and Lord!) is a campus cry of annoyance.

SHIT OR BUST

Shit as an adjective is either predictably negative when applied to any thing or person considered bad, obnoxious, unpleasant, inferior or worthless, or on the bad = good pattern, in which case it can signify excellent or first-rate. Passing on to the verb, one sees another vast assemblage. The simple verb offers the obvious moving of the bowels, as the medicos have it, as well as vomiting. In figurative terms it offers to deceive, to bamboozle, to tell lies or to exaggerate; to waste time; to act in a cowardly manner; to respond dramatically, with alarm, fear, anger, e.g. he'll shit himself when he hears this!; to annoy; to stop; to do something badly; to fail; to make a mess; and to frighten.

And like the noun it offers a variety of phrases, at least some of which may be seen as quasi-proverbial. These, for instance, use shit in its literal sense: **I could shit through the eye of a needle**, I'm suffering from diarrhoea; **shit dimes and quarters**, excrete bags of drugs (worth dimes – 10 cents – or quarters – 25 cents) after swallowing them when facing a police search; and **shit in high cotton or high grass**, live 'high off the hog' (the lucky man or woman can also **fart through silk**). To **shit in one's own backyard, on one's dining-room table** or **on one's doorstep**, on the other hand, all refer to any situation in which, foolishly, one does something that jeopardises one's existence by its proximity to one's personal, social or professional life – typically to steal from one's own workplace or to conduct an affair with an in-law or employee. To **shit where one eats** is similar, though it tends to focus on committing a crime in one's own neighbourhood. To **shit green** (where green is the image of a disturbed stomach, left in that state by one's disturbed emotions) can mean to desire, to be extremely shocked, to be enraged or to be afraid. To **shit and wish**, from the eighteenth-century proverb 'shit in one hand and wish in the other – and see which one fills up first', is a remark made to anyone who starts their sentence 'I wish … '. To **shit on someone's parade** apes the better-known **piss on someone's parade** and neither are to be admired. **Shit** (or **piss**) **or get off the pot!** urges someone to stop dithering; the term was supposedly used by then US Vice-President Richard Nixon to his boss President Eisenhower when the latter, one might feel understandably, seemed less than wholly keen to go along with Nixon's desire for him to defend the Veep's palpable corruption. In Nixon's case it was a matter of **shit or bust**, to make a last, desperate gamble, which he duly did, regaling the nation with his mawkish, self-serving and wholly mendacious 'Checkers Speech'. Eisenhower, though all too likely tempted, resisted telling him dismissively to **go shit in your hat (pull it over your head and call it flowers)**! nor indeed **go crap in your hat, go shit in a pot and duck your head, go spit in your hat!, go spit up your trouser leg** nor even **go shit in your wallet**. Finally, to **shit through one's teeth**, a particularly repellent image dating from the eighteenth century, means to vomit, to lie blatantly or, in the West Indies (where it is also found as **shit through one's nose**), to suffer or be humiliated; **shit in your teeth!** was an exclamation of dismissal.

More specific plays on defecation, this time occasioned by the stomach-churning responses to fear, offer **shit a brick, shit** (or, even less plausibly, **piss**) **bullets, shit it, shit one's load** or **pants, shit one's brains out,** or **shit tacks**. But if shit a brick (variously found as **shit a giraffe, shit bricks, shit nickels, shit peach pits, shit pickles, shit snowballs** and **sweat bricks**) is firstly a term for terror, it can also refer to a finally successful trip to the toilet after a lengthy period of constipation; its other meanings are to be absolutely delighted or to be furious. It can, in addition, work as an exclamation of extreme surprise or annoyance.

DON'T SHIT A SHITTER

The shit that underpins lying and deception, albeit figurative, is duly productive, although it seems to refer mainly to the word bullshit, nonsense: **do a lot of shitting and one's pants aren't down,** to talk loudly and foolishly. And a desire to prove the honesty of one's words can be found in **I shit you not.** The warning **don't shit a shitter** (also **don't bullshit a bullshitter**) stresses the error in trying to fool someone who deals in fooling others. To **shit on** or **over** is to abuse or to humiliate, to deal with comprehensively, to defeat, e.g. in a sporting fixture, or to talk tediously. A variation is **shit on from a great height**, which was coined in the RAF, shortly after the First World War.

Finally a few derivatives. **Shitty** (and **shitey**, **shitty-ass**, **shittypants**), literally meaning covered in excrement or generally filthy, is extended to mean unpleasant, disgusting; mediocre or second-rate; mean, malicious and nasty; tedious or futile; unwell, depressed, or guilty; bad-tempered; dangerous or incompetent. Its own derivative **shittiness** means unpleasantness, while **shitty-nosed** (from all that **arse-licking**) means sycophantic and contemptible. The **shitty end of the stick** is of course that which one would prefer to avoid. And for shit, surely the most widely used of all slang terms, I do believe that's that. You don't think so? Come on: **would I shit you, you're my favourite turd**.

IS FOR
TURD
AND TWAT
AND TITS

Let us be clear: this has nothing to do with thrushes. Not our homegrown *Turdus philomelos* (the song-thrush), not *Turdus poliocephalus* (most of which are extinct), nor *Turdus ignobilis* nor even *Turdus merula*, which is in fact a blackbird. Nor any of the 173 species of the family Turdidae.

This is about another of those words that can truly qualify as 'Anglo-Saxon'. **Turd**. The Anglo-Saxon word was *tord*, itself allegedly based in the presumed Indo-European root *der*, tear or split. Thus, the excrement is seen as being 'torn' from the body. As originally used around the year 1000, it was merely descriptive; the derogatory uses appeared in the mid-fifteenth century. By 1567, when Thomas Harman brought out his glossary of criminal cant, it was common enough to be included in his 'conversation' between two thieves. 'Gerry gan the Ruffian cly thee' curses one, and Harman translates this as 'A torde in thy mouth, the deuill take thee' (*gerry* being a variation on *jere*, a piece of human excrement, itself based on the synonymous Romani *jeer*).

As with many similar terms, vulgar rather than actual slang, turd was excluded from polite speech (and dictionaries) in the great linguistic purge that sought to clean up English by the late eighteenth century and which saw the word, if it did appear, discreetly deprived of its middle letters. As for its use to denigrate a fellow-being, that seems to have vanished, at least from written record, from the early eighteenth century to the early twentieth. It has remained off-limits although, like many of the 'milder' obscenities, it has crept gradually into spoken, if not written English, especially where, like its cognate **shit**, it refers not to excrement but to a human object of derision or dislike.

IT'S ALL HONEY OR ALL TURD WITH THEM

Turd is used for a piece of excrement, and a person who is, in other words, 'a piece of shit'. Its uses divide between the literal and the figurative, with the former often implying a predilection for homosexual anal intercourse. Thus, while **bugturd**, **turdball** and **turdburger** are used as person-to-person insults, a **turdburglar**, otherwise known as a **turd bandit**, **-puncher** or **-tapper**, is a homosexual male. (Australia's military college, RMC Duntroon, prefers **bowel burglar**.) A **turdhead** is an unpleasant or stupid person, who can be **turdish** or **turdy** (though the latter can have a literal meaning – covered in excrement – too). **Turd cutter** refers to the buttocks, **turdkicker** to a yokel or peasant and **turd-packer** (as well as **turd-puncher**, **turd-tapper** and **shit-packer**) to a homosexual. A **turd poodle** is both disgusting and stupid; neither is **a turd in the punchbowl** a term of affection. A **turd-strangler**, however, is a plumber, even if **turd-strangling**, applied to a human target, is less professional than, again, personal. To **chuck a turd** is to defecate and to **turdbird** to lie or exaggerate.

Turds seem to lend themselves to semi-proverbial phrases: **it's all honey or all turd with them** describes those whose relationship fluctuates violently: they are either the closest of friends or the deepest of enemies. **As popular as a turd in a fruit salad** is, unsurprisingly, extremely unpopular, just as **not worth a turd** (coined in the late fifteenth century) means worthless. **As fine as a cow turd stuck with primroses**, an appealingly rural image, means very fine indeed. One who **would skin a turd** is especially miserly, as is one who **would not give someone the steam off one's turds**. To **push a turd uphill** (sometimes **with a toothpick**) means to work, talk and otherwise strive unsuccessfully, against the odds. To **scare bird turds out of** is to terrify. And, as Harman used it above, **a turd in your teeth!** is the *c.*1500 equivalent of go to hell!

Finally, in an act of blatant plagiarism, I offer a couple of 'turds' from *Viz* magazine's magnificent *Magna Farta* (2008): '**Turdsearch**: The desperate hunt for reading material one embarks upon when **Mr Brown is at the window**.' And, for Dr Who fans, the '**turdis**, One of them detached, modern, portable, space-age-looking public conveniences that could well be a phonebox or small internet café.'

TWATS, TWATHEADS AND TWATTING

Twat (or **twat-hole**, **twit-twat**, **twot**, **twotch**, **twoit**, **twattle** and, as a plural **twats**, the labia) has meant vagina since 1656: it is related to *twachylle* or *twittle* which, usually spelt *twitchel*, meant a narrow passage. A dialect usage, *twatch*, means to mend a gap in a hedge. None of which, it turned out, was apparent to the poet Robert Browning (1812–89) who in 1841 published *Pippa Passes*, a mainly verse 'drama' drawing on his studies of Elizabethan and Jacobean plays and known today for its blithe assurance that 'God's in His heaven, all's right with the world.' As part of his research Browning read the poem 'Vanity of Vanities' (1660), in which he found the couplet 'They talk't of his having a Cardinalls Hat, / They'd send him as soon an Old Nuns Twat.' The coarseness of the verse was lost on the poet, who simply assumed that twat denoted some part of a nun's attire. Thus in *Pippa Passes* he wrote blithely: 'Then, owls and bats / Cowls and twats, / Monks and nuns, in a cloister's moods, / Adjourn to the oak-stump pantry.' Others were less innocent, and the lines remained a good source of schoolroom sniggering. Browning was never to be disabused of his belief: he died in happy ignorance since no-one could find a delicate enough means of explaining his error.

Squeamish Mr Browning notwithstanding (and was it not fortunate that such terms as the **browning**, for anal intercourse or cunnilingus, let alone the **Browning family**, a generic for male homosexuals, still lay a century in the future), twat is one of a number of terms that equate the vagina with a slit, which presumably for the relative accuracy of the physiology, outdoes the popular 'hole' list when it comes to finding synonyms for the vagina. **Slit** itself first appeared in the eighteenth century. Its peers include **chasm**, **crack**, personified as meaning whore as well, **cranny** (thus **cranny-hunter**, the penis), **crevice**, **gap**, **canyon**, **breach**, **ditch**, **furrow** (and **one-ended furrow**), **gulf**, **gutter**, **gash**, **slice of life** (and **agreeable rut of life**), **slot**, **trench**, **chink**, **prime cut**, **notch** and **nick in the notch**. **Inglenook**, divorced from its cosy fireside role, can also mean slit, as can **crinkum-crankum**, which otherwise has a standard English meaning of a narrow, winding passage (although **crinkum** itself means venereal disease).

As well its vagina meaning, twat can be found metonymised as a woman (also a **twotface**), as a term of abuse irrespective of gender, as the buttocks or the anus, and figuratively as something unpleasant and/or second-rate. It can be used, like such parallel terms as **fuck**, to denote a neutral term for a person, no insult intended.

From thereon the compounds are unswervingly based on the genitals. The **lick-twat** has been performing cunnilingus since the seventeenth century, while the **twat-faker** or **-masher** is a pimp. **Twathead** and **twatmaster** are terms of abuse, as is **twatman** (on the model of superhero Batman). The **twat-mag** is a pornographic magazine and the **twat-rug** a woman's pubic hair. **Twat-hooks** echo **cunt-hooks** and also mean the fingers, while a **twat-scourer** (literally, 'cunt-cleaner'), is not just an insult but also a doctor or surgeon. A **face like a bag of smacked twats** is a less than positive description of an unattractive woman. (Other less than alluring faces can resemble **a bull's bum**, **a festering pickle**, **an abandoned quarry**, **a smacked arse**, **a stopped clock**, **a stripper's clit**, **a twisted sandshoe** and **a yard of tripe**.)

To go **twatting** or **twat-faking** or **-raking** (**fake** meaning to make) means to have sex. **Twatting** is intercourse, and like **fucking** can be used as an intensifier. To be **twatted** is to be drunk, and **twatty** is to be a stupid twat. Finally, the **twattling-strings**, **twatling-strings** or **twiddling-strings** – which comes strictly not from **twat** but from dialect's *twattle*, to chatter, to talk idly – refer to the anal sphincter, especially in the context of breaking wind.

A TASTY BIT OF TIT

'You can't put "tits and ass" on the marquee! … Why not? … Because it's dirty and vulgar, that's why not! … Titties are dirty and vulgar? … Okay, we'll compromise. How about Latin? *Gluteus maximus, pectoralis majors* nightly … That's alright, that's clean, class with ass, I'll buy it … *Clean to you, schmuck, but dirty to the Latins!'*
Lenny Bruce, in the Carnegie Hall, 1961.

There is, one might agree, something profoundly sad in the fact that the mother's nurturing breast has fallen foul of the fearful strictures of linguistic morality. But there it is, **tits**, right between **cunt** and **cocksucker**, in George Carlin's list of filthy words. The OED marks it as slang and dates it to the 1920s, though Alan Bold's 1979 collection of bawdy ballads claims this supposed conversation between Queen Victoria and her daughter Louise, from 1871: 'You may whimper a bit, but on no account shit / Though he mangles your tits to a jelly.'

There are two varieties of **tit**, both with their sexual overtones. And although the better known is based on standard English *teat* and as such means the female breast (usually in the plural), the older version is in fact onomatopoeic, and implies anything small; it may have come from, and certainly echoes, such Scandinavian terms as *titta*, a little girl, or *tita*, a small fish. The original slang use, around 1550, referred to a small or half-grown horse, but by the end of the century tit meant a girl or woman, either as an insult, or somewhat better, a generic – for instance, a **tasty bit of tit**. The inference is again of size, but there may have been a link to the horse, i.e. the woman can also be 'ridden'. A **little tit**, on the other hand, was always a term of affection. The nineteenth century saw it as yet another synonym for vagina, and thus extended as **tit-bit**, which also meant a penis, a young girl and an ineffectual person. A **willing tit** was either 'a little horse that Travels chearfully' (B.E.'s canting dictionary of 1698) or a complaisant woman.

TITTING ABOUT

Teat is properly a nipple, rather than the whole breast, and thus tit, as well as meaning breast, has (originally in military use) described anything considered to resemble the nipple, e.g. a button or a small switch. The imagery of breast-feeding underlies its use as something on which one 'feeds', e.g. a hand-out such as a government grant. It also stands equally for something extremely simple and usually rewarding, especially in the context of a criminal scheme, and finally, through resemblance, for a British bobby's helmet (which last phrase itself means the glans penis). And a tit, giving the ever-popular phrase **I feel a right tit**, can be used, like so many other parts of the body, to mean a fool. Other fool-related images include **stand there like a tit in a trance, make a tit of oneself** and **look like a (right) tit**. To **tit, tit about** and **around** and **titsfart about** all mean to play around, to waste time, to act in a trivial, pointless manner. A **big tit** is an important person or one who thinks they are.

Still, it is the literal rather than figurative breast itself that creates most slang compounds and phrases. **Tit art**, **tit mags** and **tit books** are pornography, possibly softcore. The **tit-bag** or **tit pants** are a brassiere (the Royal Navy prefers **tit hammock**); **tit spanners** are hands – hardly evocative of the gentlest of affections; a **tit show** is a striptease; and a **tit-sucker** or **tit-wrench** is a weakling, as is a **tithead** (who can also be a British policeman – that helmet again) and a **tit-wank**, which also describes an act of non-penetrative intercourse in which the man rubs his penis between the woman's breasts. The **tit-kisser** is a womaniser and the **tit man** (his opposite numbers being the **arse man** and **leg man**) is devoted to **top bollocks** and attempts, with a **tit-off**, to caress them and to become **tits deep**, wholly involved, with their bearer. Their buxom, **titsy** possessor, if pleased with her figure, is **tit-proud**. She can also be metonymised as a **set** or **bushel of tits**. Ideally (well, as a masculine ideal) she'll **get her tits out** (**for the lads**). That said, the lads can do it too: act uninhibitedly, that is. Or, while she may be supermodel material, she's still a **titless wonder**. A **tit-puller**, however, is a dairy farmer and **tits on toast**, another one from the New Zealand farmyard, is pickled belly-pork on toast (gourmet note: belly-pork often has the nipples still attached). The cynical **tits and zits** refers to the hormonal world of teenage love and sex.

WRINGERS, TANGLES AND TEETH

When it comes to their appearance in phrases, tits run riot. 'All that crap, you're putting it in the paper? It's all been denied. Katie Graham's gonna get her tit caught in a big fat wringer if that's published.' Thus one-time US attorney-general John

Mitchell to reporter Carl Bernstein at the height of the Watergate scandal in 1972 (Katherine Graham was the owner of the *Washington Post*, in which 'that crap', which would bring down him and his president Richard Nixon, was appearing). It is not merely a **wringer** that threatens the tits, and thus their owner, with a problem. One can **get one's tits in a knot**, **a twist**, and **a tangle** (and someone else can put them there); they can also be **in a tight crack**. To **be** or **get on someone's tit**, **tits** or **tit-ends** is to annoy them, as well as, of a man, to pursue them sexually. This may render one **on the hind tit**, angry; on the other hand, one may **not give** either **a fish's** or **a rat's tit**. Those who fail to **keep their tits on**, or calm down, may well **suck hind tit** or **titty**, that is, be inferior, take a secondary role. The **hind tit** itself is bad, unfair treatment; the verb may also mean to toady or curry favour, while to **lick tits** is to run errands and perform small tasks. To be **off one's tits** is to be drunk, intoxicated by drugs or simply at one's emotional limit. Those who benefit from a **sugar tit**, something comforting (and used of someone desirable, as is the affectionate nickname **sweet tits**) are **living off the tit**, in luxury, although it can mean to be over-protected.

Other phrases include the early twentieth century's **all tits and teeth** (**like a third-row chorus-girl**), a woman who capitalises on her physical charms, presumably a winning smile and notable breasts, to compensate for her lack of more subtle attractions. To **go tits-up** is to die, or at least to fail, often of a project; to **go full tit** or **to the tits** both imply absolute commitment. Finally, the appearance of tits where they would otherwise be unexpected gives a variety of images of worthlessness: **useless as tits on a nun**, **a boar** or **hog**, **on a bull**, **on a hand**, **on a gumdigger's dog**, and **on a canary**.

U

IS FOR

UNDIES

Of course underwear is not really 'dirty'. Not in so many words. It can be dirty, and off it goes to the wash, but 'dirty' dirty? Well, it's in the eye of the holder, I suppose, the eye, and the caressing fingers, the drooling tongue, the snuffling nose, the placing of the female garment on the male head ... Nonetheless undies, usually as worn by women, remain 'naughty' (and where would a millennium of British comedians be without them?) and for my purposes qualifies. U is for **Undies.** (Anyway, does anyone have a better suggestion for U?)

Still, we must try to find at least a little genuine dirt. And here it is: faecal stains. Top of that list come the **skid marks**, **skiddies** or **scooter tracks**, which give the aggressive query: **do you see skid marks on my forehead?** – another way of asking 'do you think I'm talking out of my arse?' **Flotch** is a synonym, while to **blotch** (as, surely, the old school word for blotting paper) is to emit a small amount of liquid at the same time as breaking wind, hence the **blotcher**, a liquid-emitting fart that stains one's underwear. Similar problems include the **follow-through**, whereby one soils one's underwear when one believes oneself to be doing no more than breaking wind. And **Tijuana**, that byword (at least in the US) for anything cheap, nasty and thus dirty (the over-riding slur is of course a racist one aimed at Mexico) gives the **Tijuana racetrack**, stains on the underwear that result from an attack of diarrhoea, i.e. the **Tijuana cha-cha**. After which come the **Hershey squirts** or **stains**, diarrhoea or faecal stains on one's underwear due to liquid emitted when breaking wind via the **Hershey highway**. The Hershey Bar is a popular US **chocolate** bar, although the highway's UK peers, the **Bournville boulevard** and the **Cadbury alley** are not linked with such unfortunate side-effects.

KNICKERS TO YOU

And that is more than enough of that. Instead let us turn to something dearer by far to the male libido: knickers, as we Brits have it, and panties as they prefer across the Ditch. The original **knickers** was an abbreviation for the knickerbocker suit – once mandatory for convicts and defined in the OED as 'loose-fitting breeches, gathered in at the knee, and worn by boys, sportsmen, and others who require a freer use of their limbs'. They were apparently so called because of their resemblance to the illustration of the breeches worn by Dutchmen in illustrations accompanying Washington Irving's *History of New York* (1809), which he wrote under the pseudonym 'Dietrich Knickerbocker' (itself one of the names of the first Dutch families of what was then New Amsterdam).

The convict theme persists in **knickers and stockings**, a (long) term of imprisonment – one could 'get the knickers', penal servitude, possibly for life, and among the most despised of petty criminals is the **knickers bandit**, who steals female underwear from washing lines. Such thefts are also known as **snow-birding** or **snow-dropping** (hence the **snow-dropper** or **snow-gatherer**, the thief), the **snow lay** or **snow rig**, the practice of such theft. After that, knickers seem inevitably to be associated with problems: **act as if one's knickers were on fire**, to panic, to behave hysterically; to **get one's knickers in a twist** (or **get one's tits in a twist**, **get one's panties in a bunch**, **get one's knickers up one's crack** or **one's underwear in a twist**) is to become excessively agitated over a problem or situation, to worry to extremes; hence the warning **don't get your knickers in a twist**, stop getting so worried, and the adjective **knicker-twisting**, agonisingly worrying. **You come home with your knickers torn and say you found the money** indicates the speaker's inability to believe an extremely unlikely story. **I'd eat my chips out of her knickers** (or **I could use her shit for toothpaste**) or to **fancy the knickers off** are all statements of absolute (sexual) devotion, while **shut one's knickers** is to stop talking, especially as an imperative.

PANTS, PANTIES AND PARTICULARS

And in the same drawer(s), as it were, are **pants**, a word that abbreviates *pantaloons*, itself taken from the *commedia dell'arte* character Pantaloon (Panthalon in France, Pantaleone in Italy) whose costume featured a distinctive form of breeches. Pants can mean trousers but, at least in the UK, usually refer to that which lies beneath. A **pair of pants** can mean a man, but the most recent use is, thanks to Bridget Jones (she of the 'big knickers'), the exclamation **pants!**, meaning nonsense, rubbish (and itself a variation on the ever-popular **knickers!**). Written with 'the', pants symbolises the essence of a given situation or individual and as such adorns a variety of phrases incorporating **the pants off**: **kid the pants off**, **bore the pants** (or **arse** or **knickers**) **off**, **scare the pants** (or **slacks**) **off** and **take, lick, slug** or **thrash the pants off**. To **bust someone's pants** is to beat them, severely. To **get into someone's pants**, **drawers** or **knickers** is to seduce them; to **get some pants** is, of a man, to have sexual intercourse and to **give someone pants** is, of a woman, to permit it. In **short pants** (the reference being to children's garments) is to be impoverished or out of work; to **keep one's feet in one's pants** is to keep calm, to restrain one's emotions, and to **pull up one's pants** is to stop talking and interfering. To **wear** or **pull on the pants** (coined in an era when only men were thought to wear them) is to be the dominant member of a heterosexual partnership (and is often applied to the female of the duo). To **wet one's pants** or **knickers** is to panic, to lose control, to get over-excited, as well as to find extremely exciting or attractive. The exclamation **keep your pants on!** (also **hold your pants on!, keep your britches on!, diaper on!, drawers on!,** or **knickers on!**) means calm down! And, finally, a **pants man** is a womaniser, although a **pants rabbit** or **rat** is a body louse. **Panties** are merely a diminutive of pants.

To return to the distaff side, women's underwear can be **snuggies** (the idea is snug, tight-fitting, rather than any image of winter warmth), **credentials** or **particulars**, both of which can be, tee-hee!, 'taken down'. **Tighties** are also 'snug' (though **tighty-whities** are male underpants, or even a T-shirt). **Nixies** or **nicks** (and **knicks**) stand for knickers, which can also be **squirrel-covers**, giving **shoot the squirrel**, to catch a glimpse of a woman's panties or pubic hair. The revelation of female underwear gives a few more phrases: to **chuck a bridge** is to reveal the 'bridge' or crotch of the knickers; **seven-'leven**, is for a West Indian woman to sit revealing 'everything she's got'; and **a treat**, as in **give the boys a treat**, for a girl or woman inadvertently to reveal more of her body than you would otherwise see (such as cleavage by leaning over or upper thighs or underwear when getting out of a vehicle or bending down to pick something up). Coo! Revelation forms the basis of another couple of terms, neither especially female: the **brown-eye** is the anus, and to **brown-eye** (if not to sodomise) is to drop one's trousers and underwear and reveal one's naked buttocks to anyone who is watching; to **moon** or **shoot the moon** is to perform the same 'trick', often through a car's window; to press the buttocks against that window is to **press ham**.

Spiders' legs, otherwise very thin hand-rolled cigarettes, are pubic hairs protruding from the underwear. Less available in this era of thongs, is the **v.p.l.**, the visible pantie line that appeared through tight skirts or trousers. Other terms include **aggies** (a laboured play on aga*pant*hus) and the euphemistic **how-d'ye-dos**. **Free-traders** allow access through a slit in the crotch, while **passion-killers** are their antithesis: any article of women's underwear deemed to reduce the chances of (male) exploration and access to her **passion pit** with a **passion stick**, an activity that may take place in a man's **passion** or **shag wagon**.

DIANA DORS AND BRENDA FRICKERS

Which leaves just the attendant rhyming slang. The UK actress and all-purpose 'personality' **Diana Dors** (1931–84) gives drawers, as do **early doors** and **Maggie Moores**; **do and dare** is underwear; **insects** (**and ants**) are pants (thus also trousers); **grundies**, whether **Eddies** (the *Archers* character) or **Reggys** (the real-life Australian entrepreneur), rhyme with undies, just as **Alan Whickers** (the UK journalist and TV personality b.1925) and **Brenda Frickers** (the Irish movie actress Brenda Fricker b. 1945) mean knickers and **clicketty-clicks** are 'knicks'. **Harolds** rhymes with Harry Taggs, i.e. bags. **Seldom-sees** are BVDs (from the initial letters of the name of its manufacturers, *B*radley, *V*oorhees & *D*ay: sadly the popular belief that it stood for stood for 'babies' ventilated diapers' is just that: popular).

Otherwise the lexicon deals with neutral or male underwear. Less popular in an era of central-heating (let alone climate change) are **bully-woollies** or **woollies, longies, long johns, long handlebars, long handlers** or **long-handled underwear**, all meaning ankle-length, probably woollen underwear. Variations of standard underwear include **undercrackers, underchunders** (which presumably has no link to **chunder**, to vomit, unless they're really disgusting), **underdaks** (from **daks**, trousers, and ultimately from the brandname), **underdungers** and **underfugs**, both of which reflect the proximity to the anus, as do **dung hampers**. **U.B.'s** stands for underbodies. The terror of such garments is seen in **unmentionables, unspeakables, untalkaboutables, unutterables, unwhisperables, mustn't-mention'ems, don't name 'ems**, all of which can equally mean, and equally absurdly so, trousers. **Where-abouts** (i.e. wear-abouts) is a more recent and Australian version.

KECKS, KACKS AND MELVINS

More terms are **kecks** (or **kacks**, **kaks**, **keks** and **kex** – originally a Liverpudlian variation on **kicks**, the trousers); **strides**; **bingo-bag**, one's **laundry** (and thus **drop one's laundry**, to strip); **nut-chokers** or **tackleshack** (**nuts** and **tackle**: the testicles); **scants**; **scads**; **skivvies**; **tweeds** (thus **drop your tweeds**, to have sex); **didies**; **gitches** (perhaps linked to *britches*); **gruts** and **thunderbags** (the inference is of breaking wind through them). The exotic **rammies** refers to the Malayan *rami* (*Boehmeria nivea*), a Chinese and East Indian plant of the nettle family extensively employed in weaving; however, one should note the rhyming **rammy rousers**, trousers. Like kecks, **trollies** come from the northeast, where as a dialect word it meant women's drawers, and was linked to the Scottish *trolly*, any object with its length disproportionate to its width.

And whether or not the victims appreciated the wondrous jollity of it all, a number of 'games' exist, the basis of which is to grasp the waistband of the male underwear, dragging it upwards until as much as possible of the garment is lodged, painfully, between the buttocks. Among such bullies' delights are the **Melvin** (from the idea of Melvin as a quintessentially 'nerdy' given name), the **grundy** (from grundies), the **murphy**, the **wedgie**, the **shreddies** (the aim being literally to shred the offending garment) and **scanting**. To **nugget** someone is to remove their trousers and pants and blacken their genitals with boot polish (which does not necessarily have to be Nugget brand). The **puma**, i.e. 'panties up my arse', is an uncomfortable situation, but no-one's fault but one's own; one relieves it by discreetly **straightening one's hat**, i.e. tugging the fold of material free.

LOUSEBOUND AND CHATTY

Nor is everything to be found down there inanimate. Far from it. The groin, among other parts of the body, notably the scalp, can play host to a mini-menagerie, headed by the body louse or crab. So while we're ogling knickers, why not cast an eye at such of their contents, as opposed to the **badger**, **beaver** or **pussy**, that are anything but welcome.

The standard English *louse* is found in a number of slang phrases: their preference for hair gives **louse bag**, a wig or a bag worn over the hair as well as a Scottish term of abuse; **louse ladder**, both a ladder (in a stocking) and a bushy sidewhisker; (**Scotch**) **louse trap**, variously a comb, the head, the hair or a sideburn or sidewhisker; **louse walk**, a back-hair parting; and **lousebound**, a general term of abuse (literally, one who is infested with lice). The appearance of lice in dirty lodgings gives the **louse-cage** or **-trap**, a cheap hotel or lodging house, a bunkhouse or a railroad caboose (as well as a hat). A **louse house** (also **loose house** or **louse dump**) can be both a prison or a seedy hotel. To **louse up** is literally to infest with vermin or to wash one's clothes to remove lice, but its most common use is to make a mess of, to ruin (usually deliberately), to blunder or to fail; it can be used transitively: to cause trouble for someone or to make a place or situation unpleasant or nasty.

Chattels, meaning properly moveable property, typically livestock, gives **chats** – as Grose explained in 1785: 'lice being the chief livestock of beggars, gypsies, and the rest of the canting crew'. The First World War **chat-bags** were a soldier's underwear; one who was lice-ridden was **chatty** (hence a **chatty doss**, a louse- or bedbug-infested bed). A **chat parade** was a delousing session and to **chat up** was to search for lice; thus the noun **chat-up**, a search for lice.

The **cootie** is a US synonym and as such may not, although some claim it does, come from the Malayan *kutu*, a dog tick. No matter, it remains popular as the literal body louse, a bedbug, and as a general term of abuse, or an imaginary germ or 'bug', especially as a figuratively repellent quality that can be picked up from those one dislikes (thus Sparkle Hayter's 1997 book, *Revenge of the Cootie Girls*, which charts the turning of tables by a pair of persecuted high school girls). It can also describe an inexperienced, naïve young person, keen to improve his or her status. **Cootie drapes** were a style of trousers, wide and draped and thus a possible home for lice; a **cootie garage** was the hair, especially when styled elaborately; and one who is **cootie-hearted** is considered despicable.

CRUMS, CHUMS AND HAMPSTEAD DONKEYS

Crummy is a widely used term meaning second-rate, inferior or unpleasant; on the whole it is not associated by its users with **crum**, a louse, but that's the origin, and thus crummy is simply a synonym for lousy, and can also mean louse-infested. And, as a noun, crummy is a louse. Crum itself comes from crumb, a tiny fragment of bread, and the link is to the louse's diminutive size. Among US tramps the **crum boss** was a janitor in a construction camp or mission, among whose duties was de-lousing the beds; a **crum-catcher** was a comb. The hobo was also behind the nickname **Crum Hill** for Jefferson Park in Chicago. A **crum joint** was a second-rate, dirty dwelling-house, bar or club, and a **crum roll** (the assumption/slur being that it is infested with lice) a bedroll. To **put on a crum act** is to impose on another person, and to **crum up** is to boil one's clothes to get rid of the lice.

The role of the louse as it nestles next to the skin gives **body companion**, **bosom friend** or **chum**, **gentleman's companion**, **familiars** or **family**, and **lodger** (which can extend to any kind of vermin in one's home). At the same time, its speedy movements give **crawler**, **creeper**, **backbiter** and **active citizens**. Lice are known as **galloping**, **crawling**, **leaping**, **mechanised**, **mobile**, **mobilised**, **motorised**, **travelling**, **walking** and **social**

dandruff. And the early twentieth century witnessed the **Spitalfields crawl**, a reference to the insanitary conditions of housing in Spitalfields, East London, and describing the squirming action of someone who is covered in lice.

London's East End is not the only place to be linked to bodily infestations. An **Arkansas lizard**, playing on the image of the state as poverty-stricken, is a louse. And as John Camden Hotten notes in his *Slang Dictionary* of 1860, partially eschewing Samuel Johnson's notorious anti-Scottish prejudice, 'our northern neighbours are calumniously reported, from their living on oatmeal, to be particularly liable to cutaneous eruptions and parasites.' Thus, lice can be the **Scots** or **Scotch greys** (or **grays**), while the **headquarters of the Scots greys** is a lousy head and the remark **the Scots greys are in full march by the crown office** indicated that lice are crawling on one's head (i.e. crown). Equally military are the **heavy cavalry** and the **light troops**. Hotten also notes the phrase **play the Scotch fiddle**: 'to work the index finger of the right hand like a fiddlestick between the index and middle finger of the left. This provokes a Scotchman in the highest degree, it implying that he is afflicted with the itch.'

Still in Scotland is another phrase that draws attention to one who is lice-ridden: **God bless the Duke of Argyle**. It is used when one's companion shrugs their shoulders (could it be through itchiness?) and refers to a row of iron posts erected in Glasgow by the contemporary duke which grateful lice-ridden citizens were able to use as scratching-posts. An alternative etymology suggests that the posts were erected around the duke's various estates; primarily for the benefit of sheep, they were adopted by verminous shepherds. Sheep may or may not have been lousy, but **livestock** are lice, as are **pasture lice**, **Hampstead donkeys**, **saddlebacks**, **lobstertails**, **crab-fish**, **crotch-crickets** and **-pheasants** (and **Welsh crickets**), **dicky-birds, fanny-rats** and **shirt rats**, not to mention **shirt hounds, rabbits** and **squirrels**. To **read one's shirt** was a military term for checking the seams of one's shirt for lice. Other names for lice and similar creatures include **love-bugs, pants rabbits, minge** mice (from **minge**, the vagina), **seam squirrels** and **circus bees** (presumably rhyming with **fleas**).

DRIBS AND DRABS

Lice can be **black cattle** – a term also applied to clergymen, alluding to the black colour of both the insects and a clergyman's vestments, although the descriptive **black fly** refers only to a parson: 'the greatest drawback on the farmer is the black fly, i.e. the parson who takes a tithe of the harvest' (Grose). Colour also gives **silver-laced**, lousy; the **gold-backed ones**; and the **grayback**, **graycoat** or **gray one**. To **have a full hand** was to suffer both fleas and lice. **Foo-foo powder** was used in an attempt to get rid of them all. One last term is the **arithmetic bug**, so named by W. Carter in *Devil Dog* (1920) because 'they added to our troubles, subtracted from our pleasures, divided our attention and multiplied like —ll.' The troops who suffered from such attentions during the First World War were called **leathernecks**. A **leatherhead**, conversely, is yet another name for louse.

Rhyming concludes this verminous catalogue, with **boys on ice** and **white mice**, lice, and **beattie and babs**, **dibs and dabs**, **dribs and drabs**, **Sandy MacNab** (another anti-Scots slur) and **taxicabs**, which all refer to crabs. A **rat and mouse** is a figurative louse, an unpleasant person.

Y

IS FOR

VIRGIN

'**I**f they're old enough to bleed they're old enough to butcher – and if they're old enough to butcher they're old enough to breed.' So says the real man, gazing enthusiastically on the otherwise underage and unmolested girl, or indeed – for real men come in all tastes – boy (and 'if they're old enough to sit at the table, they're old enough to eat').

It will be noticed (and is anyone remotely surprised?) that neither in George Carlin's list, from which they're completely absent, nor indeed in the slang dictionary at large, do virgins get much of a play. The origins of **prick** (see under **P is for Prick**, p.173) include a word that means the centre of a target and in its turn the slang virgin exists primarily as a target for the prick and its every synonym.

If there is one term that summons up the virgin, it is **cherry** – yet once one asks why, the question remains unanswered. Cherry has been used in sexual contexts since Shakespeare's era, but the links to virginity do not appear until the twentieth century. Formerly the images were either of the supposed similarity of the black cherry and female public hair, or plays on cherry stones and **stones**, i.e. testicles. But virgins? Nary a squeak until the 1920s, when the term first appeared in the contemporary context. That said, there are earlier examples. Cherry is defined as 'a young girl' in both Trumble's slang dictionary of 1881 and Barrère and Leland's volume of 1889, where they label it 'Thieves [slang]'. On top of those we have this, entitled 'Sport and Pastime' in the *Wit's Cabinet* of 1700:

> 'My Betty let us walk and taste of a cherry; Then not be affrighted, for thus we will do, Thou shalt have my cherry, and cherry-stones too ... But Betty she tax'd him with breaking of vows: Quoth Johnny, Don't say so, my love it is true, Thou shalt have my cherry, and cherry-stones too. And this is a vow I am resolv'd to keep, For a maidenhead I will have e're I do sleep.'

It's debatable: on the one hand we have her maidenhead, but on the other his cherry and cherry-stones, obviously his testicles, which rather implies that it's the stem of the cherry that's on his mind, i.e. his penis, or perhaps its cherry-red top. Either way, it's a one-off, and it would be 200 years before it properly returned.

CHERRY-PIES AND CHERRY-SPLITTERS

Once established, cherry was quick to spread its lexical influence. A **cherry-boy** or **cherry prick** is a male virgin, and **cherry-pie** a female one (although it can sometimes simply mean any woman, as well as her vagina, especially when the woman is menstruating). In US prison terms a **cherry farm** is a jail that houses first-offenders. A **cherryhead**, meanwhile, is a male who pretends to a level of sophistication he does not have. The heavily jocular **cherry tree** is a very tall virgin. But that's it for the intact: the remaining cherry terms all relate to the end of purity. **Bust, pop, cop** and **crack a cherry** (or **judy** or **a judy's teacup** – judy being a woman) all mean to deflower, and a **cherry-buster** is a (young) man who specialises in deflowering virgins. His gay 'cousin' is a **cherry queen**. The **cherry splitter** is a penis, and the ex-virgin has **lost their cherry**. All these verbs can be used figuratively,

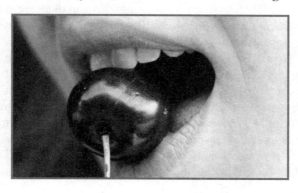

meaning to encounter a new experience. Cherry aside, to **pierce the hogshead**, **split the cup** (**split the peach** is to sodomise), **butcher**, **pierce**, **trim**, **tap** and **ease** are another set of terms meaning to deflower, and the freshly deflowered girl has a **cracked pipkin** or has been **clipped within the ring** (i.e. the vagina).

Other than its original use as virginal, cherry as an adjective is nearly always figurative: of people it means in good health, and of goods, in mint condition or brand-new. It can also mean inexperienced, new, untested, innocent or naïve. In the drug world, **cherry kicks** are the result of the first injection after a former drugs user is freed from prison. To **cherry out** is to make as good as new, typically of a car.

FROM CANNED GOODS TO SHOFUL PULLETS

From hereon in, there are no particular themes to unify those who are hymenally challenged – and yes I know, male virgins, whether as to penis or anus, obviously lack the hymen, other than figuratively. And one can dispose of them in a pair of terms: the **muffin** and the **brown berry**, which plays on the usual alliance of brown, excrement and homosexuality and the berry, which is 'ripe' and 'ready to be plucked'. **Canned goods** represents a virgin of either gender, usually female. A **greenhorn** is similarly non-specific: the term originally referred to a young animal, specifically an ox with 'green' or young horns. It was first used in a military sense, describing a new recruit, and Grose (1785) defines it as 'an undebauched young fellow, just initiated into the society of bucks and bloods'.

Following the cynical dictum above, a **young bleed** is a female virgin (and presumably only in the short term). The sixteenth-century underworld offers a trio of terms, all of them with professional overtones. **Kinchin**, from the German *Kindchen*, a small child, was a beggar's child, or any child carried by a beggar in order to excite pity. A **kinchin mort** was a young, virgin girl destined to be a prostitute or a beggar's companion – a **mort** being an unmarried woman or virgin girl who accompanied a mendicant villain (the etymology remains unknown, but one suggestion is standard English *mort*, a salmon in its third year, i.e. the popular equation of women with fish, while another puts forward Welsh *modryb*, a matron or *morwyn*, a virgin). The last of the trio is **dell**, another species of virgin who is destined to become a whore in short order. Dell may be rooted in the given name *Doll* or, in the same way that **cunt** is linked to Welsh *cwm*, a valley, could be a pun on standard English *dell*, also meaning valley. Other suggestions include Welsh *del*, pert, smart, and Lowland Scots *dilp*, a trollop.

The past also brings a couple of pullets, which are normally understood to be young hens. The **virgin pullet**, as defined by the early nineteenth-century sports journalist and slang collector 'Jon Bee' (John Badcock) in 1823, is one who while 'often trod has never laid', i.e. is no longer a virgin but is not yet a mother. Then there is the **shoful pullet**. **Shoful**, also **schoful, shofel, shofle, shovel** or **show-full**, comes from the Yiddish *schofel*, worthless stuff, rubbish and ultimately from the German–Jewish pronunciation of Hebrew *shaphal*, low. The shoful pullet was therefore that remarkably, dare one say implausible, figure the 'virgin' prostitute, whose maidenhead is miraculously renewed for each new client.

KEEPING IT FOR THE WORMS

Virgin itself offers the **virgins' bus**, 'so named satirically in reference of the chief patronesses at that late hour' (Ware, 1909), i.e. girls who have resisted male advances and take the last bus home, running westward from London's Piccadilly Circus. The **virgin vault** is a US campus residence hall for females, and a

born-again virgin a celibate homosexual man. The initial V gives a **vicky**. Following the usual calumnies that have gathered around the unfortunate Irish, the **Irish virgin** is a virgin who is deemed likely to remain one (it may refer to Irish girls who become nuns, offering up only their spiritual virginity, and that to Christ, after which one fears that they may be reduced to celebrating a succession of **Irish weddings**, i.e. masturbation). In the list of international sexual stereotypes, Rome is identified with orgies, but a **Roman engagement** is a gay term for anal intercourse with a virgin woman; this may, or quite possibly may not, be in the context of a group grope.

And that's about that. One who is **fly-blown** has been deflowered. A **plastic surgeon** – quite why one can only wonder – is the virgin herself, as is a **raw sole** (punning on the usual slang link of females and fish). **Veggie-meat** is an available but still virgin young woman (the 'veggie' is about to become 'meat'). The sixteenth-century euphemism, a **rose**, is compounded by **pluck a rose**, to deflower; until then she remains **unlaid** and is **keeping herself**. To which state the rather better-known response is, **are you keeping** (or **saving**) **it for the worms?**, as addressed to a supposed virgin and intended to shame or bluster her into intercourse; the worms in question are those, of course, that will feast on her corpse.

W

IS FOR

WORK

Work? Surely W should be for … wank. Good dirty word, lots of 'em, no problems there. Except that while wank and its many, many synonyms do indeed qualify, that's all they are. Infinite, seemingly endless synonyms. You can do, you can pull, you can polish, you can make, you can take and beat and flog and whip and pound and … you get the picture? Basically you take a hand, and you apply it to the penis (or in a very small minority of cases – slang cases that is – a finger and apply it to the clitoris, or there's a vibrator (though that doesn't seem to have entered the lexicon)) and that's it. Linguistically as well. Could there be a moral lesson? Would it remotely matter? Anyway, enough with setting out the words for wank: do it yourself is my advice. Or look at **O is for Onan** (see p.167).

So W stands for work. And what sort of work might that be? Commercial sex is what. Specifically, that much-reviled (but sometimes admired) figure, the pimp (and yes, I do note the initial letter – but P is long since spoken for). Prostitutes have popped up all over this text: seek and ye shall find. There will be some here too. But primarily it's the pimp and, as they relate to each other, his girls.

So let us start with pimp. The etymology is, and doubtless fittingly, iffy: the OED, as stern as ever, refuses every suggestion, but for once the sex/French equation may not be a cliché and the word may be linked to such words as *pimpreneau*, a scoundrel; *pimpant*, alluring or seducing in outward appearance or dress; or *pimpesouée*, a pretentious woman. The word began life around 1600 meaning one who arranged opportunities for (illicit) sex; whores didn't yet seem to come into it. And when they did, in the eighteenth century, the word remained standard English. It is only in the context of the US black pimp, a sub-culture all of its own, and considered a pretty admirable one by large sections of an otherwise impoverished community, that we find the word in slang. As the writer Touré sums it up in *The Portable Promised Land* (2002): 'this one little syllable represents a job, a mindset, a way of life, a way of walking, a way of talking, a way of dressing, a pejorative, and a high compliment.'

As the man says, the pimp – a style of walking supposedly reminiscent of a pimp. The US writer Nathan McCall explains it in *Makes Me Wanna Holler* (1994): 'My Aunt Iris … said it (i.e. the pimp) was handed down through generations from the slavery days … Some slaves were forced to walk with a ball and chain attached to one ankle. When they walked they took a regular step with the free leg and sort of hopped on the other to drag the heavy ball and chain.' (Well, possibly: after all, the hip-hop style of ultra-low-slung trousers is another example of fashion based on suffering, supposedly taken from US jails, where a prisoner is deprived of his belt, with the inevitable effect on his trousers.) It's a walk that has embedded itself in slang, characterised as the **pimp stride**, **stroll**, **strut** or **walk**, in every case a strutting style of walking, intended to emphasise one's pride, independence and masculinity. One who adopts it is a **pimper**. Less obvious is the synonym **kimible**, an exaggerated version of the walk or strut; it may come from the phrase 'arms akimbo'. To pimp is to adopt the walk – as, although no etymology exists, is **smeb**.

SIMPLY PIMPING PIMPTASTIC

After which one has a range of terms, all based on the pimping lifestyle. **Pimpable** describes a woman who is a potential prostitute; **pimp-ass** means both contemptible and, on the bad = good model, excellent; **pimping** (in fact a US campus usage) means well-dressed (also **pimpish**), doing well or is just a general term of approval; **pimptastic** means either fantastic or self-aggrandising; and **pimpy** (or **pimpo**) signifies having the characteristics/personality of a pimp. Then there is the pimp's costume, or **pimp fronts** (from **front**, a suit), the features of which include **pimp boots**, ankle or 'Beatle' boots, or **long-shoes**, presumably long and narrow footwear (and giving the **long-shoe game**, the profession and lifestyle of pimping). Such narrow, pointed shoes could also be **rat-drawn** (from a rat's pointed nose). A **pimp cane**, used originally by pimps to discipline their prostitutes, has come to mean any cane used as a weapon. The **pimp stick** or **pimping stick** is also a cane, but can describe another weapon: two wire coat-hangers twisted together to make an improvised and vicious whip to keep those ho's in line. Not that a pimp needs more than an open hand across the face to give them a **pimp slap** or **pimp smack**. Then there are **pimp shoes**, any shoes currently in fashion amongst the profession; **pimp oil**, perfume (usually strong); **pimp shades** or **tints**, dark glasses; **pimp socks**, ultra-thin nylon socks, usually with a pattern of vertical stripes; and the **pimp's turban**, a derby hat (at least when such headgear was in style). Yes, that man is **pimped down** (or **out**, or **up**). He rides a **pimp ride**, **car**, **wagon**, **pimpmobile** or **pimpillac** (as if the others aren't probably Cadillacs as well) and leans nonchalantly on the **pimp post**, the arm-rest between driver and passenger. His drug of choice is **pimp dust**, cocaine, but he'll smoke a **pimp stick**, a cigarette or marijuana joint.

There are grades of pimp. The **simple pimp** barely sustains a living. The **gorilla pimp** beats his girls, but the **sweet** or **sugar pimp** (or **candyman**) prefers to sustain that **pimp talk**, that charming (and mendacious) style of chat that enticed the girl into handing him over her earnings in the first place. The adjective **coffee-and** refers to anything seen as cheap, minimal, second-rate (e.g. the theatre's **coffee-and role**, a small part that will pay for little more than snacks, and the drug world's **coffee-and habit**, a small-time heroin habit, adopted either through grim self-control or simple poverty) – hence the **coffee-and pimp** (or **coffee-and mac**), which described a small-time pimp, whose women barely made him a living, let alone provide the high style to which he aspired.

Similarly second-rate are the **chump**, the **cigarette pimp** (his girls hardly make enough to keep him in smokes), the **popcorn pimp** – who may even be a man who claims to be, but is actually not, a pimp – and the **chile pimp** (or **chili pimp**, **chili-bowl pimp**, **chile-mack**, **chili-mack**), in which *chile*, with its link to Mexico and peppers, is used to denote anything inferior. The **promoted pimp**, however, is a senior figure, deemed sufficiently experienced to hand out advice to other pimps or to their prostitutes. The **welfare pimp** takes his girls' welfare payments – perhaps because they are failing to earn him anything better. Finally, even pimping has its bible: all US pimps claim to **work from a book** – in other words, for a pimp to run his professional life by the recognised 'rules and regulations' of the pimping life, supposedly enshrined in an authoritative – if as far as anyone knows unwritten – **Book**.

VENUS'S GAME

The beaten girls, abusive clients, potential for a serious cocaine habit and, of course, the continuing threat of jail may not sound much fun, but pimping is known as the **game** and for a pimp to **have his game together** or **have his game uptight** is both to be in full control of a situation and at the same time to define one's image by a variety of material/symbolic 'props'. These are not invariably pimping terms, but they all spring from his vocabulary: to **run down game** is to explain the principles of the pimping business, both from experienced pimps to novices and from the pimp to his prostitutes, telling them the tricks of their trade. To **kick game** is to use any means whereby one attempts to gain economic, psychological or other advantages over a rival or victim. To **lift one's game** is to improve one's situation in some way, while to **let one's game slip** is to lose control of a situation or plan. To **come off one's game**, however, is to abandon that carefully contrived pose, the **game face**. To **get in someone's game** is to interfere in someone else's business, and to **put salt in someone's game** is to interfere in another person's planned seduction. To **put game**, or **run a game on someone**, to **whip** or **whup a game on** or to **put shit in someone's game**, all mean to confuse or deceive.

All these modern terms notwithstanding, the game (or **Venus's game**) meant sexual intercourse in the sixteenth century, and expanded to include the world of prostitution (the daughters of the game) soon afterwards. A prostitute was known as a **gamester** in the seventeenth century, and the term described a pimp 50 years later.

Those who participate in the game are **players**, and player (often spelt **playa** as in rap lyrics) is one more US term, which, like pimp and mack, is capable of moving beyond its professional limits. Defined since the 1950s as anyone who uses intelligence, wit or brains to gain their objectives, whether as a businessman, politician, womaniser or criminal, the word logically means a pimp as well as a promiscuous person; a sexual cheat and a woman who is seen as enthusiastic about sex. Probably the best-known use today is **player-hater** (often 'gangsta-d' as **playa-hata** or simply **hata**), one who resents the achievements and extravagant lifestyle of a ghetto success, whether gained legally or otherwise. It started in the ghetto, but has spread far beyond these confines. The **boss player** is a thoroughly experienced, professional, worldly-wise pimp who may even transcend pimping for superior occupations; the term can be applied to any admirable figure outside the pimp milieu.

ON THE GAME

And sometimes a game is just a game. Pimps and their girls ran three in particular: the **badger game**, the **Murphy game** and the **panel game**. The badger was originally a thief who specialised in robbery on the riverbank, after which he murdered the victim and disposed of the corpse in the water. From there the word moved to describing a pimp or a thief who rifles the pockets of a man who is currently engaged with his accomplice, a prostitute, also known as a **badger**. (The accomplice was probably her pimp too, but not invariably.) Prostitute/thief teams were once common: the eighteenth-century **buttock and file** or **buttock and twang** were names for a whore who doubled as pickpocket and the man, probably a decoy who would then remove the booty, who helped her. A **down** (that is, ac-complished) **buttock and sham** (i.e. fake) **twang**, conversely, was a whore who did not add pickpocketing to her skills; in that case the man did not practise thieving either. The **twangman**, in Ireland, could also be a pimp.

The **badger game**, a phenomenon of the mid-to-late nineteenth century (at least by this name) ran thus: the girl took a client to her room, and, right in the middle of the fun, her accomplice, playing the 'outraged boyfriend' or even 'husband', would erupt into the room and threaten the appalled client with blackmail – that or handing over the contents of his pockets. There were only two winners in this temporary *ménage à trois*, and the hapless client wasn't one of them. The game spawned a variety of terms: the **badger house** or **crib**, in which it was played (**crib** being a room or house, in this case usually a brothel); the **badger man**, the male accomplice; and the **badger moll** or **worker**, the girl herself. The name, it appears, is based on the creature, which is both nocturnal and carnivorous – the prostitute too 'devours' her victims after dark.

The **Murphy game** echoes the badger variety in every way, and is probably the best-known name for the trick. The origins apparently lie in the original 'players' having lured their victim by promising them a meeting with 'a lovely woman called Mrs Murphy'. The difference is that, although it is optional, a room is not required and the 'playing field' can equally well be some dark and deserted alley; nor is blackmail involved – it is all much simpler: the accomplice simply beats the client unconscious and then robs him. That accomplice is the **cock-pimp** (specifically when posing as the husband), the **bearer-up** or **bouncer**, although the latter can more often be found in a brothel as a **chucker-out**.

Of the three, the **panel game** was the most sophisticated – or at least it required a bit of skill. James D. McCable spelt it out in his exposé of New York lowlife *The Secrets of the Great City* (1868):

> 'This method of robbery is closely connected with street walking. The girl in this case acts in concert with a confederate, who is generally a man. She takes her victim to her room, and directs him to deposit his clothing on a chair, which is placed but a few inches from the wall at the end of the room. This wall is false, and generally of wood. It is built some three or four feet from the real wall of the room, thus forming a closet. As the whole room is papered and but dimly lighted, a visitor cannot detect the fact that it is a sham. A panel, which slides noiselessly and rapidly, is arranged in the false wall, and the chair with the visitor's clothing upon it is placed just in front of it. While the visitor's attention is engaged in another quarter, the girl's confederate, who is concealed in the closet, slides back the panel, and rifles the pockets of the clothes on the chair. The panel is then noiselessly closed. When the visitor is about to depart, or sometimes not until long after his departure, he discovers his loss.'

The game was played in a **panel crib**, **den**, **house**, **joint** or **store**, which again was usually a brothel. The player was a **panel thief**, **dodger** or **worker**.

Less well-known, but doubtless equally injurious to the victim, was **crossbiting**, which predated the Murphy game by some 300-odd years. This involved the usual trio: the whore, the 'outraged husband' and the hapless sucker. A twentieth-century equivalent was the **lumberer**, a prostitute or pimp who specialises in robbing her/his clients. Finally, America's contemporary **crocodile scam**, which is more of the same – its name comes from the way the girl, like the amphibian, opens her jaws to embrace a victim.

PONCING ABOUT

If the pimp, unadorned, remains essentially standard English, then **ponce** is always slang, but again defying easy etymology. It may come from the French *Alphonse*, a given name which itself means pimp, but ponce predates that use. However it was probably popularised in 1864 when the English production of Dumas's hit play *Monsieur Alphonse* – the tale of a kept man (though not a pimp as such) – arrived in London.

Ponce in the pimping context seems to be somewhat archaic today (Colin MacInnes used it as the sole synonym in his fictionalised study of the game *Mr Love and Justice*, 1960), but **ponce about**, to act in a pretentious, affected manner (also **ponce it up**), to wander aimlessly, to live as a good-for-nothing or to waste time, and **ponce off** or **on**, as much to scrounge money as actually to live off immoral earnings, and **ponce up**, to decorate (an object), to dress up (a person), usually with some ostentation and flashiness, are all in regular use. Some link ponce to the verb pounce: the OED knocks this back, but one long-dead synonym for a pimp was **pounce-** or **ponce-shicer**.

MACK TALK

Mac or **mack** are both popular US terms that have not made it across the Atlantic, but the root, **mackerel**, meant both pimp and procuress in the fifteenth century and beyond. The word comes from French *maquereau*, which in turn came to mean pimp, but the popular link to the 'fishy' mackerel seems too easily accepted. More likely would appear the etymology put forward by Loredan Larchey, in his *Dictionnaire Historique* (1878): 'In the Middle Ages the word *macque* signified *vente*, the profession of a merchant. From this came *maquerel* and *maquignon*. The *maquereau* is nothing more than a merchant of women.' This would also fit with another possible source, the Dutch *makelaar*, a broker. The Victorian pornographer Edward

Sellon (see also under **G is for Gob**, p.85) feminised the French as *maquerelle*, presumably meaning a madam or bawd, in his book *Phoebe Kissagen Or, the Remarkable Adventures, Schemes, Wiles, and Devilries of Une Maquerelle* (1866).

Mackerel did not outlive the seventeenth century, but mack has been current in the US since at least the 1940s. (Whether 'Mack the Knife', the anti-hero of Broadway's 1950s rehash of Brecht and Weill's *Dreigroschenoper*, was linked to this sort of mack is unknown: Brecht had called him 'Mackie Messer' (German *Messer*, a knife), so maybe not – his 'real' name being, after all, Macheath.) And like pimp, mack has its own sub-set of terms. **Mack talk** (or simply **the mack**) is seductive, persuasive talk, specifically the 'chat-up' line used by a pimp to recruit a new girl. The **macman** is the pimp himself, while a **hard mack** is one who beats his girls and a **sweet mack** is one who charms them. **Mackdom** is the world of pimps and thus, by extension, of all smooth operators.

Other terms have transcended the purely pimping world. To **mack**, which means to work as a pimp, to adopt a pimp walk, or to recruit a new prostitute, can also mean to talk seductively. To **get the mack on** or **make mac with** are to make a pass at someone or to flirt. To **put the mack down** is to act in a smooth, sophisticated manner, reminiscent of the idealised pimp, and **sweet mack** can also describe anyone who deceives or tries to charm a member of the opposite sex with seductive words, or one who is a successful seducer – as a verb it means to lie or exaggerate in order to deceive, exploit or influence someone, to have sex or be successful in any context. **Macked out** (and **up**) is stylishly or flashily dressed. To **mack on** (or **to**) is to make a verbally forceful attempt to seduce a person, to flirt heavily. And **mack daddy** or **mcdaddy** (thus 'The Great MacDaddy', protagonist of an African–American rhyme of the 1950s) is not just a successful pimp or criminal but also an important, influential black man, a power in the community, a very virile, successful or skilful man and, on US campuses, anything or anybody that is considered the best. A similar black superstar is the **big willie**, described in 1996 in *Vibe* magazine as 'the strong, silent type … an old-school romantic (and) a savvy businessman … a free thinker, fluent with modern technology. He is fearless, vigilant and innovative.' Surely an etymology is not required.

Macaroni is hollow spaghetti and the original macaronis ('These merry Wags … always appear in a Fool's Coat, and commit such Blunders and Mistakes in every Step they take, and every Word they utter', as the *Spectator* sneered in 1711) were smart young men among whose affectations, subsequent to making a trip to Italy as part of the young aristo's obligatory Grand Tour, was the ostentatious consumption of this form of pasta. In pimping contexts, a **macaroni** is the middleman, usually a pimp, who stands between the client and prostitute. As a **macaroni with cheese** he is someone involved in a wide variety of activities such as pimping, drug-selling and gambling games. And the root here surely comes from mack, and not Milan. Two other terms play on mack: **magoofer** and the semi-rhyming slang **MacGimp**.

HOONS AND BLUDGERS

Another term for a pimp that has yet to penetrate the UK, nor yet the US, is Australia's **hoon**. Again it defeats the etymologists, although Sydney Baker, author of *Australian Language* (1945, 1966), suggests a contraction of Jonathan Swift's 'houyhnhnm' (the anthropomorphic horses of *Gulliver's Travels*, 1726), but unfortunately for this hypothesis, as opposed to the loutish, corrupt hoon, Swift's quadrupeds are seen as intelligent beings. It is their human slaves, the 'yahoos', who are the fools – and noted as such in dictionaries. As well as a pimp, hoon means a show-off with limited intelligence; a flashy lout or hooligan, one who drives in a dangerous, showing-off manner, or an exploit that involves 'hoonish', i.e. exhibitionist, loutish behaviour. Thus, one has the **hoon bin**, an enclosure where drunken sports supporters are detained during a match (the equivalent of the northern hemisphere's **sin bin**);

a **hoon-chaser**, a policeman; **hoondom**, the world of loutish exhibitionists; and **hoonery**, loutish behaviour.

Australia also offers **bludger**, both a pimp and a general term of abuse, usually implying that the person in question lives off the efforts and money of others and as such is used to describe a white-collar worker (from the point of view of a manual labourer, who sees such work as idling) or, in criminal eyes, a policeman.

FROM SHRIMPS TO BEAVERS

Anything as widely known as a pimp generates its rhyming slang. Thus, **blue moon**, **dish ran away with the spoon**, **egg and spoon**, **silver spoon**, **silvery moon** and **terry toon** all rhyme with hoon; ponce gives **candle and sconce**, **Charlie Ronce**, **Joe Bonce**, **Alphonse** and the semi-rhyme **ronson**; and pimp itself is a **fish and shrimp**.

The pimp, of course, is first and foremost a businessmen. As the etymology of *maquereau* makes clear, he is a merchant, a seller of women. A number of his names help underline the image: the facetiously titled **account executive** works for high-class prostitutes, presumably call-girls. Like his standard English equivalent, the **apple-monger**, meanwhile, is a dealer in 'fruit', i.e. 'ripe' females; the **apple squire** is similarly occupied. **Beaver** means the female pubic hair and offers a number of terms, including **beaver trader**, pimp; **beaver book**, pornographic book; **beaver shot**, close-up photograph of, or camera-angle on, the female genitals; and **split** or **wide-open beaver**, which is also used in commercial pornography to describe the fully exposed female genitals (sometimes held open). Man the hunter gives us **shoot the beaver**: for a man to look up a woman's skirt in the hope of seeing her pubic hair or vagina, but it isn't that sexist, and can also stand for a woman deliberately to display her genitals, usually while otherwise dressed.

SMOCKSTERS, HACKSTERS AND HUSTLERS

The smock is properly a chemise or shift and thus generically 'womankind'. Slang rendered women labelled **smocks** immoral from the late sixteenth to the eighteenth centuries and the sense promoted several compounds, among them **smock merchant** or **smock agent**, **smock attorney**, **smock tearer**, **smock tenant**, **smock pensioner** and **smockster** – all meaning pimp. **Smock Alley** was both a vagina and a street of brothels (and there was an actual Smock Alley, running off Petticoat Lane in London's East End, well known for its brothels). A **smock shop** was a brothel and a **smock toy** a lover of either sex. **Smock vermin** were whores and a **smock fair** the place they gathered. A pimp could also be a **smell-smock**, otherwise used to describe a priest, although the 'smock' in question may have been that of the Virgin Mary.

Other 'salesmen' include **salesman** itself, the **broker**, the **cash carrier**, the **crack salesman** and the **hackney**, although when this last is female, and otherwise known as a **lady hackster**, **hackney jade** or **hack**, she is usually a whore (and there must be the inevitable link to **ride**). Either use comes from the fourteenth-century hackney horse, a run-of-the-mill horse, i.e. not a warhorse or hunter, which was used for everyday riding and subsequently typified as the sort of horse available for hire. A **hole-monger** sells holes, i.e. vaginas, while a **hustler** is not just a pimp (nor indeed a whore) but anyone who uses their initiative to obtain or secure something (usually money), one who lives by their wits – hence the dictum, 'hustlers don't call showdowns': one who is on the receiving end of a hand-out does not cause trouble because that might terminate the flow of free gifts.

FROM JOCKUM-GAGGERS TO HAYMARKET HECTORS

The mid-sixteenth century **jockum** meant the penis. Thus, to **jockum-cloy** was to have sex, while a **jockum-gagger**, **jack-gagger** or **jock-gagger**, literally a 'penis-beggar', was a man who lived on his wife's prostitution. Then there are the **meat salesman** (in which **meat** means the female body) and the **muff** (i.e. the female pubic hair) **merchant**; the **nookie bookie** (from **nookie**, itself either from **nug**, to have sex, or Dutch slang *neuken*, to fuck); and the **petticoat merchant**. (A **petticoat pension** is the money a prostitute hands over, which makes her pimp a **petticoat pensioner**, though this can also merely indicate a kept man.) Money is the source of Australia's **red bob**, **red shilling**, **red deener** (a sixpence), **red penny** and **red quid**, all of which refer to the girl's daily take (and **red bob** can also be a nickname for a pimp). Why red? Possibly because of the link of red to sin, thus the guilty condemnation of the money thus earned. Finally, if **chicken** can mean a young boy or girl, then plural chickens are poultry and a **poultry dealer** is one who sells them. (The **chicken man**, however, is a buyer of such tasty delicacies, rather a seller.)

As those canes and coat-hangers indicate, the pimp may be a smooth talker, but all too often he can show himself just as ready to enforce his word with his fists. The sixteenth century's **bellswagger** was literally one who 'swaggers his belly'. A **bruiser** was more usually a prize-fighter or any form of violent man; he could also be a pimp, as was a **carrion** (i.e. flesh) **flogger**, a **flashman** or a **flash chap**, who could also be the brothel bouncer, as could a **bludgeoner** (though he was always available to play an 'outraged boyfriend' role if required). The flashman, for whom the priggish Tom Brown's persecutor and G. MacDonald Fraser's best-selling anti-hero were named, was more generally defined as a man-about-town, a loafer with no visible means of support but an endless appetite for good clothes, parties and places of entertainment; such a man lived by his wits and often off foolish women. The pimp's ambushing and robbing of his whore's client gives **carry the cosh**, to work as a pimp.

It seems paradoxical but the word **bully**, whether in standard English or slang, may finds its roots in Dutch *boel*, a lover of either sex. On those grounds it began life in the sixteenth century meaning a good fellow or a companion; its less savoury reputation followed as the century turned, and he became variously the pimp, the bouncer and even the client. Extended as **bully hack**, **bully-huff** or **bully huff-cap** (a **huff** being a blusterer or bully), he could be the brothel's hired thug or the prostitute's temporary, violent 'husband'. Last of the tough guys is the **Haymarket hector**, taking his names from the Haymarket, a centre of London prostitution, and hector, a swaggering bully, and ultimately Homer's Trojan hero.

SUBURBAN ROARERS AND WESTMINSTER WEDDINGS

The Haymarket was not the only area to give its name to pimping. It may come as an unpleasant surprise to those who live in such areas, but the term suburb was once a synonym for red-light zone. Of course the suburbs of the sixteenth and seventeenth centuries — Holborn, Wapping, Mile End, Bermondsey, and Clerkenwell — were somewhat closer to the heart of the Metropolis. These days they are pretty much in the heart of London, but not then: they were beyond the City proper and as such were home to various 'stink' industries, whether literal, e.g. tanning and leper hospitals, or figurative, e.g. playhouses and brothels. Hence, **suburb** – while not indecent in itself – came to be used in a variety of phrases, all denigrating 'suburban' life and its denizens. They include **suburb-garden**, a house in which one installs a mistress; **suburb-humour**, unpleasant humour, usually at another's expense; **suburb justice**, corrupt justice, easily amenable to bribes; **suburb-trade**, prostitution; **suburb tricks**, sexual amusements; **suburb sinner**, a prostitute; **aunt of the suburbs**, a prostitute; **suburban roarer**, a pimp or male 'heavy' in a brothel (roarer was a variant of **roaring boy**, a riotous hooligan); **house in the suburbs**, a brothel; and **minion of the suburbs**, a male prostitute. A **suburban** (or **suburban wench** or **roarer**, **suburb lady** or **suburb whore**) was a prostitute who worked in the suburbs rather than the West End of London. The **suburb trade** was the world of suburban prostitution and the **suburban-trader** a prostitute's client. And, as the sporting journalist and 'great lexicographer of the Fancy' Pierce Egan put it in his monumentally best-selling *Life In London* (1821) – home to the original Tom and Jerry – a **fancy piece** was: 'A sporting phrase for a "bit of nice game" kept in a preserve in the suburbs. A sort of Bird of Paradise!'

Perhaps the most notorious of those suburban spots was Clerkenwell, and specifically Turnmill Street (at least one address in which, a gay club, has managed to maintain its louche image into the twenty-first century). It was in Turnmill Street (or possibly in another 'red-light' district between nearby Old Street and Goswell Road) that stood a number of seventeenth-century brothels, one of which was distinguished by its give-away architecture: a **picked-hatch** (or **pick-hatch**, **pickt-hatch** or **picthatch**) – in other words a spike-topped ('picked') half-door, designed to prevent unauthorised entrance. The door went, but the image remained as a popular brothel sign. The word stayed too, giving **picked-hatch captain**, a pimp; **picked-hatch vestal** (who was definitely no virgin), a prostitute; and the phrase **go to the manor of picked hatch** (or **go to picket hatch grange**), to visit a brothel.

The sixteenth century also offered the brothel-based phrase to **go to Westminster for a wife**, meaning to visit a brothel. This was based upon the contemporary proverb: 'Who goes to Westminster for a wife, to St Paul's for a man or to Smithfield for a horse, may meet with a horse, a knave and a jade.' And despite the supposed difference indicated in the proverb, Old St Paul's Cathedral was also well-known for the raffish individuals who frequented its purlieus – and devotees of Westminster Abbey, who preferred to mock the City's cathedral, opted for **go to Paul's for a wife**. A **wife out of Westminster** was therefore one who was unconstrained by monogamy, and a **Westminster wedding**, defined as 'A Whore and a Rogue Married together' (B.E.) was similarly a visit to a whore. Less specific, but definitely urban, was the **town bull**, in standard English a bull housed in turn by each of the cow-keepers of a village. He was variously a promiscuous man or a 'whoremaster', i.e. a pimp or procurer. Synonymous are **town stallion** and **town trap**, and a very promiscuous man was **as lawless as a town bull**.

HORSES, PONIES, CHICKS AND HOS

The prostitute can – and regularly does – function in a pimp-free zone. Indeed, the pimp is an endangered species today in the UK. But pimps have a greater role in US culture, with a vocabulary to match. The girls who work for a single pimp are a **family**, a **flock**, a **string** (**of ponies**), a **nest**, a **corral** and above all a **stable** (which can also mean a girl's regular clients). The pimp is the **stable boss**, while individual girls are each a **stable sister**; to **stable up** is for a hitherto solo prostitute to join those girls working for a given pimp; it can also be used transitively – the pimp **stables up** a **ho**.

Within the stable, among the **horses** working together in harness, is a hierarchy: paradoxically the **bottom woman**, **bottom**, **bottom baby**, **bottom bitch**, **bottom ho** or **bottom lady** is in fact the most reliable and experienced of the girls; possibly one of the last (albeit unconscious) survivors of the eighteenth century's prized virtue of 'bottom', i.e. stability. Just to confuse things, **top woman** means exactly the same. Other favoured girls are the **boss**, **mama bitch** or **main bitch** (or **main chick**, **girl**, **ho**, **lady**, **stuff**, **whore** and **woman**; the pimp himself is the **main man**) and **star** (**of the line**). A **star boarder** is the best-performing prostitute in a brothel. Underlining the economics of their relationship she can also be a **share certificate**, in other words an 'investment'.

A **nothing-ass bitch** is a prostitute who will not work, or equally sinfully refuses to hand over the money earned to her pimp. **Bitch**, of course, long predates the current fashion for its use as encouraged by rap; in 1785 Francis Grose called it 'the most offensive appellation that can be given to an English woman, even more provoking than that of whore', and he cites the 'Billingsgate' rejoinder: 'I may be a whore, but can't be a bitch.' The modern **working girl** might disagree. An **old lady** can be any member of the stable but the best, as can a **sister-in-law**. A prostitute can also be a **flatbacker**, either one who specialises in quantity rather than quality in her clients, or an honest prostitute (i.e. who delivers the promised sex and neither tricks nor robs her client). In both cases she lies on her back and causes no trouble. On the whole less desirable is the **mudkicker**, from the racetrack jargon mud-kicker, a slow racehorse that gets stuck in the mud: this is a prostitute who robs rather than has sex with her client or fails, either through laziness or lack of appeal, to make enough money for her pimp; however, the word can also apply to a dedicated, very hard-working prostitute. As ever, it's the context that counts. If things really don't work out she turns into a **flat tyre**, a girl who has been rejected by her pimp – it also means an impotent man. The ideal girl is the **stomp-down woman**, the hardest-working woman in the stable. The **weekend ho**, on the other hand, probably doesn't have a pimp (she may be helping with the house-keeping) and, as her name implies, doesn't work full time. (**Weekend pussy** is a man's occasional, if regular, girlfriend; she remains an amateur.) Other freelance whores include the **orphan** and the **outlaw**, both of whom work the **open game**.

Although the prostitute appears to be absolutely under the pimp's control, the fiction persists that the relationship is her choice; thus she **chooses** or **claims** him, at which point she gives him **choosing money** to seal the relationship. He **cops for** her, entices her, and wears his extra-smart **copping clothes** in order to **cop** her or seduce her into the stable. They may then enjoy a **copping fuck** to seal the bargain, at which point he **puts her on the block** (a term that in Australia, however, means to subject a woman or a homosexual man to gang rape; thus **go on the block**, to be the subject of such an assault). The clothes she wears are **bonds** – since his money (which she will pay back on the job) has paid for them; this 'binds' the women to him.

Sometimes the relationship lasts, and he **locks her in**, but underlining the pimp philosophy is that of **cop and blow** – literally, take it and leave, in this case to exploit an unsatisfactory prostitute for as much money as possible. Exploiting such a whore is a **short-money game**, in which case the short refers to time as well as her earnings. For the girl to come up, unpardonably, with **short money**, means she's failed to meet her **trap** (from the customers she traps), the financial target she has been assigned and the number of customers she has to service; thus **trap money**, her daily earnings. It's **pimp sticks** time (these being two coat-hangers twisted to form a whip, used to chastise errant hos).

X IS FOR

X-CREMENT

Yes, we have gazed hard at **turd** and analysed **shit**, and even taken a passing sniff at **crap**, but in the world of slang there's so much more to **number twos** than that. And while I would be loathe to trespass on such peerless experts as Roger Mellie (as in *Viz* comic and the *Magna Farta*), a man who gives a new meaning to the term anally fixated and whose team of researchers have put together a detailed catalogue of **bog-trotting** action that would have the most dedicated proctologists, dare one say, shitting themselves with pleasure, we can still add our ten-pennorth. So let X stand for X-crement and let us begin.

For once, we can begin with rhyming slang, which usefully sets the scene for what follows. Shit has been dealt with elsewhere (see under **S is for Shit**, p.204) but its rhymes have not, and they are legion. First the general stuff: **bob and hit**, **brace and bit** and **tomtit**. Then the celebs: erstwhile Hollywood golden boy **Brad Pitt** (whose name also served for an armpit and a female **tit**), singer **Eartha Kitt**, the Australian jockey **Edgar Britt** and **William Pitt**, the UK's youngest ever prime minister. The former Thatcherite politician **Douglas Hurd** stands for turd, as do such monarchs as **George III**, **William III**, **Richard III** and **Henry III**. **Lemon curd**, **mockingbird** and **my word** also qualify. Crap gives **game of nap**, **horse and trap**, **pony and trap**, which itself gives a second level of rhyme, with **macaroni**, and, finally, **man-trap**. **Ali oop** equals poop, and the **muffin baker** rhymes with **quaker**, a solid piece of excrement, even if John Camden Hotten, compiling the first list of rhyming slang in the mid-nineteenth century, assumed it was simply the religious meaning that was on offer.

With shit, turd and crap disposed of, excrement still displays a couple of biggish players: cack or kak, and the alternative caca and kaka, plus poo or poop. **Cack** was a standard term, meaning to void excrement, until the sixteenth century, and whether as a verb or noun, the word can be traced back to Latin *cacare*, to defecate; *cac-hús*, a latrine, can be found in Anglo-Saxon. The word can also mean nonsense, as well as rubbish, whether literal or figurative, and is used (in Ireland) as a general term of abuse, a contemptuous term for an individual. **Cackbag** is equally contemptuous, as is **cackface**. A **cack-knacker**, otherwise **cock-knocker**, is another unpleasant or worthless person. One who is **hot cack** at something is highly skilled, the equivalent of **shit hot**, while **cack**, like shit or crap, can mean 'the daylights' and thus to **beat the cack out of** means to beat up severely. **Cacky**, which as a noun is a variation on cack, means literally covered in excrement and figuratively disgusting or second-rate. It may be that **hockie**, meaning variously human or animal excrement, semen and nonsense, is a variation. One must assume that the ultimate root of **caca** or **kaka**, excrement, is also Latin, but its immediate origin lies in the Spanish synonym: *caca*. As well as the usual alternative meaning of non-human rubbish, caca has been used to refer to drugs (see also **S is for Shit**, p.204), specifically heroin, and especially when inferior, bogus or adulterated. A **kaka queen** is a gay man whose sexual preferences involve excrement, properly designated a coprophage (i.e. a shit-eater). To **go** or to **make ca-ca** is to defecate. Cack must lie behind South Africa's **kak**, although the immediate root is the Dutch *kak*, excrement. Its figurative senses mean trouble or rubbish and to **give someone kak** is to nag them. To be **in kak** is to face problems. **Up to kak** means useless, while the exclamation **kak!** has all the meanings carried by its synonym **shit! Kakker-boosah**, which goes back to cack and the nineteenth century, means either vomiting or prematurely voided excrement. Further links can be seen in the Caribbean **kuka** or **kungse**, a piece of excrement, and the synonymous **yackum**.

POO-POO, POOPIE-PLOPS AND POOT

The reduplicative **ca-ca** suggests something of the nursery, and **poo**, with its reduplication **poo-poo**, plus **poop**, **poopee** and above all **poopie-plops**, positively scream potty-time. The origin of poo is onomatopoeic, i.e. the sound of someone going 'poo!' when, for instance, faced by a recently vacated and noisomely (and perhaps noisily) used lavatory. It is, in other words, the stink on shit. As well as the regular parallel meaning of nonsense or rubbish, the word offers a wide spectrum of compounds, all excremental. The **poohead** or **poobrain** is the equivalent of a shithead and neither lack for disdain; the **poohole** and **poo-chute** are the anus; **poo-pants** is a fool; and **in the poo**, in serious trouble. The unarguably juvenile shout of **poos and wees!** is used in New Zealand to express disapproval or disgust. As for the rest: it's a gay world out there. Poo-based terms meaning a homosexual include **poo-butt**, **poo-hammer**, **poo-jabber**, **poo-jammer**, **poo-packer**, **poo-pirate** (and **poo-pie pirate**), **poo-pusher**, **poo-stabber**, **poo-puncher** and **poo-shooter**. A **poo palace** is a gay bar. And smell, if not actually poo, also lies behind modern Ireland's **stinkies**.

One consonant away, **poop** (or **poopy**) seems to sidestep the gay world, but then falls into the usual categories. But while its origins may be no more than a variation on the dismissive 'poo!', one should also note **poop**, echoic of the report of a gun. Compounds include **poopchute** or **poophole**, the anus; **poophead** or **poopbutt**, a dullard; **poop-catchers**, underpants; and **poop bag**, a colostomy bag. **Poop-for-brains** is a generally less common variant on shit-for-brains, and means just the same, while **poop-stick** denotes a nasty individual (could there be a hint in the direction of 'stirring shit'?). **Poop-scared**, or more properly **poep-scared** since the word comes from Afrikaans and is used in South Africa, means shit-scared, just as the **poephol** is the anus and to **poep** is either to defecate or break wind. The verb **poop** is, naturally, to defecate, but it also means to shoot a gun, to hand things out and to urinate. **Poopy** is the equivalent of shitty. Finally **poot**, which is linked to French *péter*, to fart, can mean soft excrement, an unpleasant person and the anus, and, as a verb, to defecate or break wind.

BURYING A QUAKER

The colour, consistency and shape of the turd all play a role in evoking slang terms. Colour first: and that (no prizes here) is brown or at best gold. In fact the word **brown**, by itself, does not mean excrement, but the concept gives a round-up of terms wherein the brown of the anus and of its product is used as a synonym for matters homosexual. Paradoxically, the adjective brown pure and simple is just that – pure and simple, worthy, earnest, totally devoid of any double entendre or 'smut' and referring to the brown clothes popular among the sedulously moral Quakers. It is that costume that also offers us **Quaker**, a piece of excrement that is long, thin, hard and of course 'brown', and the phrase **bury a quaker**, as the *Profanisaurus* puts it, means 'to release a payload from the bomb bay'. Otherwise, brown forsakes religion for gaity.

The **Brown** or **Browning family** was, in more guarded days, a euphemism for the whole gay world (the stress being on the identification with anal intercourse), though **Admiral Browning** (originally nautical) is merely human excrement. The **brown highway**, **pipe**, **star** or **starfish** (and the **pink starfish**) are all the anus. Thus, a **brown pipe engineer** is a gay man, presumably one who goes for the active role in anal sex. A **brown shower** (on the pattern of the **golden shower**, which involves urine) is an act of defecation for sexual purposes. **Brown stuff** (also a **brown baby**) is excrement, and can refer to trouble, as in 'I'm seriously in the brown stuff', i.e. 'the shit'. That otherwise blameless freshwater fish the **brown trout** finds a new home as it 'swims' around the toilet bowl, while to **fish for brown trout** is to have anal intercourse. To **sling trout**, in a US prison, is to throw excrement or urine over another prisoner. Still in prison, though no longer brown, is the UK's **flying pasty**, a package of turds tossed out of one's cell window – the result of over-crowding and the continuing use of the grim system of 'slopping out'. To 'launch' such a package is to **fly a kite**.

CHOCOLATE, HONEY AND FUDGE

Even in the UK, where such products, albeit taking the same name, apparently fail to fulfill even the barest of EC standards, **chocolate** manages to be brown. And like brown itself, the word lends itself to the anus and those who enjoy its homosexual possibilities. The **chocolate runway**, **starfish**, **canyon** (through which one can **ride**), **channel**, **freeway** (along which one **cruises**), **speedway**, **highway**, **tunnel** and **whizzway** are all the anus. The **chocolate bandit**, **chimney-sweep** or **puncher** is a gay man; anal intercourse is **chocolate cake** or the **chocolate cha-cha** (which of course the participants can **dance**). **Honey** is the colour of the mix of piss and shit in the privy or cesspit and the concept of honey-coloured deposits underpins the **honey-bucket** or **honeypot**, a bucket used for night-soil; the **honey-cart** or **wagon**, a vehicle for collecting excrement (coined in the 1920s, it has been adopted by airlines, railway companies and other owners of public transport that provide mobile lavatory facilities); the **honey-dipper** (also **honey-digger**, **honey dripper**), a latrine cleaner; and the **honey house**, which is a privy.

Colour still underpins **gold** and **old gold** – both meaning excrement – as well as Australia's **bronze**, **bronza**, **bronzer** and **bronzo**, either excrement or the anus or posterior. In Australian prisons to **bronze up** is to register a 'dirty protest' by smearing one's cell walls with one's faeces. To be as **ugly as a hatful of bronzas** is to be very ugly indeed. A final link to colour, though equally to waste, is **dust**, which in its meaning of money seems to abbreviate **gold-dust**. Dust can also mean shit, and somewhere there must be the traditional religious equation of money with dirt.

The dried-out Quaker aside, consistency in this context pretty much invariably implies sticky, and stickiness lies behind most of the following. Thus, **flop**, which started life as a Wiltshire dialect word meaning any thick liquid, **body wax** (presumably playing on earwax) and **clart**, another dialect term meaning viscous sticky mud or filth; **in the clarts** means either in trouble, i.e. 'in the shit' or suffering from diarrhoea. **Fudge** is another of those terms that, having been equated with excrement and all matters anal (and it can also, whether with conscious racism or not, mean a dark-skinned black person), is used to categorise a gay man, who is therefore a **fudge-packer** or **-nudger**. The anus can be the **fudgepot** or **tunnel**, while to **stir** or **pack fudge** is to perform anal intercourse. To **fudge** something is to cover it with shit and to **drop** or **park one's fudge** is to visit the bog.

DROPPING THE KIDS OFF AT THE POOL

To make a brief detour, the idea of 'dropping' lies behind many of slang's terms for what it otherwise lists as **giving birth to a copper** (or indeed **a politician**) or **going off to sing 'sweet violets'**. Among them are **drop anchor** (to **drop anchor in bum bay** being to have anal intercourse – thus the **anchor man**, the subject of the sex) and **drop one's bundle**, which can also mean to panic, to lose (emotional or physical) control, to give up hope, and to give birth. To quote the authors of the unpublished *Materials for a Dictionary of Australian Slang* (1900–10), 'It has a vulgar derivation from the fact of cowards being said to perform a natural function through fright.' Too right, mate. Then there is **despatch one's cargo**, **drop off the shopping** or **drop the kids off (at the pool)**, **lay an egg** or **some cable** (often of a dog), to **drop** or **dump one's load** (which is also

defined as to reduce tension by having sexual intercourse), and to **pinch a loaf** or **pinch one off**.

More 'sticky' terms include **gick**, which is a variation on **guck** (thus, **give one the gick**, to disgust); the Scots **keech, keegh** or **keek**; **oily soil**; and **pilgrim salve** (which in seventeenth- to eighteenth-century standard use referred to an ointment, made mainly of swine's grease and isinglass). Others, capitalising on the initial 's', are **scharn**, dialect for cowdung; **scumber**, animal dung or sticky, viscous mud; **scutter** (from Irish *sciodar*, diarrhoea, and hence **tail-scutter**, a fart); and **sozzle**, from dialect *sossle*, a liquid mess. **Scat**, however, means dung or droppings, and is also listed among those terms that equate heroin with 'shit'. It also refers to defecation in a sexual context, and a **scatman** is a male homosexual. Most logical of all is, naturally, **mud**, which gives the **mud snake**, either a turd or a penis. The stickiness also underpins the use of mud to mean thick, strong coffee, opium, the heroin substitute methadone and pea soup.

It also extends to a set of terms that quite simply mean dung or emphasise the simple filthiness of a piece of excrement. Aside from **danna** (see under **K is for Khazi**, p.124) are **dub**, a Scots term that also means filth or a dirty puddle – although one must also see the simple abbreviation of 'double-you see' (W.C.); the sixteenth century's **gerry** or **jere**, from Romani *jeer*, excrement, and possibly linked to Devon's local *gerred*, bedaubed, filthy (though that adjective may have followed the noun); **dooty**, which most likely corrupts the standard English *dirty*; and the German/Yiddish **dreck**, literally excrement, which can mean excrement, rubbish or, again, heroin. The heap of dung, freshly excreted, also offers a pair of terms that call up the image of steam, doubtless stinking in its turn, rising from the still warm pile: the **steamer** (hence **clip a steamer**, to defecate), and **smoky joe**.

DUKIES, DUMPERS AND DREADNOUGHTS

And thence to terms based on size and shape. These include **pucky**, which evokes the puck, a disc of hard rubber used in hockey; the **banjo** (it can also, rather more feasibly, stand for a leg or shoulder of mutton, a shovel and a frying pan); the **Bondi cigar** (specifically human turds floating in the waters of the famous surfer's paradise, Bondi Beach, Australia); the **clinker**, in standard English a hardened mass; and the **curl**, which gives **curl paper**, lavatory paper, and **curl one off**, that is, to **back one out**. **Dukie**, **dookey** or **dukie** probably comes from Scots *dook*, the bung of a cask; the word gives **dukie-hole**, which can mean an anus or a person who is seen to resemble one. To **drop**, **do**, **blast** or **take a dukie** is to defecate. A **log** is self-evident, as is to **build a log cabin**.

Standard English *dump* means a heap, and a **dump** is an act of shitting, as well as (the link to drugs again) the vomiting that may follow an injection of heroin. One **takes a dump**, but to **dump on** is to criticise, or to pass one's troubles on to another person. The **dumper**, meanwhile, is a sexual sadist (possibly with an obsession with excrement/defecation), usually as encountered by prostitutes. The **dreadnought** ('what's the matter with our bloody shits today?') and the **moby** (from Herman Melville's novel *Moby-Dick*) are outsize pieces of excrement; so too is a **grogan**, which is also found amongst the macho cadets of Australia's RMC Duntroon as meaning a woman.

To round things off, a few terms from animal life. The **alley apple** is the 'fruit' of the horse, and as an **alley rifle** was often 'shot' at an enemy. The **barker's egg** (from **barker**, a dog) is dogshit; so too is a **hot dog**, which puns both on the foodstuff and the link between turds and 'sausages'. **Mallachy**, from the Irish *meallach*, lumpy or globular, is what the cat shat on the mat.

CLAGNUTS, GRIBBLES AND DAGS

It is a tribute to slang's infinite curiousness, and its attention to the less immediately obvious things in life – not to mention its refusal to ignore that which others might prefer to pass by – that the lexicon offers as many terms for the excrement that clings to the anal hairs as, other than basic shit, it manages for any other aspect of human ordure.

Clag is northern dialect for a sticky mass entangled in hair, which makes obviously for **clagnuts**. Another dialect term, to *gribble*, meant to remove matted wool and dung from the tails of sheep, and pieces of human shit are hence **gribbles**. **Winnits** or **willnots** (i.e. 'will not come loose'), **langballs** and **men in the rigging** are all synonyms, as is **tagnuts**, which 'tag along'. Probably the best-known, though originally in the context of an Australian sheep-shearing shed, are **dags**, a word ultimately spawned by standard English *dangle*, after taking a detour via *dag* and *daglock*, dialect terms for a lock of wool matted with excrement on the tail parts of a sheep. It was of the sheep that the term was originally used, but that would change. **Daggy** means unpleasant, while to **rattle one's dags** is to get a move on, especially as a command. And since slang can never resist a good (or in this case mediocre) pun, we find another synonym: **klingon**, which plays on standard English cling on and *Star Trek's* 'bad guys'. The word can also refer to crack cocaine addicts (who 'cling on' to every morsel of the drug) or to a tedious or unpleasant person (who 'won't leave you alone').

Finally a small punnet of berries, first among which is the **fartleberry**, the product no doubt of breaking wind. The **dillberry** or **dillball** can also be used to describe a piece of nasal mucus dripping from the bottom of the nostril and a stupid, dull or obnoxious person. The **dilberry bush** is the pubic hair, the **dilberry creek** or **dilberry-maker** the anus. The **dingleberry**, also **dingledork**, can be the usual piece of clinging excrement, someone (or something) stupid, dull or obnoxious, the vagina, or specifically the clitoris and, in the plural, the female breasts. Last is the **gooseberry**: as a piece of excrement it is relatively recent (from the 1940s on) but the **gooseberry-grinder** meant the buttocks in the eighteenth century, especially in the dismissive phrase **ask Bogey the gooseberry grinder**, in other words 'ask my arse'.

DO-DOS, JOBBIES AND SIR-REVERENCE

It is inevitable that faced by so ostensibly 'dirty' a topic, there will be euphemisms. Primary amongst these is the evasive, all-purpose **do**, reduplicated as **do-do** or modified in the canine context as **doggy-do**; **doings** works the same way. The **Gravesend twins** would be beyond meaning – unless one appreciated that one of London's main sewers has its outfall into the Thames Estuary at Gravesend, and that thus the twins are poo and pee. **Big jobs** is mainly juvenile, but a **jobbie** or **jobby** is used happily by adults north of the border; it can also mean a noxious human being, while a **jobby-jouster** is a gay man. The idea of a cake or sweetmeat lies behind two more examples, both describing a turd or pile thereof: the **toly**, from Scotland's *toalie*, a small round cake, and the **tantoblin**, also known as the **tantadlin** or the **tantoblin tart**: it took its name from the *tantoblin*, a large, round sweet tart, although the more immediate link was doubtless to dialect's *tantablin tart*, cow dung.

Finally, one of the oldest terms available to denote a lump of excrement: **sir-reverence**, **save-reverence** or **surreverence**. The term originated in the fourteenth century when it was a linguistic formality that meant 'begging your pardon' and was used, according to Robert Nares' *Glossary* of 1822, as 'a kind of apological apostrophe, when anything was said that might be thought filthy, or indecent'. By the late sixteenth century it had taken on this euphemistic secondary meaning and is surely the basis of the twentieth century's euphemistic to 'excuse oneself' and the schoolchild's cry of 'Can I be excused?' Despite its phrasal origins, it was definitely a noun. Thus Ned Ward, that indefatigable explorer of London byways, recalled in his 'Frolic to Horn-Fair' (1700): 'An Unlucky Rogue … a Ladle in his hand, Fishes up a Floating Sir-Reverence in his Wooden Vehicle, and gives it an Unfortunate Toss upon my Ladies Bubbies.' And Francis Grose, always keen to throw in a bit of arcane information, dealt with it thus in the 1796 edition of his slang dictionary: 'reverence, an ancient custom which obliges any person easing himself near the highway or foot-path, on the word reverence being given to him by a passenger, to take off his hat with his teeth, and without moving from his station to throw it over his head, by which it frequently falls into the excrement … '.

Y

IS FOR

YARD

Isn't it awfully nice to have a penis.
Isn't it frightfully good to have a dong.
It's swell to own a stiffy, it's divine to own a dick,
From the tiniest little tadger, to the world's
* biggest prick!*

Monty Python, 'Penis Song' (1983)

A yard. Oh, come *on*. A yard. I mean even the great John Holmes, a.k.a. Johnny Wadd – star of *Saturday Night Beaver*, *Up 'n Coming* and *Let Me Count the Lays* among others that one might suspect failed to require the attentions of the British Board of Film Classification – didn't claim a *yard* (you really want to know? it was allegedly 8.75 inches *flaccid*). But **yard**, however exotic four centuries on, remains one of the senior citizens of the phallic world. The word is rooted in a variety of terms, typically the Old Teutonic *gazdjo*, all of which mean a thin pole; it is also possibly linked to the Latin *hasta*, meaning spear, and even to the Italian *cazzo*, itself used in the UK, also slang for penis. Certainly the seventeenth-century **gadso** and **catso** are borrowings from the Italian original and, like a number of similar terms, mean both penis and rogue or villain. The first use comes in John Florio's dictionary of 1598. It was, of course, open to a world of useful puns: thus Thomas Dekker's *Honest Whore* (1604): 'You cut out her loose-bodied Gowne, and put in a yard more than I allowed her.' (And **loose-bodied gown** itself is a pun: the word meant a whore, and in the same play Dekker offers: 'If I go among the loose-bodied gowns, they cry a pox on me', yet another double entendre.)

And if the yard represents the penis as a stick, then slang's words for the male member are very often set in the image of some kind of **weapon**. Boys' toys, some might say, although the world of computer games doesn't seem to have come up with any images (**joystick** having come from the airforce, not the acne'd). The style is set early: 'Draw thy tool; here comes two of the house of the Montagues' warns Sampson in the first scene of Shakespeare's *Romeo and Juliet*, and receives the quick response, 'My naked weapon is out.' Other weapons include the sword, poll-axe, battering-piece and lance. Nor does one always need a simple synonym; the idea of opening or splitting is always popular – hence the **arse-opener** or **-wedge**. The **bush-beater** and **-whacker**, punning on **bush**, can also mean mugger; its origins are explained by Schele de Vere in *Americanisms* (1872): 'Originally it was a harmless word, denoting simply the process of propelling a boat by pulling the bushes on the edges of the stream, or of beating them down with a scythe or a cudgel in order to open a way through a thicket'. Also available are the **plug-tail**, the **beard-splitter**, the **hair-divider** or **-splitter**, the **cherry splitter**, the **split rump** and the **rump-splitter**. The **belly-ruffian** leaves no illusions as to its aggressiveness.

A **bow** shoots arrows (presumably of desire), although the term may refer to the sawing motion of the fiddler's bow (the **fiddle** being the vagina). And while these are not weapons as such, they are certainly echoic of violence (the eternal backdrop to sexual intercourse): the **swack**, **swipe**, **wang**, **wanger** and **wang-tang**. The **whammer** and **chopper** are tools rather than weapons, as of course is **tool** itself. Tool, with its roots in the Old Norse word *tol*, meaning to prepare or to make (the use of **tol** to mean sword is coincidental, as it comes from **Tol**edo in Spain, where it was considered that the best swords were made), and its direct ancestry in the standard English term for 'an instrument of manual operation' basically echoes the penetrative imagery of **prick** (see under **P is for Prick**, p.173). The **instrument** (**of venery**) is another synonym, and often appears alongside tool; thus this surely fanciful tale included in a book on *Witchcraft* in 1584: 'A yoong man lieng with a wench … was faine to leave his instruments of venerie behind him, by means of that prestigious art of witchcraft … He caught hir by the throte … saieng: Restore me my toole, or thou shalt die for it.' Quite what 'left behind' implies is perhaps better not researched. The idea of a tool extends to the **gulley raker** and **kennel raker**, in both cases originally applied to an implement used for cleaning filth from a gutter. The **handstaff** was that part of a flail that is held in the hands. Less obvious is **langolee**, which Partridge surmises as being from the Welsh *trangluni*, meaning tools.

FORNICATING ENGINES, GENERATION TOOLS AND NINE-INCH KNOCKERS

Pick up a tool and odds are you might be tinkering with an engine, and the mechanical world is happy to give space for the penis. **Engine** has been a popular literary euphemism from the early seventeenth century onwards, often in the context of inadequate ones that fail to 'pump' sufficient 'water' to extinguish the insatiable 'flames' of a woman's lust. It was much beloved of John Cleland in the *Memoirs of a Woman of Pleasure* (1748–9), for example when Fanny – as ever strangely literate for a simple country girl – recalls that a lover 'unbutton'd, and drawing out the engine of love-assaults, drove it currently, as at a ready-made breach'. There are a number of allied terms. Among them are **machine**, the **love** or **sex machine** (thank you, James Brown), **fornicating engine** or **tool**, **fornicator** and **fornicating member**, **garden engine** and **gardener** (no sniggers in the direction of a **hose**: the garden is the vagina), **gaying instrument**, (in an era when **gay** meant simply sexually active) and the **generation tool**, working in the **generating place**, the vagina.

The size of such engines gives the seemingly modest **inch** (but actually because it 'inches in'), the boastful **nine-inch knocker** (and let us not forget Robert Burns's poem 'Nine Inch Will Please a Lady' not to mention his 'nine-inch men' in 'Tweedmouth') and **four-eleven-forty-four**, an Afro-American term that refers to the supposed dimensions of four inches in circumference and eleven long. However, its real origins may be quite different: 4-11-44 was one of the 'lucky numbers' popularised in the 1870s among players of the numbers or policy racket, in which bettors wagered on a given number, published in the daily press and based on stock-ticker or horse-race results. It was also known as the 'fancy gal roll' or the 'Washerwoman's Number'. In 1872 the New York paper *The Galaxy* explained: 'Sometimes a mania seizes the entire fraternity of colored players to play some particular "flat gig," which is generally 4–11–44, and the numbers being sure to be drawn only after everybody has been tired out and quit betting on them, their appearance evokes a storm that is comical in its intensity when its occasion is remembered.'

SCHLONGS, PRONGS AND WANDS

Meanwhile, on the other side of the ghetto, the Yiddish **schlong** (from the German *schlange*, snake), as popularised in Philip Roth's *Portnoy's Complaint* (1969), has a certain onomatopoeic heft, while **kidney wiper**, given human anatomy, presumes impressive length. The unqualified **knocker** relates to the vagina as a door, as do **key**, **picklock**, and **knock Andrew** (though this is more likely a misprint of **nockandro**, the buttocks). **Chink-stopper** and **gap-stopper** are self-evident. **Sky-scraper** comes from the name for the topmost sails on a large sailing boat.

The image of weaponry plus the shape of the penis is further responsible for several allied groups of synonyms. To return to the stick and such terms as resemble one, one finds **stick** itself, and compounds thereof such as **gutstick**, **fuckstick**, **drumstick** and **shitstick**. Stick-shaped, but employing other imagery, are **prod**, **prong**, **ramrod**, **reamer**, **rod**, **wand** or **sceptre**, **pipe** (thus to **lay some pipe**, to have intercourse), **pole** (thus the US campus slang for sex education courses: **holes and poles**), **tube**, **pile-driver**, **pilgrim's staff**, **spindle**, **staff of life** (which puns on the phrase's usual meaning, coined in 1638, of bread or any other staple food), **shove-straight**, **spike-faggot** (no gay implication: the seventeenth century's **faggot** is a woman), **wood**, **broom-**

handle, clothes-prop, tentpeg, rolling-pin, roly-poly, plough-share and dibble (from the gardening implement, a dibbler). The pink of Caucasian penises gives copper-stick (otherwise an implement to give a stir to boiling laundry) and coral branch, as well as rubigo (an old Scots term, possibly from the Latin *ruber*, meaning red). The gigglestick, joystick and joy prong all suggest pleasure rather than pain and the wriggling stick or pole (thus to wriggle navels, to have intercourse) is presumably as pleasurable as it is simply penetrative.

Alongside these 'stick' terms are a variety of 'clubs'. These include hammer, bludgeon, club, claw-buttock, pestle (which in other contexts meant a constable's staff, although it is found here as the logical opposite of mortar, meaning vagina), life preserver (a form of truncheon or sap) and billy (either from the mid-nineteenth-century billy, a truncheon, or a pun on the billycock hat). Truncheon itself joins the list, although the sensitive truncheon is a nickname for the human nose.

PORK SWORDS AND
PILLICOCK PISTOLS

Prick, of course, relies on an image of stabbing or knifing (see under **P is for Prick**, p.173), and slang's penis lexicon has another subgroup of weaponry: the sword, knife or dagger. Among them are **sword** and **dagger** themselves, **dard** (literally, a dart) and **love-dart**, **lance of love**, **dirk**, **bayonet**, **blade**, **bodkin** (a dagger), **butter-knife** (playing on **butter**, semen), **bracmard** (a seventeenth-century term for a short broad sword and itself borrowed from the French *braquemard*), **pike** and **pikestaff**, and **cutlass**, **culty-gun** and **cutty gun** (all of which come from the Latin *cultellus*, knife – also the basis of **cutlery**). Finally, with an accent on **meat**, come the contemporary trio of the **pork sword**, **beef bayonet**, and **mutton dagger**.

Cranking up the level of weaponry, we reach the **gun**. 'This is my rifle, this is my gun,' chant the unfortunate recruits drilling in America's boot camps, their M-16 clasped in one hand, their penis in the other, 'this is for fighting, this is for fun,' or as they say in the Marine Corps: 'I don't want no teenage queen. I just want my M-16.' Sir yes sir! And don't we all love the smell of napalm in the morning. The penis as **pistol**, confirming feminism's most pessimistic stereotyping, has a venerable history: not for nothing is Shakespeare's braggart soldier boasting of his **cock** (see under **C is for Cunt**, p.32) named Pistol. Later sexual hardware includes **bazooka** (originally an anti-tank rocket launcher, first used in the Second World War), **cannon** and the Afro-American **peacemaker**, a term that springs either from the nickname of the Wild West's legendary Colt .45 revolver, or, just possibly, from the ironic nickname accorded the nuclear arsenal's MX missile. On the other hand it may do no more than abbreviate the **matrimonial peacemaker**, which dates to the seventeenth century.

While the following terms too are not weapons as such, they all suggest a definite degree of man-to-woman aggression: he

THE WIFE'S BEST FRIEND

wields the whatever-it-is while she is always on its receiving end, and any pleasure, if it's even on the cards, is purely coincident. Among them are **eye opener**, **girl-catcher**, **girlometer**, **leather-stretcher** and **-dresser** (**leather** being the vagina, as is the **leather lane**), **trouble-giblets**, **tickle-gizzard**, **tickle-toby**, **tickle-tail**, **tickle faggot**, **tickle thomas** and **bum-tickler**. The originally northern dialect **pillock**, (sometimes known as **pillicock** or **pillicock pistol**, and which like prick and dick is also used as a pejorative) dates back to the fourteenth century and gives **pillicock hill**, the vagina. The **placket-racket** uses placket to mean woman and thus, objectified, vagina; the penis as racket 'hits' her. **Enemy** may be purely literary; its implication is also quite unequivocal.

With weapons in mind comes the need to brandish them. Where else, especially in more agrarian days, than on the hunting field; hence a selection of terms which anthropomorphise the penis as a hunter. Among them are **cunny-catcher**, punning on the sixteenth-century **coney-catcher**, a conman, itself punning on **coney**, a rabbit; **Nimrod**, the 'mighty hunter' of Genesis (with an additional punning nod towards **rod**); **crack-hunter**; **cranny-haunter**; **cracksman** (no doubt he 'breaks in', although this **crack** is the vaginal one); and of course **hunter** itself.

THE WIFE'S BEST FRIEND

After such extensive devotion to the macho end of things, it may almost come as a surprise (relief?) to discover that not every term for the penis waves it, as it were, in the world's face. The point of view remains, inevitably, that of a man, but on occasion he seems capable of noticing that that there may be another person in the room and that that person may possess two X chromosomes. Such terms include **partner**, the **wife's best friend**, with whom one **shakes hands** (urinates), **good time** (as in 'I'll give you a good time ... ', although the traditional whore's come-on 'Fancy a good time ... ' obviously bears other interpretations), the **merrymaker**, the **master of ceremonies**, and the **ladies' plaything**, **treasure** or **delight**. That 'delight' calls up the etymology of the **dildo**, described by Grose as 'an implement resembling the virile member, for which it is said to be substituted, by nuns, boarding-school misses, and others obliged to celibacy, or fearful of pregnancy.' Its root lies in Italian *dilletto*, which means delight – and one can probably take the 'ladies'' as read. **Lullaby**, which 'puts one to sleep', and **lamp of light**, may be numbered amongst these gentler images. The procreative aspects of the penis are almost wholly subsumed in the sexual ones, but **child-getter**, **baby maker** and **brat-getter** do acknowledge that the pox isn't the only potential after-effect of that bit of **slap and tickle**.

Cock, **prick** and **tool** have survived, but they were once rivalled in popularity by such words as **tarse** and **limb**, as well as **tail**. They all appeared around the beginning of the eleventh century, but died out, at least in the sense of meaning penis, by respectively 1700 (tarse) and *c.*1900 (limb). **Tail** for penis appeared in the mid-fourteenth century, and Chaucer used it in the *Canterbury Tales*, but while it still plays a role in the slang lexicon – either as the buttocks, the vagina or as a generic term for women – it has not meant penis *per se* for some time. The long-defunct **pintle**, from the Anglo-Saxon *pintel*, and as such standard English from 1100 until 1720, was another variation on the prick or pin = penis model. In its prime, from the seventeenth to nineteenth centuries, pintle generated a wide range of combinations: the **pintle-bit**, **-maid** or **-merchant**, all of whom were mistresses or prostitutes; the **pintle-blossom** (a bubo or chancre, see under **D is for Dirty**, p.41); the **pintle-case**, the vagina; the **pintle-fancier** or **-ranger**, a pair of randy girls; and the **pintle-smith** or **-tagger**, a surgeon, presumably specialising in **pintle-fever**, venereal disease.

The term *member*, reminiscent of the defunct limb, is a direct translation of the Latin *membrum virile*, the virile or privy member, and has always been standard English since its first appearance in the thirteenth century. There are, however, a number of terms that use member, and which must be seen as slang, albeit of the heavily punning variety: **dearest member** (1740, used by Robert Burns), **master member**, **jolly member** and **the member for Cockshire** (with its extra pun on cock and reminiscent of such equally 'geographical' descriptions as the equally punning **County Down** or **Low Countries**, the vagina). The **member mug** is a chamber pot. The **unruly member**, however, is the tongue, a phrase based on lines 5–8 of the Epistle of St James.

JOHN THOMAS, CAPTAIN STANDISH AND OLD BLIND BOB

Surely – please tell me you are with me on this one – there are few things more repellent that the allotting to the genitals of a pet name. Unfortunately, humanity enjoys football and junk food too, so there's no accounting for execrable tastes. Fortunately, on the other hand, these pet names tend to nestle between the sheets, brought out only for one's partner (though how quite does one introduce the thing to a new friend? 'Hi, my name's John, and this ... is the Mighty Avenger.' Well, he's hardly going to call it **Tom Thumb**, is he? Tom Thumb? Think size). Nonetheless the penis has attracted a number of proper names, all of which can be categorised as general slang rather than bedroom intimacy. Perhaps the most obvious, even if one usually forgets that it is a name, is **dick**, i.e. the popular diminution of Richard, which emerged from the British Army around 1880, and is presumably a variation on another 'improper' name, the once equally popular **John Thomas**, although some authorities see it as yet another development of **dirk**. The term soon passed into general use, and one should note the First World War's cynical translation of the DSO (Distinguished Service Order) as 'dick shot off'. Perhaps the most celebrated occurrence of **John Thomas**, whose variants include **man Thomas**, **Tommy**, **Master John Thursday**, **Master John Goodfellow**, **Julius Caesar** and **Jack Robinson**, is in D.H. Lawrence's once taboo (and ever tedious) novel *Lady Chatterley's Lover* (1928), with its bucolic (some say stomach-churning) couplings of 'John Thomas' and 'Lady Jane'. The term originated *c.*1840 and remains in use, albeit somewhat self-consciously; the abbreviation **JT** is also popular. For a while it was generic for a male servant, but that barely survived the nineteenth century. **John Willie** is a similar term, which was taken up as a pseudonym by John Coutts (1902–62), one of the most fêted (if clandestine) illustrators of bondage and discipline pornography, notably in the misadventures of his painfully put-upon heroine 'Sweet Gwendoline'. The most recent is **jimmy**, straight out of hip hop, along with **jammy** (one jams it in?). **Mr Cool**, which rhymes with tool, is another recent coinage.

Other names include **Jacob**, (a reference to the biblical Jacob's ladder – up which one climbs), **Jack in the box** (which 'pops up'), **Captain Standish** (who 'stands erect'), **Don Cypriano** (another of the coinages used by Sir Thomas Urquhart (1611–*c.*1660) in his translation of Rabelais), **Jezabel** (the mind boggles) and **Dr Johnson** (probably on the model of John Thomas, and while it's top marks for effort, do we really believe Eric Partridge's suggestion that 'there was no-one Dr Johnson was not prepared to stand up to'?). The US use of **johnson** for penis emerged in the mid-nineteenth century; it is unlikely to stem from the great lexicographer but is more likely a variation on the synonyms **jock** or **jack**, although later use might have been bolstered by the champion heavyweight (and lady's man) Jack Johnson and the **johnson bar**, taken from railroad jargon.

Little Davy is not specifically 'little' and nor is **Master Reynard** a 'fox'. **Nebuchadnezzar** offers yet another pun: as recounted in the Bible, the Babylonian monarch was wont to enjoy a morsel of grass – grass is of course green, and for the Victorians **greens** were sexual intercourse. **Old Blind Bob**, **old Horney** and **old Hornington** (see under **H is for Horns**) and **old Rowley** (which also means the devil) convey a certain affectionate tone. **Old Slimey** does not, though perhaps one can see it as descriptive. **Peter** and **Robin** – used as the pet name for a servant's penis in the Edwardian porn novel *The Modern Eveline* (1904) – are linked to John Thomas; **St Peter** 'keeps the keys of Paradise' while **Sir Martin Wagstaffe** 'wags his staff'. **Roger** also means to have intercourse, and a century later the name was one regularly given to bulls (although in sixteenth-century crimspeak it meant a goose – the long neck, perhaps, rather than the bullish lusts, are what matters). **Percy** is essentially alliterative (and best-known in the Australian phrase for urination, **point percy at the porcelain**, although it was also used as the title of a deeply embarrassing film of the Sixties, and, as it happens, the name was given to *The Modern Eveline*'s incestuous brother). **Polyphemus** is taken from Homer's *Odyssey*, where he is a Cyclops, distinguished by his single eye and thus a distant relation to the modern **one-eyed trouser snake** and **one-eyed brother**. The **bald-headed hermit** abandons higher things and seeks heaven in the **cave of harmony**. Nor is a proper name obligatory: the penis has been given a variety of human 'jobs': the **customs officer** exacts his 'duty' on 'entering' **Eve's customs house** ('where Adam made the first entry'). The milkman (i.e. **milk**, semen) is usually a masturbator rather than the object of his abuse. The **rector of the females** may play on 'erect' as well as the church hierarchy, while the **solicitor general** is a definite nudge towards standard English *solicit*. Another ecclesiastic, the **vestryman**, emphasises the position of the vestry at the **entrance** of the church (which, perhaps co-incidentally, is of course a **holy place**).

SWEETMEAT, LOLLIPOPS AND MARROW-PUDDING

A quick look at G, which for our purposes stands for **gob**, will establish slang's extensive take on fellatio, or 'eating'. That which is devoured is more often than not the penis. The vagina is on the menu too, but in slang terms it's far more exotic, not to mention threatening: who said *vagina dentata*? And while we're at it, how strange of the French, in whose slang the penis is *la bite*, to make that male member grammatically 'feminine' while the vagina, *le vagin*, is 'male'. Though back this side of the Channel things are not much simpler. In 1785, when Francis Grose wanted to define our homegrown **bite**, used for the vagina, he felt it necessary to put his definition into Latin: '*secreta ( ) mulierum*'; that otherwise mysterious bracket illustrates the 'woman's secret **gap**'.

So what kind of food are we considering here? Well, it would appear that we have two categories: the sweetie and the meaty. The first offers **sweetmeat**, **sugarstick** (the logical soulmate of the **sugar basin**), **lollipop** or **ladies' lollipop**, **tummy banana**, **lunch** and **pud** (thus to **pull one's pud**, to masturbate). As well as the **pork sword**, the **beef bayonet**, and the **mutton dagger** meat terms include the simple **meat** (thus a **bit of meat**, intercourse), **beef** (to **do** or **have a bit of beef** is for a woman to have sex), **hambone**, **tubesteak**, **white meat** and **dark meat** (a woman, depending on race), **sausage** and **live sausage**, **goose's neck** and **gooser**, and **turkey neck** (particularly favoured by the writer Charles Bukowski, but also used, albeit as a simile, by Sylvia Plath in *The Bell Jar*, 1971). The purveyor of all these is the **butcher** (hence the **butcher's shop**, the vagina). His tool, the **meat cleaver**, implies that here the vagina, rather than the penis, is the flesh in question. **Schnitzel** and **schnickel** come from the German for veal cutlet and are usually encountered, since the mid-nineteenth century, in the form of Wiener (Viennese) schnitzel, coated with egg and breadcrumbs, fried and often garnished with lemon, capers and anchovies. Yum-yum as they say – and indeed they do: **yum-yum** is another term for penis, as well as for the vagina and, occasionally, intercourse. Finally there is the **crimson chitterling**, which takes us back to the useful *Modern Eveline*, wherein it may of course be no more than coincidence that the one country house to be named is called 'Chitterlings'. More carnal treats come in **marrowbone**, **marrowbone and cleaver** and **marrow-pudding**. **Gristle** is usually inedible – not here it ain't, girls. Then of course we have the **lemon**, that staple of the blues.

Plaintively, we request that our woman squeeze it; mercifully she does. The juice runs down our leg.

Still in the realm of the edible, we have the **creamstick**, although the cream in question is semen, and its modern successor, the **ice cream machine**. The **goober** is standard American for a **peanut**, and related, at least in this context, to the shape that makes the penis a **bean**. And as usual we have a bit of Shakespeare: 'O Romeo, that she were / An open et-caetera / thou a poperin pear!' says Mercutio in *Romeo and Juliet*, that repository of so much innuendo. The **poperin**, or **poperine pear**, is another case of lending a shape to the phallic synonym. The 'poperin' in question is the town of Poperinghe in west Flanders. The term may even, as Eric Partridge suggests in *Shakespeare's Bawdy* (1947), offer a second level of doublespeak, with poperin punning on 'pop her in'. **Et-caetera** is of course a literary euphemism for vagina. **Jargonelle**, an early ripening brand of pear, is another linguistic penis-substitute. It appeared in the eighteenth century and was originally limited to what gardeners condemned as a second-rate variety; it may be pure coincidence that in French the same fruit is known as *Cuisse Madame*, or lady's thigh.

FROM AARON'S ROD TO ZUBRICK

If I ask my database for definitions that include the word penis, it is delighted to oblige. But sometimes too much is not that good a thing. There are some 1106 such entries, from **Aaron's rod** to **zubrick**, and with the best will in the world, I cannot dissect or even type up the lot. But size does matter, after all, and I shall attempt at least a selection of what's on offer.

For instance the physical aspects of copulation give **jigger** (originally meaning key but also vagina), **jig-a-jig**, (**zig-zig** is a less frequently encountered variant) which means copulation (usually as offered to tourists), **do-jigger**, **jiggling bone** and

driving post. Simple physicality also offers **joint** and possibly the northern dialect **tadger** or **todger** if it comes, as some have claimed, from the term *tadge*, meaning to join. **Nag** and **bob-my-nag** both trade on the meaning of nag as horse, and thus one of slang's many equations of copulations with a 'ride'. Impotent is flaccid but flaccid is not impotent, merely resting, and the shape of the flaccid penis gives **flip-flap, flapper, flapdoodle, floater, crank, derrick** (as in a crane, which in turn immortalises the name of a long-dead hangman), **dangler** (and the **danglers**, the testicles), **dingle-dangle, pendulum** (though it just 'swings') and **dingaling** (once productive of many a giggle in Chuck Berry's song 'My Dingaling').

Since the vagina, as we know, is a dark threatening tunnel, Indiana Jones-like, the penis must get burrowing along it. Candidate number one is the **mole** (which wanders around in the dark, although a mole was for a time a promiscuous girl – but this may well be a variation on **moll**, and as such related to another unlikely term, **doll**, also more usually meaning a girl) plus its dialect cousin **mouldiworp** (literally, 'earth-thrower', and as E. Nesbit put it in *The House of Arden*, 'A friendly Mouldiwarp is a very useful thing to have at hand'). Other burrowers include the **maggot**, the **ferret** (thus **ferreting**, copulation), which turns **dung-puncher** as the **chutney ferret**, the **cunny-burrow** and **cunny-burrow ferret**, and the **mouse**. Back on the surface, and back to shape (well, sort of) music offers the **blue-veined piccolo** or **trumpet**, and indeed **blue-veined steak** (Roquefort dressing, anyone?), as well as the **flute**, usually combined as the **skin flute, living flute** or **silent flute**. (Opera lovers will regret the absence of *The Magic Flute*.) **Fiddle-bow** may have musical overtones, but fiddle here means vagina, as in the **fiddle-diddle**, where **diddle** means sexual intercourse. Neither is **whore-pipe** something one plays upon, one simply puts it in. Less tuneful, but loosely related to the 'blue veins', are **Bluebeard** (either the children's story or Henri Landru (1869–1922), a French serial killer who ended his days on the guillotine) and **Blueskin** (otherwise meaning mulatto), best-known as the nickname of the highwayman and felon

Joseph Blake, who was hanged in 1724; Jonathan Swift wrote him a memorial ballad.

Now how, given that we are looking at an aspect of the human body, could we overlook Mother Nature. And here she is, giving us **stalk**, **tail**, **root**, **man root** and **old root**. As well as **bog bamboo**, **sensitive plant**, **acorn** (that one whence great oaks grow) and **arm**. The First World War brought in the **short arm**, often found as 'short-arm inspection': once over the willie to check for clap. The animal kingdom (see also under **Z is for Zoo**, p.295) offers **worm**, **hog**, **bird**, **big bird**, **beak**, **white owl**, **cuckoo** (possibly an amplification of cock), **rabbit** (those randy bunnies) and **strunt** (in standard English the fleshy part of an animal's tail); the **pizzle**, once an animal's penis, became slang for the human variety. Assuming that **pecker** puns on beak, it, and its derivative **pecnoster** (i.e. pecker plus paternoster) also qualify here. And human anatomy itself offers various synonyms: the **thumb of love**, **stump**, **big foot Joe**, **third leg**, **middle leg** and **best leg of three**. The etymologically puzzling **tallywag** (or **tallywagger**, **tallywhacker** and **tallywock**) may be related to tail, but the original tally was a notched stick, and that image is certainly feasible. Nature itself has a role to play, and not merely penile: thus, the **pioneer of Nature**, **nature's scythe** (the penis), **nature's privy seal** (the hymen), **nature's treasury** (the vagina), **nature's duty** (intercourse) and **nature's founts** (female breasts).

Euphemistic terms were especially popular in literary use, and as such they're long gone. On the whole you're no longer likely to encounter **Aaron's Rod**, **Adam's Arsenal**, **Father Abraham**, the **confessor** (thus the **confessional**, the vagina), the **athenaeum** (from its original meaning: a group of persons meeting together for mutual improvement), or **my body's captain** (coined by the US writer Walt Whitman). Connoisseurs of olde worlde porn may well find **pego**, supposedly from the Greek *pege* meaning spring or fountain. Most euphemistic of all are those terms which fail even to identify the object in question: **dingus**, **doover** (from **doofah**, a gadget or thingummy), **that**, **the Lord knows what**, **what Harry gave Doll** and **what's** its name. **Privates** and **private property** are of course the supreme examples.

Slang can also offer a small group of terms that apply not merely to the penis, but to the whole genital area. The image is often of a **tool**-kit, neatly packed with everything required for sexual and procreative efficiency. Thus one finds **accoutrements, equipment, gear** and **marriage gear, tackle** and **wedding tackle, kit, necessaries, luggage** and **bag of tricks**. The feeling that the genitals were 'precious' is also important, giving **lady ware, crown jewels** and **family jewels**. Finally, a selection of more or less humorous terms for the penis and attendant testicles: **string and nuggets, three-piece set, meat and two veg, watch and seals** (as a meal this was a sheep's head and 'pluck' or viscera) and Gore Vidal's **okra and prunes**, as created for his novel *Duluth* (1983).

Z

IS FOR

ZOO

Poor animals. Not satisfied with wiping them out species after species, with entrapping them in zoos (which remain, however admirably organised, essentially prisons), with exhibiting them in circuses, with rendering their images grotesque and their 'speech' infantile for the purposes of Hollywood's bottom line, with raising them for our consumption in conditions that must in their cruelty be designed to render their eventual deaths a blessed release, and with every other aspect of their treatment that is justified by the conceit that of all the species, humanity is in some way the superior one, we snatch what we stereotype as their worst characteristics, and use them to embellish slang's vocabulary of sex. But so be it. The words are writ. Z is for Zoo.

And since we are making humans into animals, our zoo is arranged somewhat differently to the normal. This way for the penises, that for the vaginas, over here for whores and there for self-abuse. Come along, there's lots on offer.

The basic penis image is, as will have been guessed, the snake. It can be an **anaconda** (hence **empty** or **drain the anaconda**, to urinate) or a **pyjama python**, it can be a **worm** (hence **burp the worm**, or **snake**, to masturbate), **earthworm** or even **pantworm**. As such it offers such double entendres as this, in *Oxford Jests* (1712): 'A little slender Northern lass was ask'd, How she durst venture on so big Man? Oh, says she, a little Worm may lie under a great Stone.' The stone, dare one assume, is a testicle. The **snake** itself, often found as its common sub-species the **one-eyed trouser-snake**, gives us the **snake charmer**, a gay term for fellator, **snake gully**, the vagina, the **snakepit**, also the vagina, as well as a gay bar, a brothel (alternatively a **snake ranch**) or a non-specific 'red-light' area. To **take one's snake for a gallop** allows one either to masturbate or urinate. Finally the somewhat menacing **black snake**, often modified as the **Alabama black snake**, is the black penis. The Alabama version could once also be found in deep south prisons, as a particularly vicious whip. While an **eel** is not strictly a snake, it's got the look, and thus an **eel-trap** or **eel-skinner** is a vagina.

HOW'S YOUR BIRD?

The idea of pecking or snuffling around, of sticking one's nose (or beak, or proboscis) into some kind of hole underpins a number of animal images. One cannot be more literal than **pecker**, i.e. that which pecks and is in standard use a beak. If recorded use is to be believed, pecker was used as a figurative term for courage and 'guts' some years prior to its adoption as the penis and hence a generic for sex in general, but the chronology of such synonyms as **balls** tends to suggest it is only a matter of what's on record. Pecker offers the **pecker check**, a health check, looking for symptoms of VD; **pecker cheese**, smegma; **pecker snot**, semen; and **pecker tracks**, sperm left on a sheet or other similar object after intercourse or, usually, masturbation. The **pecker palace** is a room in a US prison set aside for conjugal visits. To **stick one's pecker in** is not in fact sexual, it just means to interfere; and **keep one's pecker up**, which ultimately is, has come to mean to stay cheerful, despite possible adversity.

What possesses a pecker – human males apart? A bird, of course. And the simple **bird** (plus **birdie** and **dickybird**) is another 'beaked' penis. It can also mean the vagina (as well as **birdbath**, hence **bird-washing**, mutual cunnilingus) and fellatio. To **beat** or **jerk one's bird** is to masturbate, to **get one's bird in a splint** is to get into (painful) difficulties, and to **eat**, **gobble** or **swallow one's bird** is to fellate. **How's your bird?** is a greeting, while the dismissive response **not on your bird!** means 'in no way!' or quite impossible. A **bird taker** enjoys anal intercourse from the passive end while a **bird in a gilded cage** represents a (gay) man's crotch in a pair of expensive trousers. To **cop a bird**, often used of a prostitute, is to fellate. The **blackbird** offers another avian name for the penis (there is no racial implication), while **cockatoo**, **cockerel** and **chanticleer** (from French *chante clair*, sing clearly, best-known as the name of the cockerel in the fable of 'Reynard the Fox') all play unashamedly on **cock** (which albeit primarily a tap, remains intimately connected to the herald of the rural dawn). The **robin** might suggest a 'red-breast' but it's another phallus, and to **pull one's robin** is to masturbate. The **dicky-bird** is juvenile, but it stands up as required, and a **naughty dicky-bird** was a whore.

Of less interest to the twitchers (although of much more to the butcher's slab) are the **goose** and **goose's neck**, and the **turkey-neck**. To **have a bit of goose's neck** is to have sex, while to **come one's turkey** is to masturbate. A **turkey gobble** is fellatio in Australian prisons, thus a **turkey gobbler** is a fellator/fellatrix. Finally, the **maribou stork**, another penis, and the key, for the ignorant among us, to the title of Irvine Welsh's collection of short stories *Maribou Stork Nightmares* (1995).

FROM DINOSAURS TO DONKEYS

Beaks aside, more nosing around comes with the **anteater**, variously a circumcised penis and the man who has one; it can also signify an erection. The **dinosaur** mixes male bravado, i.e. the supposed dimensions (and could it have teeth?), with a supposed resemblance to a dinosaur's neck and head. The **dragon** is doubtless seeking its dungeon. The **dragon upon St George**, however, allies the mythical beast to the vagina: the phrase evokes a position of sexual intercourse in which the woman is on top of the man. The **ferret**, like the animal, burrows into holes and to **walk one's ferret** is to masturbate. The **weasel** is another burrower (and the term was used to mean a lecher in the seventeenth century); to **grease the weasel** is to have sexual intercourse. Next to burrow along is the **mole** plus the **mole–catcher**, the vagina, and next door to him the **mouse**. Somewhere between the burrowers and the snakes is the **lizard**, giving such phrases as **bleed**, **choke**, **lift**, **gallop** and **whip the lizard**, all meaning masturbate, and to **drain**, **squeeze**, **leak** or **flog the lizard**, to urinate. To **give the (old) lizard a run** is to have sex, and if that's too much to hope, manipulation of the saurian offers yet more masturbation images including **pet, squeeze, stroke** and **milk the lizard**. Similar effects can be achieved by **milking the anaconda, maggot** or **moose**. The **maggot** is itself another 'burrower'.

The **toad** has no obvious penile characteristics – other than that it puns on toad in the **hole**. The **hog, hogger** or **hogleg** (otherwise a name for a large **pistol**) all offer a porcine contribution, while the **hog's eye** can double as the anus or the urethral hole in the penis; the **hogs-eye man** is a womaniser. Given its standard definition as the small intestines of animals, especially pigs, the **chitterling** or **chitterlin** usually indicates a flaccid penis, but it can manage an erection. Long before it became the stereotype of the wily Chinese, a **pigtail** was a roll of coarse tobacco (and linked to the sailors who both smoked and wore one); it was also a penis.

To take in a few more animals: **horsemeat** plays on **meat**, and the general image is of size; the **horsecocked** individual has a large penis, also known as a **horse's hangdown**. Still in the stable is the **charger** and **bob-** or **billy-my nag** (**nag** being a horse, and indeed a woman and as such intimately linked to any image of **riding**). **Donkey-dicked** is of course another image of penile magnificence (a **donkey yawn** is a large vagina, and having one is to be **cow-cunted**) and the **mule**, while perhaps less impressive, does at least evoke the organ, size notwithstanding. For a man to **muledick** is to copulate aggressively and violently; to **ride the mule** is just to fuck. At the same time a mule can also indicate an impotent man (not to mention an unattractive woman). To **lope one's mule** (or **pony**) is to masturbate, while to **water one's mule, horse** or **pony** is to urinate. To range from one end of the canine scale to another, both the **chihuahua** and the **St Bernard** can represent the male appendage; it will surprise no-one to find that the former is of less than average size and the latter a good deal more. **Rover** is another term, used by the South African gay world. **Cony** (in its standard form meaning a rabbit) is used as a play on **cunny**, i.e. **cunt** (see under **C is for Cunt**, p.32) and the **coney-catcher** is a logical name for a penis. The variant **cunny-catcher** makes the title even less ambiguous. Still lapine are the **jack rabbit** and the **live rabbit**, both underpinned by its 'jumping up' when excited. The rabbit also gives to have a **bit of rabbit pie** and to **skin the live rabbit**, both to have sexual intercourse, which latter also describes a man peeling back his foreskin. And if the **monkey** is the vagina then the **monkey spanner** (which 'unbolts' it) is the penis; to **touch the monkey's head** is for a woman to place her fingers on a man's penis and to **slap the monkey** is to masturbate.

SPITTING THE WINKLE AND STROKING THE BEAVER

While fish and the water they occupy are usually linked to femininity (see under **L is for Ling**), the penis gets its share of the slab. Not exactly fishy, but certainly allied to the sea, is the **seal**, which seems to have been given its further meaning by the poet John Donne (1572–1631). It covers, as it were, the waterfront, meaning variously the vagina, the penis and, in the plural, the testicles. (All that claimed, the seal may in fact be the one that requires sealing wax.) **Moby Dick** is rhyming slang for **prick** and/or **dick**; he is also (however fictitious) a very large whale. Down several sizes come the **lobster**, the **snapper** and, even smaller, the **tiddler** and the **winkle**. To **spit the winkle**, for those of us who have sadly missed the delights of **riding the plank** is an Australian surfie term that is defined as to squirt water from one's anus. Surf City, eh? Well, as the lyrics say, 'all you gotta do is just wink your **eye**'.

So, as we know from **L is for Ling** (see p.137), the vagina's main link to the animal kingdom is the world of fish. But there are some leftovers. Setting aside the wonderfully negative **mark of the beast** (where the **beast** is the devil rather than an ugly female), this list is headed by that industrious creature, the beaver. **Beaver** means the female pubic hair and offers a number of terms, including **beaver trader**, the pimp; others include **beaver book**, a pornographic book and **beaver shot**, a close-up photograph of, or camera-angle on, the female genitals. Also used in commercial pornography is **split** or **wide-open beaver**, the fully

exposed female genitals (sometimes held open). Such images enhance the appeal of **beaver flicks**, porn films. Man the hunter gives us **shoot the beaver**: for a man to look up a woman's skirt in the hope of seeing her pubic hair or vagina (such a peeping tom is a **beaver shooter**); but it isn't that sexist, and can also stand for a woman deliberately to display her genitals, usually while otherwise dressed. The **beaver palace** is a brothel, the **beaver cleaver** the penis. A masturbating woman can **brush** or **beat her beaver**, while to **stroke the beaver** is to have heterosexual intercourse.

MUFFBURGERS AND MICE

Stroking involves **fur**, and while the animal has long since departed, fur, of no matter what origin, is naturally linked to the pubis. The **furbelow** puns on the standard English *fur below* plus standard *furbelow*, an adornment to a dress or other garment; itself ultimately from *falbala*, a trimming for women's petticoats, scarves and the like. It was first adopted to describe the kind of garment worn by a prostitute, thence by metonymy to the woman herself, and from there to the pubic hair and/or vagina. Modern uses gives us **furburger** (or **muffburger**, both which of course can be 'eaten') and the **furry hoop**. Still thinking of fur and its stroking, comes **kitten** or **kitty**, smaller versions of the **cat** and the cognate of **pussy** (for both see under **M is for Motherfucker**, p.144). As well as the vagina and various terms implying a young or inexperienced girl, the kitty has also been a pint or half-pint pot and the junior member of a gang. Possibly linked to kitty, but perhaps a nod towards the chocolate Kit-Kat bar, which comes in sizes offering two or four 'fingers', is the **kit-kat shuffle**, itself a two-fingered version of the all-male **five-finger shuffle**. Whatever the root, it describes female masturbation. Feline imagery comes with the **tabby**, based on the *tabby cat*, a striped variety, and *tabby*, which originally meant striped or watered silk (which was first produced in the Baghdad suburb of Attabiy). The word was first used in slang in the seventeenth century to denigrate an old woman and since then has denoted a prostitute and a pretty girl. But it's the tetchy, gossipy **old biddy** image that has lasted. The seventeenth century also coined **tabbyism**, the tendency to act as a querulous, interfering old woman.

When it is seen as a small creature making its way through a confined space the **mouse** is defined as a penis, but when the accent moves to its fur and softness, then it changes sex and becomes the vagina. It was first used to mean a woman in the sixteenth century, although it seems somewhat contrary to the creature's retiring image to find that such a woman was specifically a prostitute or any other female arrested for brawling in the street. Still female, and rather more in character, it has meant a timid, weak or effeminate man, and by extension a homosexual and thus a fellator. It can also refer to a wife (and thus the **mousetrap**, marriage) or a vagina. The mouse was also a girl who accompanied Australia's equivalent to the UK's Fifties Teddy Boy. A **titmouse** is also the vagina. The **nest in the bush** or **bird's nest** both emphasise the female pubic hair (in gay use it can also mean both a hairy chest and pubic hair that links the crotch to the navel; facetiously this extends to mean a woman's breasts). A **duckpond** is another vagina (and how can one resist the **duck-fucker**, eighteenth-century Royal Navy slang for the man who takes care of the poultry on board a ship of war?).

BUMBLEBEES, BARRACK HACKS AND BARN OWLS

For the rest, the vaginal menagerie is pretty much at random (as already hinted at under **R is for Ram**, p.190). There is the **cushat**, a wood pigeon or ring dove (reminiscent of the **soiled dove**, a whore, and the **dovecotery**, a brothel), the **bumblebee** (another one of those threatening vaginas with a 'sting in the tail'), and a **dog's mouth**, which is more than usually tight. The **growler** may appear to echo the dog, but it's rhyming slang – in other words, a **growl and grunt**. The **pig-bite** offers another synonym. The **civet** or **civet-cat**, a creature somewhere between a fox and a weasel, is best known for the musky odour that certain of its glands give off. That musk is used in perfumes and is traditionally viewed as overtly sexy. From there one finds civet-cat used to denigrate a woman seen as too (threateningly) sexy, notoriously delivered by Virginia Woolf (1882–1941) who displayed perhaps less than wholly unshakeable feminist solidarity when she described her fellow-writer Katherine Mansfield (1888–1923) as one who 'stinks like a civet cat that had taken to street walking.' (Get back, as they said in other days, in the knife box!)

Snakes usually summon the penis, but the **rattlesnake canyon** underlines male terror of what lurks 'down there', while the **serpent socket** again acknowledges the penile shape. A **horse-collar** is a vagina that is considered larger-than-average (quite what 'average' may be is another story, could it reflect on a smaller-than-average penis?), while a **pigeonhole** is a tight one. A **trot** (another variation on the horse) can be an old hag, a young whore or, again, a vagina. Horses and riding underpin **barrack hack**, a military term that is defined as a horse available to any soldier in a barracks; in this case she is a prostitute and, like the animal, is available to anyone who wishes to 'ride'; more ambiguously the term was also applied to a woman who regularly attends military balls. Finally, the dialect term **madge**

howlet, a barn owl, is used in slang to mean the female parts, which are otherwise known as **Madge Howlett**, **Madge-owlet**, **madge**, **Margerie Howlet**, **Jennie Howlet** and **howlet**; **madgyland**, or **maggyland**, is the world of prostitution.

TORMENTING THE TROUSER TROUT

In our next cage, a brief survey of the use of our furry friends as used for the purposes of masturbation. Other than those animal-linked terms mentioned above, one may **gallop the antelope** or **maggot**, **slap** or **pump the monkey**, **tug the slug**, **skin** or **strangle the goose**, **gander**, **snake** (or **stogie**: sometimes a cigar is just a penis) and **milk the cow with one udder**. Those achieved, one can start again: other terms include **pump the python**, **ride the dolphin**, **rope the goat**, **shake** or **tease the weasel**, **shemp the hog**, **shoot (the) tadpoles** (from the 'tadpole'-like shape of sperm), **spank the turkey**, **take the monster for a one-armed ride**, **teach one's dog to spit**, **tease one's crabs**, **torment the trouser trout** and **torture the tentacle**. To **walk the dog** possibly reflects the up and down hand movements that are used in making a yo-yo 'walk the dog'. Rhyming slang offers a **Brahma bull** (i.e. **pull**) and a **monkey spank** or **piggy bank** (i.e. **wank**).

Although, as far as is yet known, the oldest profession has no outposts among the animals, it is in naming prostitutes that we find an especial delight in borrowing from nature. Given her innate 'flightiness', it is logical to begin with those that equate her to some form of **bird**, at its simplest a **bird of the game**. Other working birds include the **cuckoo**, the **guinea bird** (her price), South Africa's **goosie**, the **partridge** and the **nightingale** (also the eighteenth-century army's word for a soldier who cries out during a flogging or one of the under-world's synonyms for an informer: they both 'sing'). The **jay** or **jaybird** is noted for its noisiness and bright colouring, and for its boorishness towards other birds. One might have suspected that **polly**, usually allied to parrot, would evoke the same image, but no, it's a nickname for Mary, and thus **moll**, who is of course a whore herself. A **lone duck**, **dove** or **mouse** was a former 'kept woman' now turned common prostitute and working either from her own room or in a house of assignation. The **wren** was a girl who specialised in army camps and to **spin a wren** is to dance with a (pretty) woman; there is no evidence of her being particularly small.

FARMYARD FROLICS

The farmyard offers **chicken**, which has had a wide variety of uses in feminine contexts, including that of a prostitute, and thus this exchange from F. Pilon's play, *He Would be a Soldier* (1786): '*Sir O.* Why, what the devil, man! Aren't you content with one of my chickens, but you must have my old hen in the bargain? *La O.* Old hen! *Sir O.* Yes, my Lady; when I had you first you were no pullet.' And **hen** (plus **hen of the game** and **hen of the walk**) too serves as a whore, as well as a woman (usually over 30, which in the sixteenth century, when it was coined, meant at best middle-aged), and a mistress, girlfriend or even wife. With women, of whatever moral standing, hen gives a number of compounds: among them the **hen–cock**, an effeminate or homosexual man; a **hen coop** or **roost**, a brothel; **hen-fest**, a women-only party or gathering; **hen fight**, a fight between two (or even more) women; **hen fright**, a man who is dominated by his wife; **hen hussy**, a man who is seen to be over involved in household affairs and similar 'women's concerns' (in dialect the term refers to a woman who minds the poultry); and **hen mill** or **hen pen**, a women's prison. From birds of the game to game birds: the **quail** and the **snipe**. The former is allegedly an amorous creature, hence its reinvention as a name for a prostitute in the seventeenth century; the inference tends to be a young woman, even underage, and a **San Quentin quail** is defined as a girl below the age of consent: sex with her will have one jailed, and the recipient of one's own new name: **Chester** (**the Molestor**). The snipe had no positive image and its first use referred to a lawyer, and his 'long bill'. And while the gay use of quail refers to a pretty young man, the gay world's snipe is a male prostitute or one who befriends homosexuals to acquire money, especially by robbing them. Avian imagery also offers Australia's **crow**. However, beware such false friends: the word abbreviates standard English *chromolithograph*, a picture printed in colours from stone. Although the term is uniquely Australian, it originates in the comparison by US writer Francis Brett Harte (1836–1902) of an over-dressed, over-made-up prostitute with a chromolithograph – both are colourful and flashy, but neither resembles natural beauty. All that said, one should not overlook the Italian *cornaccia*, which means both a crow and a 'loose' woman.

Still on the farm one finds **heifer**, and thus **heifer-den**, a brothel (a **heifer paddock** was a girls' school). Mid-sixteenth-century Scotland's **kow clink**, a whore, presumably refers to cows as well, and the modern verb to **cow it** means to work on the game. One of the stranger terms is **goatmilker**, which exists in standard English as a name given to the bird *Caprimulgus europæus*, from a belief that it sucks the udders of goats. In slang it has meant both the whore and her stock-in-trade, the vagina. The goat is another one of those animals that's seen as horny, and to **play the goat** is to copulate energetically; the **goat's jig** is intercourse, while the **goat's genolickers** (an Irish variation on the **dog's ballocks**) meant the real thing or ultimate example. A **goatskin** is a long foreskin and to **look goats and monkeys at** is to gaze lecherously at or to leer. A **goat-fuck** or **goat screw**, however, is merely an instance of chaos.

The farmyard cockerel inspired the **cockatrice**, properly a hybrid monster with the head, wings and feet of a cock, terminating in a serpent with a barbed tail. And people would *pay* for this woman's favours? The cockatrice leads to the **stingtail**, in whose dubious (and diseased) honour Ned Ward noted in *Hudibras Redivivus* (1705–7) that: 'For am'rous Joys, we always find, / Leave a repenting Sting behind.' The

cockchafer appears equally unappetising: the word has meant a prison treadmill (yes, its movement 'chafed one's cock'), as well as a whore, the vagina and the sort of woman who today would be dismissed as a **cockteaser**. In standard use it is a beetle, popularly known as the maybug: the *cock* element expresses its size (relatively large), while the *chafer* or *chaffer* is a beetle, itself from various Teutonic synonyms, which possibly go back to roots meaning to gnaw or describing any animal enclosed in scales or husks. The **ladybird**, an insect with a far more attractive image, is another hooker, although the word probably refers more to the 'bird' group than to the spotted ones.

LIFE'S A BITCH

The exploitation of animals in slang is too great for complete exploration, even in the limited sphere of sexuality. But before departing the imagery, and indeed this whole brief overview of slang's 'dirty department', it is right that we draw to a close with a word that in many ways – in its casual, unquestioning sexism, its blithe side-stepping of political correctness, its cruelty, its reverse anthropomorphism, and dare I suggest its inventiveness and range of application, is an excellent example of my beloved slang.

So let us finish with **bitch**.

Like the then acceptable **arse** (actually **ars**), the first record of the standard English *bitch* is in Abbot Aelfric's glossary of Latin to Anglo-Saxon, produced in AD 1000. It translates *canicula*, a small female dog. The word's more immediate etymology remains a problem: the Anglo-Saxon word may have come from a Teutonic form, the Old Norse *bikkja*; it may on the other hand have been the origin of such forms. There seems to be no relationship, or not one that is yet known, to the French word *biche*, which means both a bitch and a fawn. For slang's purposes bitch is listed as a derogatory term from the early seventeenth century, before which it presumably had been standard English but probably only by default and one would assume it was equally derogatory, or as the OED terms it, 'opprobrious'. The first recorded example comes sometime just before 1400, in a piece of invective in the *Chester Plays*: 'Whom calleste thou queine, skabde biche?', which for all its spelling, and the use of **quean**, a loose woman, not to mention **scabbed**, syphilis-ridden, has a strangely modern feel.

By the time Francis Grose added it to the word-list that made up his *Classical Dictionary of the Vulgar Tongue* in 1785 he could term it 'the most offensive appellation that can be given to an English woman, even more provoking than that of whore', and he cites the 'Billingsgate' rejoinder: 'I may be a whore, but I can't be a bitch.' That said, the seventeenth-century verb to bitch was to frequent whores; it could also mean to back down through cowardice and not until the 1920s do we find an example of the modern use of bitch, to complain, to gossip behind someone's back. Or almost so; in Ned Ward's *Compleat & Humorous Account of Remarkable Clubs* (1709) one finds: 'A Leadenhall Butcher would be bitching his Wife, for not only opening her Placket, but her Pocket Apron to his Rogue of a Journeyman.' It is hard to discern any alternative meaning. Nonetheless, after that the meaning seems to vanish for a couple of centuries. In short the original use implied disapproval of the woman's sexuality, e.g. a bitch in heat; today's use focuses on her personality.

RIDING THE BITCH'S SEAT

Aside from the basic derogative, the noun **bitch** can mean a whore, or the queen in playing cards or in chess, and can be used as a general derogatory term of address to a woman or any female creature. The current use, which appears to cast a blind eye on the derogatory background and with the seemingly interchangeable (and many would say even more unpleasant) **ho,** is used to define any female, including one's allegedly best-beloved girlfriend. It emerged in the US black community in the 1970s, and its current popularity is very much rooted in that of rap music, no lyric of which seems complete without it. Still 'female', bitch has been used of the male host at a campus tea party and for the middle back seat in a car (at least a big American one), i.e. where a woman is 'supposed' to sit. This gives the phrases **sit** or **ride bitch**, **ride the bitch's seat**, **ride punk** or **ride pussy**, all of which refer to taking the middle of the car's back seat or the pillion on a motorbike. So threatening is such a seat, it appears, that the phrase **no bitch!** has been developed to counter it: no bitch! delivered in response to a claim of **shotgun!** ('I want to sit next to the driver') means 'I won't ride in the middle of the back seat.' Hey, gang, it's Johnny. Boy! is he a wild one! 'What are you rebelling against, Johnny?' 'Well, I don't like sitting in the back seat … '.

Used of a man, bitch implies submissiveness, cowardice, weakness and, by sterotyped extension, outright homosexuality. To **make someone one's bitch** – always a man-on-man interaction – is to dominate them; the term began in prison where the **bitch**, alternatively a **punk**, is the weaker 'female' partner of a 'macho' prison homosexual. (Neither of them may persist in these roles after they are freed.) The bitch can also be used of any object or person, irrespective of gender. It can mean something or someone considered extraordinary or surprising, an otherwise unspecified object, or creature, a person, neither in a necessarily negative sense nor especially aimed solely at women, nor used solely by men; it can denote an exceptionally skilled person. In prison use, other than the gay sense, it can be a long prison sentence, specifically a **big bitch**, a conviction under any crime that carries a mandatory life sentence or a sentence so long that it is an equivalent; or a **little bitch**, a sentence that while not quite so great, is still depressingly protracted. A bitch can be a problem, a complaint, anything unpleasant, difficult, or problematic; it can be anyone, irrespective of gender, who complains or makes (what are perceived as) unfairly negative comments. It can simply be a thing.

GETTING THE BITCH ON

Bitch lends itself to a number of compounds and phrases; they are almost all based on either femininity or its extension, effeminacy. The **bitch booby** was a rough, unsophisticated country woman (and a 'military term' according to Grose); **bitch's wine** was champagne, supposedly preferred by women drinkers; and a **bitch bath** is a 'bath' in which the usual water is replaced by an application of cosmetics, masking the dirt rather than removing it (such a marginal 'wash' is not dissimilar to the **ho splash**, although that uses water, even if it only touches the **PTA**, the pussy, tits and armpits). A **bitch's bastard** is a term of abuse (specifically aimed at more than usually vicious prison officers), while the modern US campus's **bitch-boy** can either be used to denote a fool or as a term of affectionate address between friends. A **bitch fight** was a gay term for an argument between two homosexual men; the **bitch lick** is a hard blow; while a **bitch slap**, across the face, denotes one's contempt for the target: a real man would have earned a clenched fist and a punch. The **bitch hammer** is the penis. Further gay uses include **bitch's Christmas**, Hallowe'en; a **bitch's blind**, a gay or bisexual man's heterosexual wife, and as such a predecessor of the modern **beard**; and a **bitchery**, a bar frequented by homosexuals. A **bitch** or **bitching party** was a nineteenth-century occasion: either a campus tea party or party composed solely of women, some of whom, perhaps, may be assessed as **bitch squeaks**, telltale and garrulous. One who **stands bitch** is either the hostess at a tea party or simply makes the tea. In the Caribbean a **kitchen-bitch** (or **kitchen crumb** or **key**) is a man who hangs around the kitchen instead of going out and doing 'man's things'. **Bitch water** is cologne (the assumed effeminacy of even the most anodyne form of male cosmetic); **bitchweed** is any form of adulterated or second-rate marijuana; **Bitchville** is a notional state of cowardice; and **bitch tits**, mocking the primping Schwarzeneggers of this world, refers to the bodybuilder's over-developed pectoral muscles. In neutral terms **like a bitch** and **as**

a bitch are both phrases of intensification; a **bitch-on-wheels** is an extreme example, someone or something infinitely superior.

To **get the bitch on** is to yell at someone, to criticise, or to nag, as is to **pitch a bitch**, which can escalate to causing a full-scale disturbance, even a fight; it can also mean to leave. To **go bitch** is for a man to act in an effeminate or cowardly manner, while to **go bitchcakes** is to lose one's temper, and to **go bitching** meant to go out looking for whores. To **pull someone's bitch card** is to correct them by moving from words to actual force – the image is of challenging the bitch in them. To **make a bitch of** is to blunder, and to **flip a bitch** (or **flip a dick**) is to make an illegal U-turn: the image is of the lousy female driver; no matter – she messes up like that and her man will **stamp a bitch**: hit her hard enough to leave the imprint of his rings in her flesh.

Slang. You gotta love it.

* * *

And we do. we surely do. But hang on a moment. Isn't there something missing? A kind of lexical spot-the-ball as it were. You know it should be there, but ... And indeed, check the cover, this book has a title. *Getting Off at Gateshead*. But of city nor indeed phrase – and you can check – as yet nary a mention. Let us make amends.

Slang doesn't do medico-Latinisms, those most up-market of euphemisms. Thus *coitus interruptus*, literally 'intercourse interrupted', will not be found amongst its headwords. Nor too, although my predecessor Eric Partridge, bound by his own avowed squeamishness and the linguistic gelding of his time, did feel it safer to include such Latin definitions – rather than using simple English – such as the *membrum virile* (the 'virile member', i.e., the penis), and *pudendum feminae* (the vagina and literally 'that which is fit to be ashamed of of a woman') not to mention *foeminam subagitare* (to fuck, but properly rendered to 'lie illicitly with a woman' – and used as such in Francis Grose's slang dictionary of 1785). But no more. The removal of the penis sometime during what were once termed 'the paradise strokes' (and which prophylactic act, according to the sexologist Havelock Ellis, may have been the correct interpretation of 'the sin of Onan' rather the generally accepted one of masturbation), is as much a guarantor of efficient contraception as the pious Catholic's wagers on Vatican Roulette, but like much to do with copulation, it has established a role in the counter-linguistic lexicon. The phrases that describe this inefficient and un-satisfactory process almost all suggest a journey completed before its proper terminus. *Coming*, as it were, before one has actually *arrived*. Thus **getting off** or **out at Gateshead**. They cover the UK, and even appear in Australia. And nearly all reflect a slower, statelier, Bradshaw-regulated era of travel in which mighty engines, their massive pistons finally stilled, a last gusher of steam pouring from their thrusting chimney, deliver the sated traveller at that final, climactic stop. ('The

08.57 stands at Paddington and the game's afoot, Come Watson, come,' as the Master possibly didn't say.)

Strangely enough the London termini and their adjacent halts play no role is this nomenclature. There is no premature descent at Watford, Reading or Clapham Junction. One must assume – doubtless incorrectly – that every metropolitan coupling, as it were, achieved its ultimate destination. But the image is prolific elsewhere. Thus one 'gets off' or 'gets out' at **Gateshead**, the station prior to Newcastle; at **Broadgreen** or **Haymarket**, both stations adjacent to Edinburgh Waverley, **Edge Hill**, before Liverpool Lime Street, **Paisley**, before Glasgow, **Fratton**, before Bristol Dockyard (and thus mainly a naval term), and at Australia's **Redfern**, which leaves one a stop short of Sydney Central.

There are other terms for *coitus interruptus,* and they too seem to orginate in the age of steam. **Leaving before the gospel** assumes a regular attendance at church, while **firing a shot across the bows** recalls some Hornblower-esque encounter. Or one has the eighteenth century's **make a coffee house of a woman's cunt**: a term that is defined by Grose, never a man to resist a pun, as 'to go in and out and spend nothing'. He also offers **make a lobster kettle out of someone's cunt**. The kettle boils the hapless crustacean to death, and it also turns it from blue to pink. The lobster would around the end of the nineteenth century, and then but briefly, be slang for the penis, but not in 1785. Quite how the phrase evokes delayed ejaculation remains elusive. And Grose, sadly, is not telling.

One last point. Gateshead, the origins of which apparently lie in the words 'goat's headland', and which boasted an abbot as early as 623, lies on the southern bank of the River Tyne, opposite Newcastle upon Tyne. There are doubtless many reasons for the traveller to alight there. And doubtless many do. Or did. For while it is hard to admit this, the phrase being this book's title, but lexicographer's task is truth, and the truth is this: at least when travelling to Newcastle, one can no longer descend at a single stop's distance. Today there is but the MCE: the Metro Centre. A trip thence from, say, London, requires as many as three changes. The station, notes a guide, is 'unmanned'. Indeed.

So now you know. And are you happy? After trudging though these 315 pages of analysis and information (albeit as regards the world of several thousand allegedly 'dirty' words). Possibly not. And that is apparently just as should be. To throw in another chunk of Latin and to focus on the primary topic of those pages, *poste coitum omne animal triste est.* 'Every bloke's miserable after a shag.' Or so they say. But, as one regularly finds when faced with the authorship of a 'deathless' quote, just who is this 'they' anyway. Majority fingers gesture towards one of the 'pseudo-Aristotelian' philosophers (i.e. those who wrote their own works under the real Aristotle's name), in whose *Problems* 955 a 23 it states 'After sexual intercourse most men are rather depressed, but those who emit much waste product with the semen are more cheerful'. What the 'waste product' entailed one has no idea. But anyway other fingers opt just as keenly for the pioneering physician Galen (*c.* AD 130–201) who offers the same concept, but with the addition *praeter mulierem gallumque*; 'except the woman and the cock.' Given that the good and Greek doctor presumably eschewed English-language puns on 'cock', this suggests another sneer at woman's supposed sexual insatiability. It is reassuring to see that slang's prejudices are not merely broad, but of such long standing.

And that really is that.

Nuf ced.

BIBLIOGRAPHY

Barrère, Albert and G. Leland, Charles, *A Dictionary of Slang, Jargon and Cant* (2 vols, 1889)

'Jon Bee' (John Badcock), *Slang: A Dictionary of the Turf, the Ring, the Chase, the Pit, of Bon-Ton and the Varieties of Life* (1823)

Carey, H. N., *The Slang of Venery* (1916)

Cotgrave, *Dictionary of the French and English Tongues* (1611)

Downing, W.H., *Digger Dialects* (1919)

Farmer and Henley, *Slang & its Analogues* (6 vols, 1890–1904)

Florio, John, *New World of Words* (1598)

Folb, Edith, *Running Down Some Lines* (1980)

Gent, B.E., *A New Dictionary of the Terms Ancient and Modern of the Canting Crew* (c.1698)

Gold, R.S., *Jazz Lexicon* (1968)

Grose, Francis, *Classical Dictionary of the Vulgar Tongue* (1785, et seq.)

Hall, B.H., *College Words* (1856)

Harman, Thomas, *A Caveat for Common Coursetours* (c.1566)

Hotten, John Camden, *A Dictionary of Modern Slang, Cant, and Vulgar Words ... by a London Antiquary* (1859 et seq.)

Nares, Robert, *A Glossary* (1822)

OED, *Oxford English Dictionary* Online Edition

Palsgrave, John, *Lesclarcissement de la Langue Francoyse* (1530)

Partridge, Eric, *Dictionary of Slang & Unconventional English* (8th edn, 1984)

Pretty, A.G. (ed.), *Glossary of Slang and Peculiar Terms in Use in the A.I.F. 1921–1924* (unpub.; ed. 2003 Amanda Laugesen, Canberra, Aus.)

Rodgers, Bruce, *The Queens' Vernacular* (1972)

Trumble, Alfred, *Slang Dictionary of New York, London and Paris* (1890)

Ware, J. Redding, *Passing English of the Victorian Era* (1909)

Williams, Gordon, *A Dictionary of Sexual Language and Imagery in Shakespearean and Stuart Literature* (3 vols, 1994)

INDEX

bucker 195
buckess 195
bucket of shit 212
buck fitch 195
buckish 195
buck nigger 195
buck nun 195
buck of the first head 195
buck party 195
buck's night 195
buffalo piss 180
buff the wood 61
bug 122
bug-chaser 122
bugger 73
bugger-all 209
bugturd 223
build a log cabin 274
bull gism 112
bull fuck 112
bull gravy 112
bullhead clap 45
bull piss 180
bull's bum 225
bullshit 206
bully 261
bully hack 261
bully-huff 261
bully huff-cap 261
bully-woollies 235
bum 17, 108, 200
bum-banditry 93
bumblebee 48, 303
bumbo-claat 30
bumbo-cloth 30
bum cloth 30
bum-faker 200
bum-fighter 200
bumfuck 55
Bumfuck, Egypt 134
bump pussies 152
bum-ranger 200
bum-shaver 200
bum-tickler 200, 285
bum-worker 200
bungler 65
burn 52
burner 52
burn one's poker 52
burn one's tail 52
burp the snake 297
burp the worm 296
bury a quaker 270
bury one's bone 94
bury the bone 60
bush 280
bush-beater 280
bushel of tits 228
bush-whacker 280
bust a cherry 243
bust-maker 200
bust someone's pants 233
butch 184
butcher 244, 290
butcher's shop 290
butt-chuckler 171
butter 115–16, 284
butter-and-egg man 203
butter-boat 115
butterbox 115

butter-knife 284
buttery 115
buttock and file 253
buttock and twang 253
button worker 198
buy queen 187

C

caca 268
ca-ca 268
cack 143, 267, 268
cackbag 268
cackface 268
cack-knacker 268
cacky 268
Cadbury alley 231
cafeteria 132
cake-eater 197–8
California house 134
Camp 184
Candle and sconce 258
candy-maker 116–17
candyman 250
canned goods 244
cannon 284
can of piss 181
canyon 225
capon 65
captain 29
captain's log 130
Captain Standish 288
cardboard box 48
cardinal 27
carousel 132
carrion flogger 260
carry one's arse 19
carry the cosh 261
carsey 125
carsi 125
case 125
case-fro 125
case-house 125
case-keeper 125
case-vrow 125
cash carrier 259
cat 149, 197
catalogue queen 187
cat bar 150
catch an oyster 143
catch arse 18
catch shit 211, 213
catch wood 60
cat-eating-shit 211
caterpillar's raincoat 121
cat fight 150
cat flat 150
catfood 150
cathouse 150
cat-lamb 150
cat-lapper 150
cat-nest 150
cat o'mountain 150
cat on a testy dodge 150
cat party 150
cat-scrap 150
cat-shop 150
catso 279
cat's piss 180
cat that cracks the whip 197

cat-wagon 150
cavaliers 61
cave of harmony 289
cawsy 125
cazzo 279
Cecil 162
central cut 121
centre of attraction 120
chaffer 202
chamber music 136
chanticleer 297
chapel of ease 133
charger 299
Charlene 160
charley 136
charley whitehouse 136
Charlie Ronce 258
charver 202
charvering donna 202
charvering moll 202
chasm 225
chat-bags 237
chat parade 237
chats 237
chatty 237
chatty doss 237
chat up 237
chat-up 237
chauver 202
chauvering cove 202
chauvering omee 202
cheater 121
cheeky-arsed 14
cheese 65
cheeseman 198
cheese tube 198
cheesy 198
cheesy head 198
cherry 242–4
cherry blossom kiss 31
cherry-boy 243
cherry-buster 242
cherry farm 243
cherryhead 243
cherry kicks 244
cherry out 244
cherry pie 27
cherry-pie 243
cherry prick 243
cherry queen 243
cherry splitter 243, 280
cherry tree 243
Chester (the Molester) 306
chew fish 140
chicken 189, 199, 260, 305
chicken-butcher 199
chicken-chaser 199
chicken dinner 199
chicken-eyes 199
chicken-fancier 199
chicken-freak 199
chicken-hawk 199
chicken inspector 199
chicken man 260
chicken-man 199
chicken of the sea 86
chicken rustler 199
chicken with a basket 94
Chic Sale 134
chihuahua 299

child-getter 286
children 118
chile-mack 251
chile pimp 251
chili-bowl pimp 251
chili-mack 251
chili pimp 251
chink 225
chink-stopper 282
chism 112
chitterlin 299
chitterling 64, 299
choad 145
choadsmoker 95
chocolate 231, 271
chocolate bandit 271
chocolate cake 271
chocolate canyon 271
chocolate cha-cha 271
chocolate channel 271
chocolate chimney-sweep 271
chocolate freeway 271
chocolate highway 271
chocolate puncher 271
chocolate runway 271
chocolate speedway 271
chocolate starfish 271
chocolate tunnel 271
chocolate whizzway 271
choke a darkie 134
choke the lizard 299
choose 265
choosing money 264
chopper 280
chow 92
christening 136
chuck a bridge 234
chuck a turd 223
chucker-out 253
chuck you, Farley! 84
chump 249
chunder 235
churn the butter 115
chutney ferret 293
cigarette pimp 249
circus bees 240
ciss 165
cissie 165
cissy 165
civet(-cat) 303
clackers 23
clagnuts 275
claim 264
clam 120, 142
clam chowder 142
clam-diving 120, 142
clam jam 142
clam-jousting 120, 142
clam juice 120, 142
clam jungle 120, 142
clam smacker 120, 142
clam spear 120, 142
clap 48–9
clap-clinic 49
clapier 49
clapoir 49
clappers 23
clappy 49
clap-shack 48
clapster 49
clap-trap 49

hambone 290
hammer 283
hammock 30
Hampstead donkeys 239
ham shanker 169
handicap 49
handle cranker 169
Handsome Harry 198
handstaff 280
hang an arse 14
hanging johnny 64
hank freak 171
hard 58–9
hard bit 59
hard mack 256
hard-on 59
hard-up 59
hare-finder 202
harolds 235
Harry Monk 114
hat 37
hata 252
have a bit of beef 290
have a bit of cock 39
have a bit of fish 140
have a bit of goose's neck 298
have a bit of quimsy 190
have a case with 125–6
have a full hand 240
have a paper asshole 21
have a shit 207, 213
have a trout in a well 141
have balls 25
have it away 106
have it off 106
have it up 106
have one's balls in the fire 26
have one's balls twisted 26
have one's balls under one's chin 26
have one's brains in one's bollocks 24
have one's cock on the block 39
have one's shite 206
have one's shit together 215
have someone by the balls 26
have someone's balls for breakfast 26
have someone's shit on a stick 213
have the rag on 28
Haymarket hector 261
head 91
head artist 91
head chick 91
head-fuck 77
head gasket 121
head hunter 91
head job 91
head jockey 91
headquarters of the Scots greys 239
head queen 91
head worker 91

heat 53
heavy cavalry 239
heifer 306
heifer-den 306
heifer paddock 306
hell 149, 209
helmet 122
hen 305
hen-cock 305
hen coop 305
hen-fest 305
hen fight 305
hen fright 305
hen hussy 305
hen mill 305
hen of the game 305
hen of the walk 305
hen pen 305
hen roost 305
Henry III 267
hen-whipped 152
herbalz 118
Hershey highway 231
Hershey squirts 231
Hershey stains 231
hide the salami 170
high 53
Hilda Handcuffs 184
hind tit 229
hitch-hiker on the Hershey highway 16
hit one's shit up 215
hit some shit 213
hit the piss 181
ho 263, 310
hobby horse man 196
hockie 118, 268
hog 293, 299
hogger 197, 299
hogleg 299
hog's eye 200, 299
hog's eye man 200, 299
ho jockey 199
hold your pants on! 233–4
hole 89, 192, 300
holemonger 200–1, 299
holer 200–1
holes and poles 282
holy place 289
holy week 30
honey 271
honey-bucket 271
honey-cart 271
honey-digger 271
honey-dipper 271
honey dripper 271
honey house 271
honeypot 271
honey wagon 271
hoon 257
hoon bin 257
hoon-chaser 257–8
hoondom 258
hoonery 258
hoosegow 134
hoover 89
hopper-arsed 13
hop-pole 109
hormone queen 187
horn 54, 62, 101, 103
hornbag 104
horn-child 103

horn-colic 104
horndog 94, 104
horner 103
horn-grower 103
horn-headed 103
hornies 104
hornify 103
horniness 104
horn-mad 103
horn-madded 103
horn-madness 103
horn-maker 103
horn-merchant 103
horn movie 104
horn pills 104
hornpipe 104
horns 100–4, 194
hornsmoker 104
hornsmoking 104
horns-to-sell 103
horn-work 103
horny 103
horse 43, 196, 263
horse and trap 49, 267
horsecocked 299
horse-collar 303
horsemeat 299
horse piss 180
horse-pox 48
horse's handbrake 61
horse's hangdown 299
hose 94, 281
hose job 94
ho splash 311
hoss 196
hot 52, 103
hot-arsed 14
hot cack 268
hot dog 274
hot hello 118
hot milk 116
hotshot 200
hot-tailed 53
hot tuna! 141
hough! 72
house in the suburbs 262
house of easement 133
house of office 133
house of wax 130
how-d'ye-dos 234
howlet 304
how's it bouncing? 106
how's it hanging? 106
how's it shaking? 106
how's-yer-father 122
how's your bird? 297
huby 64
huff 261
hug the porcelain god 132
hum job 88
hummer 88
hump-me pumps 83
hunk 194
hunter 285
hustler 259

ice-cream 116
ice cream machine 291
ice job 88

icing queen 96
ick-for-brains 212
Ida 161
Ilie Nastase 130
in-and-out 74
in a shit 213
inch 281
in crapper's ditch 128
Indiana 161
in for the plate 53
inglenook 225
inhale the oyster 143
injection 112
in kak 268
ink in one's pen 65
insects (and ants) 235
in (the) shit 208
in someone's arse 15
instrument (of venery) 280
insurance policy 121
in the clarts 272
in the crapper 128
in the poo 269
in the shit 213
in your arse! 19
Ira 161
Irene 161
Irish confetti 119
Irish dip 63
Irish disease 63
Irish fortune 63
Irish horse 63
Irish inch 63
Irish promotion 63
Irish rise 63
Irish toothache 63
Irish toothpick 63
Irish virgin 63, 246
Irish way 63
Irish wedding 63, 246
Irish whist 63
iron hoof 158
iron jaws 87
it 105–9
Italian 44
Italian tricks 44
itch, the 51
itching 51
Ivy 161

jack 63, 84, 170, 288
jack, the 50
jacked up 50
jacket 121
jack-gagger 260
jackhammer 61
jackhandle 61
jack-house 126
jack in the box 48, 288
jack it up someone's arse 108
jack off 170
jack-off 170
jack rabbit 300
Jack Robinson 288
jacks 126, 130
jack tar 84, 86
Jacob 288
jacque's 126
jag-off 170

For Richard Milbank
With very sincere thanks for more than a decade's unwaveringly staunch and
wholly invaluable support whether on the professional or the personal level.

First published in Great Britain in 2008 by
Quercus
21 Bloomsbury Square
London
WC1A 2NS

ISBN 978 1 84724 608 0

2 4 6 8 10 9 7 5 3 1

Typeset by Two Associates
Printed and bound in Great Britain by Clays Ltd, St Ives, Plc

Picture credits:
p.5 © dwphotos; p.10 © Lukasz Kulicki; p.16 © Michael Ledray; p.22 © Gary
James Calder; p.29 © Marlene DeGrood; p.32 © Victoria Alexandrova; p.35 ©
Mykhailo Kalinskyi; p.41 © James Blinn; p.45 © Timothy Passmore; p.52 © IRA;
p.56 © VR Photos; p.63 © maxstockphoto & Subbotina Anna; p.66 © Lev
Dolgachov; p.76 © Najin; p.85 © Wallenrock; p.96 © Cora Reed; p.100 © Niclas
Aberg; p.105 © George Allen Penton; p.107 © Marie Cloke; p.110 © Lana
Langlois; p.117 © Paul Cowan; p.124 © Bob Hosea; p.133 © janr34; p.137 ©
Sergey Rusakov; p.140 © Alex Kotlov; p.144 © Vladimir Melnik; p.150 ©
Brendan Howard; p.154 © Shaber; p.164 © Quayside; p.167 © Inc; p.173 © Lori
Carpenter; p.176 © Tom Grundy; p.183 © Heath Doman; p.191 © John Kirinic;
p.196 © Nick Stubbs; p.204 © ollirg; p.219 © Anke van Wyk; p.221 © Byron
Carlson; p.227 © Lushin Sergey; p.230 © GoodMood Photo; p.234 © istihza;
p.241 © lebanmax; p.243 © Raluca Teodorescu; p.247 © studio_chki; p.250
© Stephen VanHorn; p.266 © Bridget Zawitoski; p.272 © Justin Horrocks; p.278
© Uwe Bumann; p.283 © Pablo Eder; p.295 © IntraClique LLC; p.301 ©
Vladimir Chernyanskiy; p.311 © Oleg Kozlov